DATE DUE

APR 1 0 2013	
NOV 0 6 2017	

BRODART, CO.   Cat. No. 23-221

State Out of the Union

STATE OUT OF THE UNION

ARIZONA AND THE
FINAL SHOWDOWN OVER
THE AMERICAN DREAM

JEFF BIGGERS

NATION
BOOKS
New York

Copyright © 2012 by Jeff Biggers

Published by Nation Books, A Member of the Perseus Books Group
116 East 16th Street, 8th Floor
New York, NY 10003

Nation Books is a co-publishing venture of the Nation Institute and the Perseus Books
Group.

Books published by Nation Books are available at special discounts for bulk
purchases in the United States by corporations, institutions, and other organizations.
For more information, please contact the Special Markets Department at the Perseus
Books Group, 2300 Chestnut Street, Suite 200, Philadelphia, PA 19103, or call
(800) 810-4145, ext. 5000, or e-mail special.markets@perseusbooks.com.

Designed by Timm Bryson

Library of Congress Cataloging-in-Publication Data
Biggers, Jeff.
  State out of the union : Arizona and the final showdown over the American dream /
Jeff Biggers.
    p. cm.
  Includes bibliographical references and index.
  ISBN 978-1-56858-702-8 (hardback)—ISBN 978-1-56858-704-2 (e-book) 1.
Arizona—Politics and government. 2. Immigrants—Legal status, laws, etc.—Arizona.
I. Title.
  JK8216.B54 2012
  320.9791—dc23

                                                        2012025285

10 9 8 7 6 5 4 3 2

In memory of Nathan Allen,
Navooch, thvum knei

With rebellion thus sugar-coated, they have been drugging the public mind of their section for more than thirty years; and, until at length, they have brought many good men to a willingness to take up arms against the government the day after some assemblage of men have enacted the farcical pretence of taking their State out of the Union, who could have been brought to no such thing the day before.

This sophism derives much—perhaps the whole—of its currency, from the assumption, that there is some omnipotent, and sacred supremacy, pertaining to a State—to each State of our Federal Union. Our States have neither more, nor less power, than that reserved to them, in the Union, by the Constitution— no one of them ever having been a State out of the Union.

ABRAHAM LINCOLN, MESSAGE TO CONGRESS, 1861

CONTENTS

Barrio Viejo. (Photo courtesy of Steve Silverman, Digital Fine Art Creations.)

Homecoming

"Are you American, Abuelo?"

"No, I'm not American, I am not Mexican. In fact, I think I am no longer Yaqui. Shit, I can't tell you nothin' for real. I'm nowhere now.... You see, boy, these people up here around us are so mixed up now that no one belongs, even though this is their country, our country. Do you see?"

ALFREDO VÉA JR., *LA MARAVILLA*

Ofelia Rivas settled into a chair in a warehouse collective of artists on the outskirts of Barrio Anita in Tucson.

For more than a decade, she had carried stories from her indigenous community on the US-Mexico border in an old van donated by a punk band, in an attempt to get the rest of the country to recognize a steel-tooth partition that had torn apart her people.

In her fifties, Rivas spoke in the unaffected way of many of the O'odham elders who had educated me on the history of the Sonoran Desert—and my place in it. Over the past forty-odd years, ever since I first crossed the Arizona border in the backseat of my Dad's '60 Chevy, as freckle-faced and hopeful as the other kids along the "Sun Belt" highway, I had maintained a love-hate affair with a state I still didn't quite understand.

Rivas pressed her long skirt, and then pointed out the window and said we were within walking distance of one of the original water tanks that persuaded a detachment of Spanish soldiers to establish their presidio here in 1775. O'odham and Hohokam ancestors had inhabited the area for thousands of years. The spring in an O'odham village at the base of a west-side volcanic hill, referred to as "A" Mountain, gave the city its name: Chuk-son, Toixon, Tucson. Like the Hopi villages along the mesas in northern Arizona, the Old Pueblo is arguably one of the oldest continually inhabited settlements on the continent.

Across more than 4,400 square miles in southern Arizona, the Tohono O'odham reservation is nearly as large as the state of Connecticut. Yet only seventy-four miles have mattered to the rest of the world: the line of demarcation between the United States and Mexico. But that line did not define the O'odham or their territory. With the signing of the Gadsden Purchase in 1853, which effectively established today's border on June 30, 1854, an arbitrary line of division ran across the vast O'odham lands, breaking up the tribe's centuries-old territories in the process. Not that they were ever consulted or considered.

"We didn't cross the border," Rivas began. "The border crossed us."

That refrain, now common among O'odham and historic Mexican American families, took me back twenty years. In 1991, after living away for a decade on the East Coast and in Europe, I returned to southern Arizona to do a walkabout and work on an oral history project. Guided by O'odham archaeologist and poet Nathan Allen, I retraced the confines of the prehistoric Hohokam empire in the Sonoran Desert (the northern Mexico state of Sonora and southern Arizona), which had collapsed in the fourteenth and fifteenth centuries. Allen's father, who had served as Governor George Hunt's chauffeur in the early 1930s, had come from the Tohono O'odham village of Ce:dagi Wahia, or Pozo Verde, which now stood behind a militarized wall on the Mexican side of the border. His mother had come from an Akimel O'odham village near the Gila River, just south of Phoenix.

Beyond any scholarly pretensions, I also saw the project as a way of reconnecting to the Grand Canyon State and learning more of my own history.

Like Arizona Governor Jan Brewer, I had arrived in Arizona in 1970, sporting a pair of bell-bottoms and a Hollywood vision of the Old West. While Brewer and her growing ranks had left California, my parents had joined a new wave of migrants who were abandoning our ailing Coal and Corn Belts to reinvent ourselves in a state that had always burned in our imaginations as the final frontier for the great American Dream.

In an 1865 letter to the *New York Tribune,* Arizona promoter and future territorial Governor Richard "Slippery Dick" McCormick essentially depicted a vast and empty land waiting to be occupied: "I recommend Arizona to our discharged volunteers, and to all unemployed persons who seek a wholesome climate, and a new and brief field for energetic industry. To all who are ready to labor, and to wait even a little time for large success, it is full of promise. The day cannot be distant when it will occupy a first rank among the wealthy and populous States."

A century later, while we quickly donned cowboy boots and gave up our corn bread and catfish for green corn tamales and enchiladas, McCormick's "promise" still resonated for migrants like us, who came with the understanding that we could remake the state in our own image. Just as the Spanish friars cultivated their olive trees and the American pioneers seeded their cotton and citrus trees, my Dad planted a lawn of Bermuda grass in the sand like the rest of our neighbors. The giant saguaros that framed the photos of our transplanted home in the Sonoran Desert may have stretched across the border into Sonora, Mexico, with a lesson of desert resiliency and adaptation, but for most newcomers they remained like window dressing, not harbingers of a sustainable environment.

Within a short time, I found myself on a morning TV talk show, most likely because of my Howdy Doody red hair and chatty interest in cowboys, discussing our school's celebration of Arizona history. Our appointed roles on the program were clear: "First came the Indians," announced one kid, "then came the Spanish and Mexicans," added another, and finally I stood: "And then came the Anglos." I carried out the rest of the conversation in the present tense.

While my 1970s childhood in Tucson saw the election of the state's first and only Mexican American governor, witnessed labor leader Cesar Chavez bring international shame on his native state's treatment of migrant workers with a "fast for love," and celebrated Tucson's "Queen of Rock," Linda Ronstadt (who came from one of the city's pioneering Mexican American families), newcomers like me, in the unfolding New West's suburbs, military bases, and strip malls, found it more convenient to stand at the doorstep of our adopted state as modern-day pioneers and not consider the meaning of its conflicting cultures and ancient history.

Only by accident did I learn, for example, that much of Tucson's history had been removed, literally. My Dad's second office in town was housed in a narrow old adobe in the Barrio Viejo of Tucson. As director of litigation of the Pima County Legal Aid Society, one of the first legal cases for his section joined a community effort to stop a misguided highway proposal, named after the Butterfield stagecoach route, that would have demolished the remnants of Tucson's most historic Mexican barrios. In those early days following our arrival, my brother and I loved to wander the backstreets around my Dad's office, beguiled by the Sonoran adobe architecture and the last remnants of street life around Barrio Viejo and Barrio Libre.

"Perhaps the humble appearance of El Hoyo justifies the discerning shrugs of more than a few people only vaguely aware of its existence," Tucson author Mario Suárez wrote in 1947, in his pioneering fiction work about barrio life. "Yet El Hoyo is not the desperate outpost of a few families against the world." The first author to use the term "chicano" in modern literature, Suárez seemingly captured our initiation into a land beyond our own imaginary atlas: "Chicano is the short way of saying Mexicano," he wrote. "It is the long way of referring to everybody."

Whether "everybody" was willing to embrace Tucson's deeply rooted cultures was another matter. The National Book Award–winning poet Ai (Florence Anthony), who often explored her mixed ancestry (including Japanese, African American, Choctaw, and Irish heritages), once mused in an interview on her upbringing in Tucson's Barrio Viejo: "So I have a real early connection to Mexican culture, which I enjoyed having, and I think it added to my life to have it."

I'll never forget my Dad walking us over to a nearby empty lot, a vast field strewn with the wreckage of bulldozers and construction equipment. Under the guise of urban renewal, more than eighty acres of the surrounding historic barrio—the most densely populated Mexican American, O'odham, and ethnically mixed neighborhood in the state and region—had been razed in an unabashed act to rid the city of its "slums" as part of urban renewal. "Urban removal, more like," my Dad said, shaking his head.

"Just as we collect shards to put together the pieces of Hohokam history," Allen told me one day, "we must do the same for our contemporary times." As a child, he had been sent to the Phoenix Indian School, a notorious boarding school that sought to separate tribal children from their cultures and language, and effectively "take the Indian out of the American Indian."

On one of our first outings, the O'odham elder took me to the concrete remains of the Butte Japanese internment camp on his Gila River reservation, where thousands of Japanese and Japanese Americans had been detained for three years. At one point in the mid-1940s, it ranked as the fourth-largest city in Arizona.

"Wax on, wax off," Allen mused, referring to a famous line in the popular *Karate Kid* film. Noriyuki "Pat" Morita, the American-born star and Oscar nominee, had been imprisoned as a child at this internment camp, as well. For Allen, the camp was just one episode in Arizona's (and our nation's) long and twisted history of anti-immigrant policies.

"As a native, I've never understood the reasoning of so-called nativists," Allen told me on one trip in the mid-1990s, when a contentious debate over deportation and immigration policy once again placed Arizona in the national headlines. It made me wonder: so far from the symbolic transit station of Ellis Island, had the borderlands actually been the nation's burning ground over entry into the American experience?

After the signing of the Gadsden Purchase, Allen's and Rivas's families moved across the borderline with little thought, passing the quaint marble and iron border obelisks or ranch fences en route to their native villages, work, ceremonies, and social occasions. Still, the issue of citizenship and certain rights for the O'odham were never codified.

"My father fought in the 1960s to get O'odham support for his community on the other side of the border," Rivas began. "He was called a Sonoran O'odham. He worked on ranches and in the mines."

Less than four months before homeland security was irrevocably changed on September 11, 2001, a delegation of Tohono O'odham tribal members journeyed across the United States on a campaign to "Make It Right." When they arrived in Washington, DC, they met with members of Congress and petitioned for a change to the Immigration and Nationality Act that would recognize tribal credentials as official accreditation for citizenship rights.

According to the delegation, 7,000 out of the 24,000 Tohono O'odham had no birth certificates; an estimated 1,400 lived south of the border.

"I don't have a birth document," Rivas told me.

The events of 9/11 derailed any discussion on crossover border rights. Legislative efforts by Arizona Congressmen Raúl Grijalva and Ed Pastor for citizenship rights never made it through House committees. The militarization of the border had already been launched in the mid-1990s, as part of President Bill Clinton's Operation Gatekeeper, a measure flanking the passing of the North American Free Trade Agreement (NAFTA) that fortified border security at the main corridors of migration and shifted the journey of undocumented migrants into the more remote and deadly stretches of the O'odham desert. "The current policies in place on both sides of the U.S.-Mexico border have created a humanitarian crisis that has led to the deaths of more than 5,000 people," noted an ACLU report on the fifteenth anniversary of Clinton's policy. "Because of deadly practices and policies like Operation Gatekeeper, the death toll continues to rise unabated despite the decrease in unauthorized crossings due to economic factors."

For natives like Allen and Rivas, the cycles of conquest had been followed by our modern-day cycles of deportations, "amnesties," and now militarized efforts like Operation Gatekeeper. Every twenty years or so, border security and "illegal" immigration issues were rediscovered by political opportunists whenever the economy weakened, a war ended, or election time heated up.

I had experienced this phenomenon in Arizona as well, though far from the US-Mexico border. When I lived in Flagstaff in the mid-to late 1990s, I directed a literacy center in northern Arizona, dealing mainly with immigrants working in the tourist and service industries on the vast Colorado Plateau, which stretches from the Grand Canyon to the Navajo Nation. While the ponderosa pine forests in the northern part of the state couldn't have differed more in landscape from my adopted Sonoran Desert in southern Arizona, the machinations of immigration politics transcended the geographical borders of the state—and our shared *linea* with Mexico. My phone rang one night with an urgent call. "*La migra* is planning a sweep," a desperate voice told me in Spanish, referring to immigration agents. "Tell your students."

Earlier that week, hundreds of undocumented workers in the Phoenix suburb of Chandler had been rounded up as part of a surprise crackdown in Latino neighborhoods that brought widespread denouncements and civil rights lawsuits. The best line: when a Mexican American store clerk was questioned for her "papers" by a police officer, she naturally responded, "I've got toilet paper, writing paper, and newspaper—what kind do you want?"

By the time Arizona passed the controversial SB 1070 "papers, please" immigration law in 2010, which requires law enforcement officials to check residency status during an encounter with any suspected undocumented immigrant and makes it a state crime to be caught under Arizona's sun without proper residency documents, more than 1,200 National Guard troops had joined ranks with hundreds of transplanted Border Patrol agents on the O'odham reservation, spiraling out in what looked like a prolonged military operation in an unnamed war. The escalation of the drug smugglers, which had been part of borderland rustling for decades, turned deadly.

When construction began on the steel fence near her home, less than a mile from the border, "I couldn't sleep at night," Rivas recalled. "They worked at night—all of the scraping, rocks being crushed. Sounded liked screaming. I would sit all night listening to the screaming. Like Mother Earth screaming. They were putting these metal things in her, and we don't know how to pull them out. They put them in concrete, and told us we are now in two different countries."

One of the more outspoken O'odham against the military buildup, Rivas founded O'odham Against the Wall and began to document Border Patrol agents' abuses, including harassment of local residents, as well as the impact of the new fence and checkpoints on traditional O'odham, who were prevented from crossing the border for religious ceremonies.

"It's a frightful thing for elders, who don't speak English," Rivas said. "They make you feel like a criminal."

In 2010, with the Tea Party in control of the state legislature, State Senator Russell Pearce and Governor Brewer took the encroachment of O'odham boundaries one step further in a extraordinary assertion of states' rights over tribal sovereignty. Dismissing Indian gaming compacts and rights, Pearce tore into the Obama administration for blocking his role in the state's lawsuit against the US Department of the Interior to halt an O'odham casino on tribal land just outside Brewer's adopted home turf of Glendale.

"It is an outrage that in America today the Federal Government can swoop in, crush the state's rights to dictate what happens in their boundaries, and ignore the will of Arizona voters," Pearce said in a press statement. "It is with total disregard and disrespect for the State of Arizona that this Administration acts."

Sovereignty, apparently, did not apply to indigenous people in Arizona. The nativists trumped the natives.

Pearce drew another line in the sand: "Obama has apparently decided that in this family of the United States, Arizona is the black sheep and he will stop at nothing to crush anything the good people of Arizona want. Obama has thrown democracy out the window—he's taunting Arizonans by saying, 'don't care how you voted, what I say goes all through this land.' Here the Fed's are sticking their nose in a State's rights issue."

Returning from a traditional O'odham ceremony, Rivas was stopped once by a Border Patrol agent. He shouted at her to prove her citizenship: "Are you from the US or Mexico?" Taken aback, she answered, "I'm O'odham, on my own lands. You should prove who you are." The agent pulled out his gun, Rivas said, and then held it to her head. "Are you a US or Mexican citizen?" She looked at him. "I'm O'odham."

Rivas lit up a tobacco-rolled cigarette and swatted at the first waves of smoke. She recognized the reasons I had come home again, what drove that never-ending search to reclaim the history of our homelands and consider what it means today. To ask the question: What has happened to Arizona?

Not that conflicts over statehood and anti-immigrant fervor have ever wavered since the earliest days of Arizona. More than a century ago, carpetbagging Arizona politicians bucked a US House committee's recommendation to conjoin Arizona and New Mexico as a single state in 1906. Their reasoning: "Arizona is America, New Mexico is Mexican," and their fear over the political reality that New Mexico's Mexican American Republicans would outnumber Arizona's Anglo Democrats. Acting with "indignation that was as much racist as righteous," venerable Arizona historian Thomas Sheridan noted, the future state locked down its front-page role in the national headlines as the final frontier of an exclusionary American destiny. Arizona preferred not to become a state in the union rather than acquiesce to a "different race"—or as a US senator from South Carolina added, "a cry of a pure blooded white community against the domination of a mixed breed aggregation of citizens of New Mexico, who are Spaniards, Indians, Greasers, Mexicans, and everything else."

To understand Arizona today, I had to go beyond a nostalgic version of Arizona's frontier past, and revisit the stories Allen shared when we stood at the remains of the Japanese prison camp, in order to ask the question: were we once again slogging through another battle in an unfinished, century-old cultural war over who would be the gatekeeper of the American Dream, or had we truly reached a pivotal moment in Arizona's showdown with the federal government over states' rights?

The recognition of this often conflicting history—or, in fact, denial of it by new ranks of interlopers intent on rewriting Arizona's place in the greater American experience—begged another question: did the headlong descent of our forty-eighth state into its current states' rights and anti-immigrant spasm mark a defining shift for our country, or was Arizona simply a rogue state following a divisive historical trend that dated back to efforts of transient politicians to drag the US-Mexico borderlands into the Confederacy, derail Arizona's entry into statehood in 1912, and carry out cyclical deportations and ethnic conflict?

Such questions did not stop at the state's borders, of course. "In the nation's capital and around the country, however, political leaders should be worried that conditions in Arizona will spread nationwide," *Roll Call* editor Morton Kondracke had warned. "The failure of Congress and two presidents to enact immigration reform is plunging the nation into an ugly future. Call it the Arizonification of America."

Yet to understand the Arizonification of America, it was essential first to understand the history of Arizona.

"To undo a mistake is always harder than not to create one originally, but we seldom have the foresight," Eleanor Roosevelt had said during her visit to the Japanese camp on Allen's Gila River reservation in 1943. "We have no common race in this country, but we have an ideal to which all of us are loyal: we cannot progress if we look down upon any group of people amongst us because of race or religion."

Once again, after a decade of living out of state, I found myself coming home to Arizona, as a new generation of social-media-savvy youth and political veterans struggled to pull the state back from the brink and undo what they perceived as the mistakes of a runaway legislature that still questioned its place in the union. Roosevelt's historic reckoning that placed Arizona on the front lines of American progress had never seemed so elusive.

"Welcome back to Chuk-son," Rivas said.

Three Sonorans blogger David A. Morales.
(Photo courtesy of Chris Summitt, Summitt Photography.)

INTRODUCTION

The Three Sonorans Prophecy

Make no mistake, we are living through the most important time in Arizona's history. What makes this time so pivotal goes much deeper than what is going on with the controversial issues of today. More important is the cause of what is going on, and why.

THREE SONORANS BLOG, JULY 2010

His real name was David Morales, but he was known as Abie—although a legion of dedicated readers simply identified him with his controversial Tucson blog moniker, Three Sonorans. Our first meeting took place at a sports bar on Speedway Boulevard, where I had often cruised in my high school friend's souped-up racecars as a youth, when Tucson's grand crossroad was hailed as the "ugliest street in America" by *Life Magazine*. Within days, I found myself riding shotgun on Morales's online updates and attacks on the state's political mayhem, as he maneuvered the quickly changing media highways.

Few knew he had been an accomplished doctoral student in mathematics at the University of Arizona or that he had grown up in the once-hardscrabble town of Marana, when cotton farms still defined the area's stretches of desert. His father, a Vietnam vet and copper miner at the nearby BHP mine in San

Manuel, had served as a Republican member of the town council in the late 1980s and early '90s. By the time Morales entered the University of Arizona in 1997, the shrewd town leaders had annexed the unincorporated tracks of suburban sprawl and golf courses and big-box strip malls that stretched along the I-10 corridor, and locked their fate to that of Tucson.

One late spring night on the UA campus in 2010, with only the cubicles in the science and math buildings lit up during the after-hours, Morales found his attention wandering from the equations on his computer screen. Arizona had become the "focal point" in the nation, in his mind, and "the butt of late-night jokes." What the heck had happened? Did people really know about these Arizona legislators, Morales wondered, who had been allowed to write and pass the state's controversial SB 1070 "papers, please" immigration law?

The mathematician turned to his computer screen and started thumping on the keyboard. He logged on to his MathGeneRation's Weblog. Instead of an analysis of a theory or formula, he began to compose a different kind of blog entry:

> This is a story you should all know.
>
> I think this story is very telling, and since no one else is covering it, I will. And what I write can be used by any news source, because a story this sexy should be on the news! I will keep it short and simple. This is a story about Steve Montenegro who lives in Arizona. Who is Mr. Montenegro? Mr. Montenegro is a pastor of a Pentecostal church in Phoenix. He is also an immigrant and was born in El Salvador. Most of his church congregation are so called "illegal aliens." . . . Mr. Montenegro, despite being the spiritual leader of a group of good God-fearing Christians, and deriving an income from these same people, is also a politician. But not just any politician! Mr. Montenegro is also a member of the Arizona state legislature.
>
> What party affiliation do you think the person described above has? You would be wrong if you guessed Democrat, because Representative Montenegro is a hard-core Republican, and lately has taken to the airwaves to voice his support for Russell Pearce's SB1070.

Once Morales posted his blog, his life would never be quite the same. Some would add: Tucson would never be the same. Within a month, surprised by the response and encouragement, he transferred his blog to the *Tucson Citizen* website, an unpaid operation at the city's longest-running newspaper, which had folded its print edition in 2009. It had been founded in 1870 by Richard McCormick, the "prince of carpetbaggers" and eventual territorial governor of Arizona, who had used his former wartime newspaper skills to promote the mining and merchant interests of a virtual oligarchy in the territory. Now, it seemed, the Gannett-owned *Tucson Citizen* was in the hands of a gaggle of volunteer bloggers.

On January 8, 2011, a blog posting from Morales's portable phone brought down the *Tucson Citizen* server. Seated at a Pima County Democratic Party meeting one Saturday morning, he had been taking notes on a special resolution against HB 2281, the state legislature's thinly veiled ban on Mexican American Studies in Tucson, which equates the critical pedagogy approach of teaching Mexican American history and literature to the "overthrow of the government," and the fostering of resentment, ethnic solidarity, and division. Outraged by the unfounded accusation, the Tucson Democrats declared that Mexican American Studies "should not only be left as-is but should be expanded to include more ethnicities and cultures in every school throughout Arizona."

Then Morales received an urgent text. After confirming with a couple of other Democrats who had also received the message, he quickly posted his blog entry: "Gabrielle Giffords shot in head in Tucson." Picked up by Google news, the *Tucson Citizen* site reportedly crashed within minutes, setting off local and national news investigations.

As the blogger noted the next day, the Giffords tragedy was strangely but inextricably entangled in the Mexican American Studies and immigration conflicts. One of the slain, federal court judge John Roll, had been assigned to hear the case of the Mexican American students and teachers in Tucson challenging the constitutionality of the state ban. Roll had also received death threats two years earlier when he presided over a multimillion-dollar suit filed by undocumented immigrants who had been abused by an Arizona vigilante on the border. On the same day of the shooting, someone had coincidently vandalized the Cesar Chavez Building on the University of Arizona campus, which houses the Social Justice Education Project and the Mexican American Studies program.

Morales's tall, robust figure, scraggly beard, and camera had become a fixture at Tucson political events. He always wore one of his trademark hats— a beret, a Panama hat, a ball cap—and stood on the right side of the room, holding a video camera that had become an extension of his identity over the past year. He carried his cellphone in his other hand.

Within a year, more than 1 million viewers had logged on to read Three Sonorans. From its ardent followers in southern Arizona's Latino, liberal, and youth communities, to business and political power brokers, it had become the bookmarked must-read on Arizona politics and immigration issues. It had also drawn its fair share of enemies from both sides of the aisle. The blog was an equal-opportunity muckraker, as critical of the compromises of liberals and Democrats as any ploys by Tea Party extremists. More important, it marked the entrance and evolving power of a new generation of social-media-savvy voices that would transform Arizona's SB 1070 state of the union.

With the themes of "Desert, Science and Hot Dogs," the Three Sonorans blog issued a prophecy in the dog days of the "SB 1070 summer" with an audacious headline: "The Rebirth of Arizona."

After a brief overview of the 2008 election of President Barack Obama, the appointment of former Arizona Governor Janet Napolitano to head the Department of Homeland Security, and the ascension of Jan Brewer to power, and then the subsequent fallout over SB 1070, Morales addressed the national implications of Arizona's brewing showdown.

> Due to the events of the last two years, Arizona is now being forced to confront an issue that is about to be awakened nationwide in a larger scale very soon, and that is the issue of xenophobia and racism. In this election year Arizona will head in one of two directions. The first direction is down the path we are on now, and bills will be passed that include denying citizenship to persons born here in direct violation of the 14th amendment, along with other racist bills. The second direction will be a new path, one that will lead to a rebirth of Arizona. Ari-

zona has changed a lot in the last century, and the demographics have drastically changed. There was no international border when Arizona became a state, nor was there Border Patrol. Go back a few more decades and Arizona was in a different nation. A lot has changed, but this election will determine a crucial question. Will we be able to live as a diverse society in peace, or will xenophobia consume us?

Governor Jan Brewer and President Barack Obama in Phoenix.
(Haraz Ghanbari/Associated Press.)

CHAPTER ONE

ARIZONA V. UNITED STATES

But at a time when our discourse has become so sharply polarized—at a time when we are too eager to lay the blame for all that ails the world at the feet of those who happen to think differently than we do—it's important for us to pause for a moment and make sure that we're talking with each other in a way that heals, not in a way that wounds.

PRESIDENT BARACK OBAMA, JANUARY 12, 2011,
TUCSON, ARIZONA

ARIZONA GONE WILD

Thousands packed McKale Memorial Center that day. An overflow crowd lined the nearby football stadium, where jumbotron screens flashed the entrance of President Barack Obama, former Arizona governor and Department of Homeland Security Chief Janet Napolitano, Attorney General Eric Holder, and Governor Jan Brewer. Televised nationally, the historic event had been staged as a moment of unity in the country, with Arizona as its symbol: *Together We Thrive: Tucson and America.*

As the nation gathered to reflect on the gunning down of Arizona Representative Gabrielle Giffords, which left six dead and thirteen injured in Tucson on January 8, 2011, the president beseeched his fellow citizens "to come together as a people, Republicans, Democrats, Independents," and "find common ground, even as we're having some very vigorous debates."

Not everyone in Arizona, however, was on board with the president.

Declaring that President Obama was engaging in "jihad against America," Arizona's new State Senate president, Russell Pearce—the self-proclaimed architect of the state's controversial SB 1070 immigration law—had told an earlier national conference, "I can tell you that the best thing about 1070 is that Obama may not be visiting Arizona because we actually require papers now." In other words: Welcome to Arizona. Now go home.

With the most radical Tea Party faction in control of its legislature, Arizona had not only dislodged Sarah Palin as one of the most reliable political jokes on late-night TV shows—in fact, Arizona nativists attempted to persuade her to join their cause as a new homeowner in Scottsdale—but had set in motion one of the most alarming challenges to federal authority in modern history. As a precursor to a new era of politics, Arizona's never-ending parade of gun-toting sheriffs, prophecy-quoting fringe politicians, and carpetbagging "you're one of us" mavericks defiantly unveiled their vision of a states' rights paradise for the Tea Party and extremist forces across America.

For all the reprimands from the national editorial boards, and all the nationwide protests that erupted in noncompliance, and all the boycotts enacted against Arizona's vital tourist industry, perhaps nothing stung more than Jon Stewart's tribute in the spring of 2010 on *The Daily Show*: "Arizona is the meth lab of democracy."

There were some dandies. In one of the first bills after the Giffords incident, the Arizona state legislature declared the Colt Single-Action Army Revolver—the Connecticut-based pistol that had been used against Native Americans in various nineteenth-century territorial campaigns—as the state gun. Bereft of any concealed gun laws, you could legally lug that Colt or a lighter semi-automatic into any saloon and knock back a whiskey in all its Wild West glory. Despite the contradiction, the legislature also hammered out a law supporting state financing for the production of a Tea Party–inspired "Don't Tread on Me" license plate.

Conservative states across the country were not simply watching Arizona's ludicrous legislative antics; the Grand Canyon State, once ridiculed, was emerging as the bellwether of rebellion, and its actions were suddenly turning into blueprints for legislatures from Alaska to Alabama.

When a banner rippled at the grand opening of the Lime Fresh Mexican Grill in Florida with bare-faced taunting—"So authentically Mexican we couldn't open a store in Arizona"—the terrible irony was being played out that same day in the chain's other location, in Alabama, where the passing of a copycat (if not even more draconian) immigration law had triggered a frantic exodus of undocumented residents from the state's schools and farm communities. The fields of sweet potatoes sat empty in Alabama.

The joke was still on Arizona.

In neighboring Georgia, Pearce's public endorsement for that state's copycat fast-track legislation helped push its hard-liner immigration bill into law two months after Obama visited Tucson. Arizona got the credit. "We are at the front of the parade," Pearce told his constituents, "and we have changed the debate in Washington, DC."

Even Prince William County in Virginia, which had instituted a similar ordinance requiring law enforcement officials to check the residency status of suspected immigrants three years before Arizona—only to see it quickly repealed for constitutional violations—faltered in its trailblazing role in comparison to Arizona, whose law uniquely sparked international upheaval.

The Arizonification of America, however, had other casualties. On the same day the president spoke in Tucson, an estimated thirty thousand immigrants without proper papers sat behind bars in detention centers across the country, while the Obama administration's Secure Communities policy stayed on pace to set an annual record of nearly four hundred thousand deportation cases. Among the five thousand immigrants who had died attempting to cross Arizona's brutal deserts since the nation ramped up its border strategies in 1994, someone had most likely lost his life on that day.

Beyond the National Guard troops deployed in a massive buildup of heavily armed Border Patrol forces and the billion-dollar boondoggle of a virtual wall lining the border with Mexico, federal enforcement policies had more in common with Arizona than most people knew or cared to acknowledge. Far from the border, the "immigration war" had spilled into "secure communities" and neighborhoods and schools across the nation.

Perhaps Pearce was right. Hundreds of laws and anti-immigrant resolutions had been introduced or passed in nearly twenty-five states since SB 1070 became a slogan. While others in the nation may have shared Arizona's powerful mix of nativist fervor, constitutional revisionism, and passion for federal rollbacks and criminal retribution, no other state had injected the lethal combination of such policies into the legislative debate like Arizona's Tea Party legislature since the anti-immigrant Know-Nothing movement in the mid-nineteenth century.

And arguably, no other contemporary state (or politicians like Pearce and Governor Brewer) had waged such an obsessive campaign over immigration and border security—almost to the point of being written off as a raving relic numerous times. Not that the defiant governor or white-knuckled Pearce, a conservative former deputy sheriff with a long history of personal conflicts and scandals, were originals. Their ranks followed a well-worn trail of frontier justice in Arizona. Embracing a century-long state tradition of stirring the "brown scare" and invoking cyclical episodes of immigrant roundups and deportation during economic downturns, Pearce and fellow Fox News media darlings, like Maricopa County Sheriff Joe Arpaio and Governor Brewer, had managed to beat the drums of borderland fear long enough to gain national attention. In turn, Fox News presented the border issue as America's "third war," placing Arizona on the level of the Iraq and Afghanistan conflicts as a national security crisis.

With the backroom help of the American Legislative Exchange Council corporate lobby and the extremist Washington, DC–based front group the Federation for American Immigration Reform (FAIR), Pearce had introduced his beloved immigration bill with the fanfare of an annual pageant since 2005—only months after his son, a police officer, was shot by an undocumented immigrant in the Phoenix area.

Pearce understood the makings of the media, that perception counted as much as reality. Despite the fact that his state's crime and immigration rates were at their lowest in decades, according to FBI Uniform Crime Reports, the Tea Party president and his flankers managed to keep the fear of imminent invasion and spillover from the Mexican drug war simmering at the gates of the border. They adopted a mantra that had been coined thousands of miles away by a former George W. Bush administration law enforcement agent, but that now fit their cause like a brand-new cowboy hat: "attrition through enforcement." They railed against the social costs of immigration while refusing to admit the huge benefits of having undocumented workers contribute to Arizona's economy and tax revenues, the loss of which would amount to an estimated $48 billion, according to a Center for American Progress study.

Instead, as argued by conservative Arizona Representative Ben Quayle, the transplanted son of former Vice President Dan Quayle, "statistics and averages might mean something to government bureaucrats and analysts in Washington," but facts didn't overrule politics for those living on the border—or corporate lobbyists and politicians making laws inside the State Capitol.

Writing in the *Social Contract Press*, published by FAIR founder John Tanton—which the Southern Poverty Law Center determined "routinely publishes race-baiting articles penned by white nationalists"—Pearce laid down the gauntlet in his justification of Arizona's extremist moves: "It will do no good to forgive them because millions more will come behind them, and we will be over run to the point that there will no longer be a United States of America but, a North American Union of open borders. I ask you what form of government will we live under? How long will it be before we will be just like Mexico? We have already lost our language; everything must be printed in Spanish. We have already lost our history since it is no longer taught in our schools. And we have lost our borders."

The tipping point came in the spring of 2010: when a tragic shooting took place on the US-Mexico border in southern Arizona—the still unsolved murder of rancher Robert Krentz in Cochise County—Pearce played his trump card and rammed through his beloved legislation soaked in the memory and nonstop media coverage of the rancher's death. Within weeks, Governor Brewer didn't simply sign Pearce's SB 1070 into the books; she immortalized Arizona's groundbreaking punitive immigration measure as the front line in Pearce's even greater battle to defend the American Dream.

Using the broken immigration system as the crisis that tied the binds of all Americans, Pearce and his Arizona minions thrived on the very paradox of President Obama's address in the wake of Tucson's shooting: a nation divided.

In a country that had emerged from a bloody revolution and Civil War over the right to migration and mobility and to preserve the sacredness of our union, Arizona politicians like Pearce and Brewer stripped the scab from an unhealed wound over civil rights with their separatist invective, and dragged their border state into the national battlefield over the rights of law-abiding Americans and Latino immigrants to pursue the American Dream.

"Until the passage of SB 1070," former state senator Alfredo Gutierrez noted, "the anti-immigrant hysteria that has seized the country has supported legislation that specifically targets the undocumented. By making anyone who is 'reasonably suspicious' of being an 'illegal,' [SB 1070] targets the entire Latino community in Arizona. As recent history has shown, they will find an enthusiastic audience in the post-Confederate South."

Indeed, Arizona had conjured a massive following of supporters across the nation—and as far as Europe, where even Italian fascists and northern separatists alike offered their support for SB 1070—far beyond the issue of immigration. Galvanized by Arizona's defiance, Tea Party legislators were introducing similar bills over immigration as well as the control of guns, natural resources, education, and health care.

Arizona went one step further in standing up to a White House led by a man with, many residents believed, a questionable birth certificate. To be sure, Arizona Secretary of State Ken Bennett threatened in a live radio interview in the summer of 2012 to keep President Obama off the ballot in the state until Hawaiian officials verified the existence of Obama's birth certificate.

Within two weeks of the president's somber January 12, 2011, challenge to the country, Pearce announced his intentions to introduce a bill that would nullify "existing federal statutes, mandates and executive orders" deemed unwarranted by a state committee. As longtime *Arizona Republic* columnist E. J. Montini noted, the measure would give Arizona the right "to secede without officially doing so."

On the heels of Pearce's declaration of the sovereignty of states' rights, the Arizona legislature took its show of defiance globally, considering a bill that would prohibit "courts from considering international law or legal precepts of other nations or cultures when making judicial decisions."

Imbued by Brewer's signing of a bill in the spring of 2011 establishing an armed force to deploy at her discretion, the Tea Party–led Arizona state legislature doubled down on its "make Arizona its own country" campaign in

2012 by reintroducing its elusive but cherished nullification legislation, and passing a bill that called on the federal government to relinquish control over publicly owned land, including national forests and monuments.

But maintaining their power over those boundaries also concerned Pearce and his Tea Party ranks, as well as the state's notorious attorney general, Tom Horne. In a transient state with large retirement and seasonal communities, where more than 30 percent of the population was Latino, the rapidly changing non-Anglo majority of students in Arizona schools was emerging as the greatest threat in a demographic shift that transcended immigration issues for the state's nativists.

The Tea Party's darkest nightmare was a cautionary tale for the Southwest, and for the rest of the nation: the latest census proved that native births in Arizona, not immigration, accounted for one of the fastest-growing Latino populations in the country. With the nation's highest "cultural generation" gap—83 percent of the aging population was categorized as Anglo, and 57 percent of the children came from Latino families—Arizona had watched the state change from 72 percent to 50 percent non-Latino in the past two decades. Horne and Pearce, among other Arizona leaders, understood what the rest of the anti-immigrant elements of the Republican Party feared: across the nation, as more than fifty thousand Latinos turned eighteen every month, the voting ranks were inevitably shifting—or "browning," as Arizona observers were apt to say.

In an attempt to crush the nation's only high school program in Mexican American Studies, which had been held up as a nationally acclaimed model for churning out unusually high rates of graduates and college-bound Latinos and for notably alleviating the achievement gap that hampered education efforts elsewhere, the Arizona hard-liners conjoined SB 1070 with an accompanying law that effectively banned the program under the guise that it allegedly promoted "the overthrow of the United States government," ethnic "solidarity," and "resentment toward a race or class of people." Pearce declared that studying Mexican American history and literature in Tucson's program was the equivalent of sedition.

Pearce dropped another bombshell on the heels of the president's visit that would serve as further foreshadowing of the 2012 elections. In a direct clash with a 1982 Supreme Court decision, he sought to deny K–12 education to undocumented children and require medical facilities to verify citizenship before granting services—the bill was soon replicated in Alabama. Another bill rejected the Fourteenth Amendment guarantee of birthright citizenship to children of undocumented workers.

Six months later, on the eve of the dedication of the Martin Luther King Jr. memorial in Washington, DC, Horne stunned the nation by making Arizona the first state to file suit to strike down parts of the Voting Rights Act.

Arizona gone wild? Perhaps, but it had also gone viral.

Far from being a solitary rogue state, Arizona emerged as a quintessential training ground for manufacturing a shock crisis in order to ram through an extremist agenda. Arizona's immigration troubles also served as a convenient distraction from other homegrown disasters: the state economy was in ruins, with the worst structural debt in the nation; the foreclosure crisis had left an estimated one out of six houses unoccupied after a real estate binge; and uncontrolled development had brought the state to the brink of irreversible water and environmental crises.

"The immigrant community became the scapegoat for every social and financial issue, and there were those who expertly used to it divide communities and voters," US Representative Raúl Grijalva told me in his Tucson office near the University of Arizona in the summer of 2011. "You're poor because they're here. You don't have a job because they're here. The environment is getting trashed because they are coming over. The security of your neighborhood is worse because of them. They're all drug smugglers. I tell people: the criminalization of immigrants was key in this whole 1070 battle."

In a defining moment of the desperate economic times, the Arizona legislature even sold some of its Capitol buildings in 2010 in a fundraising-leasing stunt.

Even when the extraordinary Wisconsin uprising against the anti-union policies of Tea Party Governor Scott Walker took place in the spring of 2011, Governor Brewer elbowed her way back onto the Sunday TV talk-show circuit to make sure Arizona didn't play second fiddle to any other state rebellion. (Arizona leaders not only trumpeted the state's union-busting "right to work" policies; they also boasted that the state had stripped public school teachers of any tenure rights. By the spring of 2012, the legislature would launch its own assault on public unions.) On ABC News, Brewer defiantly declared, "We believe that the federal government just needs to get out of the way and let us run the states."

For Arizona's Tea Party legislature, the issue itself was almost secondary to the principle of state rebellion against federal control. Would Arizona draw a line in the sand at the production of light bulbs or firearms or immigration policy? Introducing a bill to exempt incandescent light bulbs made in Arizona from federal regulations, State Senator Frank Antenori—who drew the ire of the national media when he chastised Giffords for blocking media access to her less than eight months after her shooting—admitted that his main intent was to instigate a lawsuit with the federal government over the US Constitution. Light bulbs, guns, Mexican immigrants—it didn't really matter.

Brewer preferred guns. The governor signed the Firearms Freedom Act, which allows weapons and ammunition manufactured in Arizona to be sold in the state without federal registration or regulations. Responding to the criticism that the deadly drug war in neighboring Mexico was being supplied in large part by virtually unregulated Arizona gun shows, Brewer warned Washington politicians not to "get between Arizonans and their constitutional rights."

Brewer, a California transplant who had ironically inherited her position when former Democratic Governor Janet Napolitano was elevated from her post to head up the Department of Homeland Security, reveled in her head-on confrontation with federal authority—especially with President Obama. She had already emerged as the first state leader to "play chicken with the Obama administration," according to the *Washington Post*, by passing a bill that requested a federal waiver from certain Medicaid requirements.

Another bill required federal environmental inspectors to register with the sheriff whenever its representatives entered one of Arizona's fifteen counties. *Forbes* columnist Osha Davidson declared this new bill could be summed up in three words: "Stay outta Arizona."

THE OTHER ARIZONA

Since the election of President Obama in 2008, episodes like this had typified news coverage of Arizona, prompting furious debate among the nation's pundits and inviting laugh lines from late-night personalities. But while Brewer and fellow anti-immigrant demagogues dominated the headlines, the truth was that Arizona was also home to a resilient base of progressive and liberal leaders who had worked tirelessly to rescue the state from radical right-wing interlopers, political carpetbaggers, and corporate powers over the past century.

If anything, the state's cycles of history had taught "the other Arizona" one lesson: at a certain point, the extremists will overreach and serve as the catalyst for their own demise.

Nearly a century ago, Arizona's first governor, George W. P. Hunt, warned his fellow Arizonans that a different kind of national showdown was taking place in their state—one that might even resonate more today with the vast majority of Americans than Arizona's spells over immigration. "The working class, plus the professional class, represent 99 percent," Hunt said in 1916. "The remaining 1 percent is represented by those who make a business of employing capital." Made from a copper mining camp in rural Arizona, Hunt's admonition riled Wall Street as much as Occupy Wall Street and other recent uprisings have reframed the national debate over corporate influence in contemporary times. As Hunt put it, "It will be a happy day for the nation when the corporations shall be excluded from political activity and vast accumulations of capital cannot be employed in an attempt to control government."

Long before Hunt and his labor shock troops ushered in one of the nation's most progressive state constitutions in 1912, the clash over Arizona's vast natural resources, its native and immigrant labor ranks, and its rooted inhabitants and carpetbagging business interests had not only placed the border region on the front lines of American politics but also helped force our nation to come to grips with its fundamental commitment to civil rights and democracy. It had hardly been a hundred years of solitude.

"It's about raw political power now," Grijalva told me in his Tucson office, nearly a century after Hunt's pioneering clash with fringe politicians on the bankroll of corporate interests. Cupping his hands around a walrus mustache similar to the one that had made Hunt famous, Grijalva let out a sigh and then went on. "The attitude is, I'll take you over the cliff if I have to, unless I get my way."

Grijalva, chair of the House Progressive Caucus, was referring to the Republican showdown on the debt ceiling crisis in the summer of 2011, which compelled his colleague Gabby Giffords to make a breakthrough return for a vote on the floor of Congress. Grijalva had taken a leading role in holding President

Obama and the Tea Party–beholden Republicans accountable for their intractable demands. His leadership had transformed the Progressive Caucus from a symbol to a force to be reckoned with. With legacy programs like Medicare, Medicaid, and Social Security (along with other "bedrock pillars of the American success story") placed at risk for the sake of a "manufactured crisis," Grijalva appeared on national networks and called on the president to lift the debt ceiling and not bow to a handful of "unappeasable right-wing radicals."

Grijalva knew all too well that a similar upheaval was brewing on the home front.

The veteran Tucson politician and activist was no stranger to such extremist power plays, especially when it came to Arizona. And no one had taken it on the chin—both locally and in the national media—like Grijalva, whose frank, no-nonsense talk and "Pancho Villa mustache" had served as a convenient target.

"I'm wondering if we look at the map of Congressman Grijalva's congressional district, if we haven't already ceded that component of Arizona to Mexico, judging by the voice that comes out of him," Iowa Congressman Steve King told Fox News in the aftermath of the SB 1070 signing. "He's advocating for Mexico rather than the United States and against the rule of law, which is one of the central pillars of American exceptionalism."

"Our state has always had an independent streak," Grijalva said. "Conservatism is not the issue—national leadership has come out of this state for decades. But we were used to conservatives like Barry Goldwater: blunt, libertarian, hawkish, but not punitive. Now we have this punitive strain. That's the one that began to transform Arizona. And it's an aberration. A lot of us didn't notice that things were beginning to change and we were becoming a petri dish for a lot of national interests to come into Arizona and use the state as an experimental ground."

I had first met Grijalva as a high school student more than three decades ago, when I did an internship with a fellow Pima County supervisor. The mustache had grayed, but his frank demeanor and determined energy had always seemed emblematic of Tucson's rooted Latino community, which was forever adapting to and fending off the changing politics of the transient region. The son of a migrant worker, Grijalva had cut his political teeth in the Chicano movement in Tucson in the late 1960s and '70s; by 1974, he had made history by winning a seat on the school board. Following a stint as a county supervisor, Mr. Grijalva went to Washington in 2002 after legendary Democratic Representative Morris K. Udall (who was beset with Parkinson's disease) retired, and new southern Arizona congressional seats fell into play.

If only Udall and Goldwater were still around to dress down the Tea Party today. In an often-told story of the two towering icons and their mutual distaste for fundamentalist strangleholds on politics, both men were disgusted by the campaign of right-wing Moral Majority leader Jerry Falwell to halt the nomination of Arizona judge Sandra Day O'Connor to the US Supreme Court in 1981. Senator Goldwater, "Mr. Conservative" himself, announced that every Christian should line up and "kick Falwell in the ass." To which Udall replied, "That's a good idea, but it wouldn't accomplish anything because Falwell is a good Christian and he would simply turn the other cheek."

If only such unsparing humor could return to Arizona.

The other Arizona. Not that the media gave it much more than fleeting attention—or an occasional shout-out to Grijalva, who, despite his growing clout on Capitol Hill as one of the most respected progressive voices in Congress, could barely keep up with the 24/7 barrage of TV appearances and media obsession over Arizona's bottomless pit of right-wing talking heads, from Pearce, Brewer, Arpaio, and Horne to a booming rogue's gallery of legislators and their daily gaffes and scandals.

The competition was stiff. State Senator Sylvia Allen got the "world's worst person" ball rolling in 2009 when she mocked concerns over the safety of uranium mining, especially considering her claim that the "world was six thousand years old" and no harm had been done in the preregulatory dinosaur age. State Senator Lori Klein simply wanted to make a point about Arizona's wondrous gun rights when she pulled out her raspberry-pink .380 Ruger and drew a bead on the chest of a Latino reporter in 2011, and she told national TV that Republican presidential contender Herman Cain had wrongly been accused of sexual harassment because he had never bothered her and she was an attractive woman. Only months before, the former majority leader in the State Senate, Scott Bundgaard, made national news when he invoked his legislator's right to immunity when he hit his ex-girlfriend in an altercation on the side of a Phoenix highway. This wasn't quite as funny as when State Senate Appropriations Committee Chair Don Shooter draped himself in a serape and sombrero, with a half-empty bottle of tequila in hand, as the Arizona legislature voted down the extension of federally funded jobless benefits.

In the summer of 2011, in one of the most important blows to campaign finance reform in the nation, hardly any media took much notice when the US Supreme Court struck down Arizona's progressive Clean Election program, which had allotted campaign dollars for state candidates.

The battle to transcend the headline-grabbing exploits of the right wing in Arizona proved to be a formidable task for Arizona's liberal ranks. But it also marked the beginning of a movement by social-media-savvy Latino youth, increasing ranks of retiring liberal baby boomers and a revived progressive community to tell their side of Arizona's story through blogs, video productions, and exploding social networks on Facebook. In the aftermath of SB 1070 and Giffords's shooting, in fact, the nation was reintroduced to a truer reflection of the borderlands' deeply rooted multicultural and progressive politics—not the worst but the best the state had to offer.

But would the media go beyond the sensational clips of the state as a bastion of gun-toting, racist, and hate-filled Tea Partiers and secessionists?

Funny enough, one story the media did cover widely was largely a political prank. Galvanized by the national outcry over SB 1070, the "Baja Arizona" movement emerged in the spring of 2011 to "establish a new state in Southern Arizona free of the un-American, unconstitutional machinations of the Arizona legislature and to restore our region's credibility as a place welcoming to others, open to commerce, and friendly to its neighbors."

The insurgents scored a sizable amount of TV time for their cause—in essence, to give Brewer, Pearce, and Arpaio a taste of their own absurdity. "Forget calls for unity and common ground," NBC News reported. "The former Democratic Party chairman for Pima County is so fed up with Arizona's conservative politics that he wants the county to secede and form a fifty-first state in southern Arizona." Reporting from a gathering at a bar in Tucson, *The Economist* even attempted to provide a historical context for the public relations revolt. "This idea of Baja Arizona is not new," the British magazine noted. "Some trace it back to the Gadsden Purchase of 1854, when America bought from Mexico a strip of land south of the Gila River that was not included in the earlier cession after the Mexican-American war. More recently,

the Midwestern snowbirds and others who flooded into Arizona mainly settled in Maricopa, making it politically dominant and distinct."

Former Democratic Party chair Paul Eckerstrom managed to get in the last
word on a coveted NPR interview: "If we do this vote, at least we can send a
message not only to the state legislature but also to the rest of the nation to
tell the rest of the nation that not everybody in Arizona is crazy."

In that respect, Grijalva—and a handful of other veteran activists, commentators, journalists, and Democrats—became the de facto spokespeople
for "the other Arizona," as a new era of activists and political leaders began to
take the lead in a post–SB 1070 Arizona and speak out against the state's increasingly strident rhetoric, civil rights violations, and anti-immigrant policies, and bravely confront the seemingly invincible stranglehold of power by
Pearce, Brewer, and Horne in the State Capitol; rogue law enforcement agents
like Sheriff Arpaio in the streets; and Tea Party extremists and interlopers on
the airwaves.

"When Gabby was shot," Grijalva said in his office, "there was this sense
we were under siege. And it gave in to a painful pause, which also gave folks
time to come together. We said to ourselves, We can't be afraid of this."

Grijalva moved his chair closer to the table. "The American Dream will be
defined by a combination of the deeply rooted and newcomers, but not at the
expense of people who have been here. You just can't come into a place that
has deep historical roots and try to craft it into a Midwestern town or a California suburb or an Eastern city. You can't just treat Mexicans as hired help."

In the end, Grijalva felt laws like SB 1070 and the anti–Ethnic Studies HB
2281 had brought the issue of race and racism "front and center" to the nation.
"It forced our state to deal with racism, which no one wants to deal with. But
it also gave us the chance to tell the untold story of immigration and the benefits it has on the nation."

By extending tolerance and recognition of the state's native Mexican heritage and immigrant communities, Grijalva honored a local tradition that
stretched back centuries, predating the state's inception and even territorial
history.

In a land that had been continually inhabited by indigenous people for centuries and now includes twenty-two sovereign Indian reservations, the first
non-native (illegal immigrant) to enter Arizona was an African Moor scout

and slave—most likely a Muslim—who led the first Spanish expedition in the 1530s. The commander who founded the Tucson presidio in 1775 on behalf of the Spanish Crown had been an Irish immigrant. Historians often hailed Charles Poston, a Renaissance man and Kentuckian who sided with Lincoln and the Union, as "the father of Arizona." Poston was arguably the first founder of an "American" community in the territory; his nearly utopian Tubac mining settlement was established in the 1850s as a place with "no law but love," and peopled with immigrants from around the world. When a brigade of Texan Confederates occupied Tucson in 1862, a singular Mexican immigrant merchant held up the honor of the American Union.

Decades later, as the territory of Arizona grappled with statehood, it took Mexican American and immigrant copper miners to inspire the labor forces that ensured passage of one of the nation's most progressive state constitutions—even as they were left out of it. Half a century later, Arizona native Cesar Chavez led the United Farm Workers in one of the most important civil rights movements in the country. Fellow Arizonan Lalo Guerrero, the "father of Chicano music," would provide much of its pop culture soundtrack. In the 1980s, Tucson became the center of a national sanctuary movement to provide refuge for undocumented immigrants fleeing the US-funded wars in El Salvador and Guatemala.

In modern times, while Arizona's woodpile certainly didn't lack for a supply of corrupt politicians and impeached governors, its statewide politics were largely shaped by centrist Democratic governors (including, in recent years, Bruce Babbitt and Janet Napolitano) and common-sense Western conservatives like Paul Jones Fannin and Ernest McFarland. In the mid-twentieth century, Udall, a liberal giant who served thirty years in the House and became one of the nation's most powerful environmental advocates, embodied the state's progressive yet independent Western spirit. (Udall left a political legacy of his own. His son Mark is a senator from Colorado, and his nephew Tom is a senator representing New Mexico.)

Although Udall called himself a "one-eyed Mormon Democrat from conservative Arizona," the conservatives in his era had little in common with today's extreme right-wing political leaders in Phoenix. I cut my political teeth with Udall in 1981, as a seventeen-year-old intern on Capitol Hill, and I will never forget our conversations in Washington, DC, over his defiance of liberal

Democrats with his opposition to gun control. Udall, who waged an unsuccessful presidential bid in 1976, told a Harvard crowd during his campaign, "I don't claim total courage; I don't claim total wisdom."

"The political landscape had shifted such that the word 'conservative' was meaningless today in Arizona," Arizona author and historian Gregory McNamee told me in the days after Giffords's shooting. "Barry Goldwater, Fannin, McFarland—those were conservatives. And although they believed in a kind of small government, they were not stingy or shy of putting government to work to do social good," McNamee added. "McFarland, for example, had a major role in getting the GI Bill through. Those people look like progressives today, and their GOP descendants would scorn them as liberals. Today's GOP descendants are not conservative or anything of the sort, but instead right-wing extremists. There's a big difference between conservative and right-wing radicals."

With the territory of Arizona still two years away from its birth, President Abraham Lincoln had warned the nation about a "sugar-coated" rebellion brewing in the South and the "farcical pretence of taking their State out of the Union" in 1861. Such a sentiment had now emerged among a new generation of Latinos and the growing ranks of allies and longtime Arizonans fed up with the Tea Party–led state blustering.

Just how far out of the union were today's right-wing extremists in Arizona?

When a federal judge struck down critical parts of SB 1070, namely the obligatory police check of immigration status, and the Ninth Circuit Court of Appeals upheld the decision, Pearce, Horne, and Brewer's fledgling administration recognized their historic opportunity to take that question—and their states' rights battle against the Obama administration—to the US Supreme Court in the spring of 2012: *Arizona v. United States.*

In its claim that Arizona, under the framework of SB 1070, "seeks to interpose its own judgments on those sensitive subjects," namely national security, law enforcement, foreign policy, and the rights of law-abiding citizens and aliens, the Obama administration's brief before the Supreme Court subtly recalled the states' rights rebellion in Lincoln's era. "The word 'interpose' is a yellow flag in the history of state and federal relations," the *New York Times* told its readers on April 24, 2012, the eve of the Supreme Court hearing. "The southern states claimed a right of 'interposition' as a basis for secession before the Civil War, and they resurrected the idea in the 1950s."

Alongside that historic court date, another battle was playing out in the national court of public opinion.

Arizona was no longer alone. Tens of states, hundreds of city councils, thousands of schools and public facilities, and untold millions of bloggers, readers, businesses, and consumers who dealt daily with the reality of immigration and immigrants, and civil rights and racial profiling, attempted to make sense of a 250-year-old migratory tradition that had emerged in Arizona as the final showdown—or show—over who has the right to the American Dream.

There was just one unforeseen wrinkle to Arizona's extremist strategy.

Though large-scale protests against SB 1070 had once lined the capital streets with more than a hundred thousand ralliers and then faltered, Pearce, Brewer, Arpaio, and Horne had no idea that their actions would give rise to a game-changing shift in Latino activism and electoral involvement, newfound alliances and civil rights movements, and to the rebirth of a progressive tradition of activism, to reclaim the state from its extremist interlopers—or, rather, to bring Arizona back as a state in the union.

The Tucson Citizen, February 14, 1912.
(Photo courtesy of David A. Morales.)

CHAPTER TWO

TO BE OR
NOT TO BE A STATE

Americans are made up from every nationality except Mexicans. Germans, Italians, French, and all nationalities are called Americans.

SENATOR ALBERT BEVERIDGE,
DISCUSSING ARIZONA STATEHOOD IN 1902

IT HUMILIATES OUR PRIDE

Kicking up dirt-floor passion on a brisk December day in 1905, the crowd packed the territorial fairgrounds in Phoenix as if it were a rodeo. More than three thousand bona fide citizens stood in line, most of them brought in by train, courtesy of the cheap railroad lobby that steered their cause and bankrolled their political leaders. Their cause was clear: Arizonans didn't want to become a state in the union, not so long as their fate would be combined with neighboring New Mexico. It was not an issue of allegiance to the United States; it was an issue of allegiance as a certain entity.

"The objection by the people of Arizona, 95 percent of whom are Americans, to the probability of the control of public affairs by people of a different race, many of whom do not speak the English language, and who outnumber the people of Arizona two to one."

So began their resolution. A stout man raised a megaphone to his lips. The resolution against jointure was read, and as he came to the final lines the grandstand rose as one—or 98 percent. "Arizona's population is distinctly American, composed of people from all parts of the United States and the best type of immigrants from other countries." New Mexico, on the other hand, included "centers of population" where the native people were of "Spanish descent," rendering "decided racial differences between the people of Arizona."

The resolution numerated Arizona's reasons to remain out of the union: "The radical and irreconcilable difference in laws, legal customs—in Arizona, all jurors were obliged to speak and understand English. Unlike New Mexico, that had no limitations on citizen participation in their judicial system, territorial Arizona steadfastly defended its rules: No interpreters were allowed in the courtroom; Arizona's courts are conducted entirely in English."

For the assembled crowd, history was an additional witness to their cause; Arizona pioneers had "wrested" the land "from the control of the savage Apache," and they were redeeming the great natural resources from the deserts and mountains. They had earned the right to be on their own. (Indeed, the "people of Arizona" seemingly overlooked Native Americans altogether; they were not and could not become citizens.)

In many respects, Arizonans in 1905 saw themselves in the tradition of the original Tea Partiers, a self-professed "population that is intelligent, patriotic, and sincerely devoted to the Constitution and the principles of liberty as set forth in the Declaration of Independence—the peers of any people under the flag," ready to throw off the yoke of tyrannical man's dominion.

In this case: the tyranny by Congress and its intent to place Arizona into joint statehood with New Mexico.

"Arizona is not asking Congress for statehood," the defiant residents stated, jutting out their chins in search of Eastern affront. "She is asking only to be left alone with an opportunity to work out her own destiny within her own boundaries and with her well-organized American institutions. Inspired by those courageous American ideals which have made the winning of the West possible, the people of Arizona have no fear of the future."

Ever since Arizona was created as a territory in 1863, its residents had desperately wanted to ask Congress for statehood. Over the next three decades the discussion for statehood may have simmered on the back burner in Washington, DC, but it burned in the small but growing pioneer settlements. In 1891, when the territory sought to "blaze forth a new star in the galaxy of States," its display of American patriotism still fell short of the doubts over the true "Americanization" of Arizona's residents.

To be sure, in the 1890s, this was not simply an issue of the "Americanization" of Mexicans and Mexican immigrants. In fact, it was more of a question about the territory's large population of Mormons, whose outlawed tradition of polygamy lingered in the minds of outside observers and Eastern politicians.

Such a sentiment, or the lack of an "enabling act," didn't stop a group of Arizona boosters from holding their own "Constitution Convention" in Phoenix in 1891. In attempt to assuage concerns over Mormon encroachment from Utah, they incorporated a loyalty oath. The rest of the framework for statehood was equally brash, if not as ambitious and defiant. Silver would be the legal tender, contrary to national policy, and "all natural streams and lakes within the boundaries" of Arizona would become property of the state. Lotteries (a tradition in the Mexican communities) would be banned, and gambling (the domain of the Anglos) would remain legal.

"Some of the extremists and fanatics who succeeded in placing an anti-Mormon test oath on the statute books of Arizona," wrote the *Deseret Weekly* Mormon newspaper in Salt Lake City, "are moving in the same un-American direction again."

It didn't matter. Statehood was shot down. But it didn't stop another convention two years later. All in vain.

Far from a home for lone cowboys on the range, by the 1890s Arizona territory was the dominion of absentee corporations, a vassal colony of natural resources divvied up by the barons of the Southern Pacific and Santa Fe railroads and the copper industry. Not that this was any secret: as Yolanda LaCagnina wrote in her history of Arizona's struggle for statehood, "Corporations controlled the legislature." Company representatives fraudulently tampered with elections, bribed the territorial politicians, and kept any legislative initiatives in check—especially in the realm of taxes—and even had a hand in the appointment of federal judges. One copper company "fixer" was known as "the Corruption Bureau of Phoenix."

Arizona Senator Barry Goldwater once joked about the appointment of the military hero and "pathfinder" John C. Fremont as governor. A failed railroad promoter, among other entrepreneurial disasters, Fremont had accepted the top position in Arizona in 1878, according to Goldwater, so that the "family fortune might be restored in mining speculations."

"One of the most potent arguments advanced against Arizona statehood by some congressional leaders at this time," LaCagnina surmised, "was the inability of the people to govern themselves wisely."

Although the lawlessness of Tombstone (the town too tough to die) may have beguiled the nation's readers with its chronicles of crime, it was corruption that dogged the territory's dreams of statehood—at least, according to critics in Congress. There was another sticking point: Arizona's undeniable Democratic majority threatened the Republican Party's control over Congress; there were plenty of reasons to avoid adding two more senators to the fray.

"Statehood has been denied to Arizona because of sectional prejudice, ignorance, imaginary partisan policy, and pure selfishness," charged territorial Governor Nathan Murphy in 1899. "The latter reason exists in the fact that our Eastern brethren are unwilling to divide legislative representation in Congress. They refuse to grant to their brothers, Americans of the West, who are their equal in every respect, the same privileges under the Constitution which they enjoy."

By the late 1890s, though, both the Democrats and Republicans included Arizona statehood in their national platforms.

But not everyone saw the benefit in statehood. Fearful of greater tax responsibilities—especially a bullion tax for the extraction industries—and more restrictive labor policies, the powerful absentee corporate interests staved off statehood as long as possible. One of Arizona's governors eventually noted that a Scottish mining firm operating in the territory paid more in taxes to the British Crown than to his own government.

The growing but still powerless workforce in Arizona understood this. "Laborers, farmers and small businessmen became convinced," LaCagnina wrote, "that only with the attainment of statehood would the mines and railroads pay their just share of taxes." Yet the move toward statehood slumped along at the pace of a tortoise crossing the Sonoran Desert.

Ironically, the corporate barons invested in Arizona found an ally in Senator Albert Beveridge, an Indiana Republican whose leadership over the Senate Committee on the Territories allowed him to lord over the fate of the West at the turn of the twentieth century with the omnipotence of a medieval authority.

Although he was a self-proclaimed "progressive" at heart, one who took up the crusade against child labor, and a Midwestern renegade who eventually broke with his Republican Party to join Theodore Roosevelt's third party, Beveridge was an unabashed imperialist who viewed the Western territories with contempt.

In his notable speech on the Senate floor in 1900, "In Support of an American Empire," he clarified his view that self-government "does not always mean self-government." It depended on who was doing the self-governing. "Self-government is no base and common thing to be bestowed on the merely audacious. It is the degree which crowns the graduate of liberty, not the name of liberty's infant class, who have not yet mastered the alphabet of freedom. Savage blood, Oriental blood, Malay blood, Spanish example—are these the elements of self-government?"

While his speech addressed the Philippines, Beveridge would have included Arizona in that alphabet of infants, especially when it came to American rights and citizenship:

> Mr. President, this question is deeper than any question of party politics; deeper than any question of the isolated policy of our country even; deeper even than any question of constitutional power. It is elemental. It is racial. God has not been preparing the English-speaking and Teutonic peoples for a thousand years for nothing but vain and idle self-contemplation and self-admiration. No! He has made us the master organizers of the world to establish system where chaos reigns. He has given us the spirit of progress to overwhelm the forces of reaction throughout the earth. He has made us adept in government that we may administer government among savage and senile peoples. Were

it not for such a force as this the world would relapse into barbarism and night.

In 1904, the debate over governing Beveridge's perceived savage and senile peoples reached a low point when Arizona once again dominated the national headlines. Outraged that a Catholic priest had allowed Irish orphans from New York City to be placed among Mexican American families in the copper mining settlements of Clifton-Morenci, armed vigilantes rounded up and abducted the children in an extraordinary act that the US Supreme Court eventually upheld as a legally required intervention. In a letter to the *New York Times* on October 31, 1904, Arizona resident Mariano Martinez challenged the underlying assumptions of the armed kidnapping in terms that still resonate today over who is truly "American":

> The heads of these Mexican families and their children were born and raised in Arizona under the American flag. They are able to write and speak both the Spanish and English languages, and they do not butcher it as do your so-called "Arizona Americans," who are composed of Swedes, Norwegians, Serbians, Canadians, and Dutch, who have been shipped from the old country to work our mines and make out of this portion of the United States a dumping ground. The majority of the "Arizona Americans" are not even entitled to cast a vote because they have not been in this country long enough. Probably the only claim you have to call them "Americans" is that they have blue eyes, red hair, a face full of freckles, and long feet. The "low-down" Mexicans whom you refer to [we didn't by the way] are nearly all native-born American citizens and voters, as the great register of Graham County will prove. They have absolute respect for law and order. They know that the United States has laws which must be respected, and that it is strong and able to enforce them, without having to resort to mob violence, like your so-called "Arizona Americans."
>
> My parents were born in this Territory. I was born and raised in Tucson, Arizona. I was educated in the public schools, and I always considered myself an American, though of Mexican parents. Since I have

read your editorial about the assault on the Sisters by the mobs of Clifton and Morenci, I have been wondering whether I have a right to call myself an American citizen and to vote the Democratic ticket next November or not. The heads of the Mexican families you refer to are in the same position as myself.

In the case of Arizona's fate, Beveridge had made a three-day tour of the proposed state earlier in 1902 in his capacity as head of the Territorial Committee, and was less than impressed when he found "desert and cactus instead of alfalfa fields and orange groves." As one prospector noted, Beveridge saw barren hills and insurmountable mountains, not the gold and silver and copper inside them. If anything, Beveridge dismissed Arizona as nothing more than a "mining camp."

Unlike the copper mining industrialists, Beveridge couldn't be bothered with the bounty of Arizona's natural resources. Its residents concerned him. Overwhelmed by the inferior Mexicans, in his eyes, the West was not civilized like the East. He made his point by combing the barrios in Tucson and Phoenix for "Mexican loafers" who did not speak "American," reminding his colleagues that English literacy was crucial for citizenship—and statehood.

Arizona's territorial delegate, Mark Smith, one of the biggest cheerleaders for statehood, blasted Beveridge for his hasty sojourn and for his obsession with "scouring the town to see whether some Mexicans could not be found who could not speak English."

Not that Smith was outraged over Beveridge's blatant racism; in Smith's mind, the Mexicans simply didn't matter enough to be counted.

But that outrage over regional discrimination dissipated when Beveridge forced Arizona cheerleaders to look in the mirror. In 1904, he introduced a bill for joint statehood with Arizona and New Mexico. Whether he viewed it as a compromise between Republican-leaning New Mexico and the Democratic stronghold of Arizona, Beveridge's solution to the ethnic concerns in the West was wedded to an apparent experiment in eugenics. Given that New Mexicans were "not of the blood and speech" of the rest of the country, he proposed joint statehood as a way to "Americanize the whole mass of population within these Territories." Sort of the blended family approach to statehood:

"Not Arizona the little, but Arizona the great; not Arizona the provincial, but Arizona the national; not Arizona the creature of a politician's device, but Arizona the child of the nation's wisdom."

That nugget of marital wisdom from Washington, DC, fell on the deaf ears of the political class behind the statehood measure, and the railroad and mining companies, who didn't simply fear that "union with the Territory of New Mexico would make property insecure and progress impossible in Arizona" but trembled at the thought of a Mexican American majority that could place greater tax burdens or labor restrictions.

Beveridge's curveball was a game-changer.

For the Arizona statehood movement and growing ranks of laborers, the desire to break free from the stranglehold of absentee corporations and their carpetbagging sycophants was suddenly derailed by fear of the New Mexicans. As one legislator in Prescott mused, Arizona was no longer "insane" about statehood.

Nonetheless, the Senate amended the joint statehood bill with the stipulation that it had to be accepted by people in the territory first. Hence the grand fiesta at the Phoenix fairgrounds in 1905. Casting off any statehood campaign, the Anti-Joint Statehood League became the only game in town.

The Arizona territorial legislature was ready with its answer about joint statehood: "We insist that such is without precedent in American history. It threatens to fasten upon us a government that would be neither of, by, nor for the people of Arizona. It humiliates our pride, violates our tradition and would subject us to the domination of another commonwealth of different traditions, customs and aspirations."

In essence: Arizonans were Americans, and New Mexicans were Mexicans, and if the Eastern members of Congress couldn't recognize that, then Arizona didn't want to be part of the United States.

It didn't take long for the officials to tally the votes on election day in November 1906: Arizona voters overwhelmingly opposed the measure—16,265 to 3,141—while their counterparts in New Mexico overwhelmingly supported it. (Of course, the number of Spanish-speaking Mexican Americans and immigrants in Arizona who were denied the chance to vote remained another issue.)

Not everyone was happy, especially Mexican and immigrant copper miners, who had already begun to agitate on behalf of the budding state.

THE OPENING GUN OF STATEHOOD: MEXICAN-MADE

If something happened to Arizona between the late 1890s and 1905 to debunk Beveridge's view of "Mexican loafers" and give rise to an anti-Mexican attitude that threatened to negate statehood ambition, one might look for clues in the mining camps of Clifton-Morenci in 1903.

Within forty-eight hours of a new eight-hour workday law, copper miners in Morenci walked out of the pits and launched a strike. Their demand: daily wages should not have been reduced from a ten-hour to an eight-hour day.

The new law was actually aimed at Mexican and immigrant labor, including large ranks of Italians. According to historian Joseph Park, the "rush to build feeder railroads into the copper districts" between 1900 and 1910 "and the resultant upturn in production brought thousands of Mexican workers into Arizona," tripling the number of immigrants from "the two preceding decades combined." In the process, the influx of lower-wage immigrant earners undercut the political clout and wages of Anglo miners. The first union (for Anglos), in fact, had emerged in the mining town of Globe in 1896, but it had yet to command much of a following or place in the political arena. Neither were these workers the leaders of the first labor walkout in Arizona. The future state's first and defining major labor rebellion was "Mexican made" in 1903, as pioneering historian Rodolfo Acuña noted, along with the critical involvement of Italian laborers and help from an assortment of "Dagoes, Bohunks, and foreigners of different kinds, but no whites at all," according to one labor organizer. Three thousand five hundred workers walked off the job.

Without any union representation, the Mexicans and Italians worked closely with *mutualista* societies, fraternal organizations that had emerged in many Mexican communities, such as Tucson, where the Alianza-Hispano-Americana had been founded in 1894 as the first national Latino organization to confront ethnic discrimination and "offer new hope, new courage, new expression, new faith to the people."

As unions like the Western Federation of Miners watched from the side-lines, the immigrant miners defied the copper company guards, and then stood up to the detachment of armed Arizona Rangers. President Theodore Roosevelt eventually sent in the US Cavalry—more than 230 soldiers—and National Guardsmen as reinforcements in what was emerging as the largest armed showdown in the West since the Apache wars. Reportedly armed, as well, the miners faced down a state of martial law.

In many respects, the uprising served as a wake-up call for the ambivalent unions, who viewed Mexican Americans, immigrants, and "contract" laborers in particular as a threat to Anglo laborers and wages. In truth, in most mining camps the Mexican laborers were paid half the wage of Anglo miners, which served as an effective strategy by the companies to debilitate any organizing efforts.

One Western Federation representative sent back a report from the Clifton-Morenci conflict: "There has always been a peculiar condition exist-ing at this camp, which up to the present has always made it particularly diffi-cult for the Western Federation of Miners to get a foothold, these conditions being that the company make [sic] a distinction between the wage of its dif-ferent employees on account of nationality."

The courageous Mexican-led strike in Morenci changed the dynamics for the union rep. The action not only inspired the unionists, but convinced them that it would be "beneficial, not only to our unorganized brothers, who are struggling for the principle we content for," to work together for the Western Federation of Miners.

Mother Nature had other thoughts. It was not the mighty US Cavalry or gun-slinging Arizona Rangers or even national union support that brought the strike to a head. A massive downpour and subsequent flood literally wiped out many of the hillside communities, and took fifty lives in the process. The strike was shattered by confusion and misery. Once the community recovered from the deluge, some of the strike leaders were arrested and imprisoned. The workers returned to the pits. They were broken, their strike in ruins, but they had clearly made Arizona and the nation aware of the far-reaching im-plications of their warning shot against the copper barons.

It also revealed to laborers—and their union representatives—the extent that absentee corporations and their lackeys in the territorial and federal governments would go to crush any rebellion. A famous photo of the Arizona Rangers at the mine became immortalized in the annals of history.

For historian Joseph Park, the strike was "the opening gun of a long series of skirmishes between labor and management with Mexican workers as a major issue." It also marked a new era of Anglo and Mexican cooperation and "a significant decline in anti-Mexicanism," though the issue of "alien labor" remained an insurmountable problem. Park notes: "In fact, really serious troubles were just beginning. Contract systems for alien Mexican labor were established during both World Wars and the government ultimately resigned itself to legalizing what it could not prohibit. The mines continued to be affected. For every empire built in Arizona upon high-grade ore, ten empires were built by men who discovered low-grade ores and a fortune in Mexican labor."

Although it would take more than a decade to see real unity among the miners, the strike in the Clifton-Morenci camps both strengthened and challenged a new era of critical labor activity. Whether the Anglo leaders wanted to acknowledge it or not, the labor movement had officially been launched in Arizona, and with it would come statehood.

THE PEOPLE OF ARIZONA UNDERSTAND THIS PERFECTLY WELL

Arizona's great defender was a fellow Westerner, Senator Robert Owen from Oklahoma, who held sway in an emotional filibuster speech for what seemed like an eternity to his colleagues in the spring of 1911. Owen was forthright, provocative, and convincing—but, in the end, not convincing enough.

Owen held up Arizona as an exemplar in an age when "hideous exposés of crime, of graft, of municipal knavery, of vice, and the other results of such government have become an appalling national calamity."

His charge transcended the issue of statehood. Once again, Arizona was in the forefront of a national discussion over who would control the American Dream and on what terms; and that discussion came down to Arizona's vision of a future untethered to the powerful sway of corporations, expressed through a seemingly radical new constitution.

For the Oklahoman, Arizona's constitution was the grand battle over the power of corporations, the captains of finance, what Owen termed "the commercial oligarchy" in the United States. With twenty states considering a special

recall amendment to their constitutions, the statehood of Arizona also became the litmus test for Congress.

Owen pounded the podium and declared that Arizona's fate was "an overwhelming issue throughout the United States," and then he admonished President William Taft not to rebuke the territory for merely "being progressive."

"The people of Arizona understand this perfectly well, and they are determined to protect their government against the corrupt processes that have
scandalized and now dominate so many States of the Union, and which so
strongly influence Congress itself." Owen recounted Arizona's role as a vassal
colony for corporate ventures: "Through corrupt practices, the public moneys,
the public lands, the public properties, have been invaded for private benefit."

There was only one solution for such a land of corruption, and it was contained in the Arizona constitution: the right to recall public officials would
"put the political boss and the political machine out of business; it has ended
private graft ... buying of votes, the coercing of votes. ... It has made legislative and administrative officers responsive to the public will." And such a right
became the crux of Arizona's acceptance as a state.

Even New Mexico was dragged back into the debate. Referring to that territory's "corporate-written" constitution, Owen explained that the difference
between Arizona and New Mexico transcended political parties or ethnic
conflict; it was a battle between "reactionary and retrogressive," no different
from the early revolutionary conflicts between Tories and Liberals. Between
a constitution to "promote corporate power and greed" and a constitution to
"promote the rights of men, of human liberty, and of human happiness."

Owen roared: "The real issue in this contest between Arizona and New
Mexico is whether we shall permit a State controlled by special interests to
be admitted and deny the admission of a State whose government is controlled by the people."

In the end, explaining why he refused to give up the floor and yield, Owen
did what any self-respecting senator of the day would do—he leaned on Abraham Lincoln's legacy: "I must stand with anybody that stands right."

What was right and what was politically possible were two different matters in 1911. With President Taft in the White House, Arizona's hopes for
statehood seemed as plausible as ever. In the summer of 1910, in fact, Taft
had authorized the Arizona Enabling Act, which provided the necessary

funds to convene a state gathering to draw up Arizona's constitution for ratification. Strangely enough, Taft had final veto authority over the makeup of the constitution.

The president forewarned the state seekers of that power on a trip to Phoenix: "If you want to be certain that I'll veto your constitution, just go ahead and put the judicial recall into it."

What Taft didn't realize, however, was that the right to recall public officials went beyond any desire for statehood. Instead, it marked the insurgent role of the labor movement in the territory and its entry as a power player in statehood politics. Since the Clifton-Morenci copper mine strike in 1903, subsequent uprisings had taken place in other mining camps in Arizona—and just across the border in Cananea, Mexico, in 1906—by Mexican, immigrant, and recently arrived Anglo miners, and had bolstered their resolve to use the statehood battle as a way of wresting control away from outside corporate interests. By the summer of 1910, unionized miners had joined with the trade and crafts unions (such as carpenters, blacksmiths, typographers, and railroad workers) and founded the Labor Party to agitate specifically for a more progressive state constitution.

Samuel Gompers, the legendary head of the American Federation of Labor, set the scene in Arizona: "For a generation Arizona has been at the mercy of Federal Judges, Governors, and office holders, appointed from Washington at the dictation of the railroads and mining interests. The people were helpless and knew it. They were mercilessly exploited by Big Business— literally *robbed*—(there is no other word), political corruption was an accepted thing; the corporations ruled and the development of the Territory was impeded. With the chance to make a constitution and gain self-government through Statehood the hour of opportunity struck for the people."

Far from being removed from the rest of the country, Arizona's labor movement served in the vanguard of the populist crusade of progressive Democrats like William Jennings Bryan, whose longtime tirades against the undue influence of railroad barons and corporations underlined his 1908 presidential campaign slogan—"Shall the People Rule," which could have been the theme of labor's battle over the making of Arizona's constitution.

While no towering labor or union leader emerged in Arizona, a plain-speaking banker, merchant, and territorial legislator from the mining camp of Globe reluctantly stepped forward to become a champion for labor and an unflappable opponent of industry meddling in the Constitutional Convention. Selected as president of the convention as a compromise between the Democrats and Republicans, George W. P. Hunt would go on to become the most important political figure in Arizona history.

Hunt first entered Arizona on foot as a teenager in 1881, tugging along a burro with his meager belongings and a desire to reinvent himself in the American West. His family had lost most of their farm and fortune in Missouri during the Civil War. Self-educated, tireless, and ambitious, Hunt did a stint in the mines and then worked his way up the merchant ladder in Globe until he became president of a mercantile company. But the businessman never lost contact with his fellow laborers. "Many an uncouth miner has words of wisdom to fall from his lips," he once mused.

Hardly radical, Hunt was elected as a Democrat to the territorial legislature in 1892, and quickly saw that "controlling influence" was in the hands of the railroads and the mining industries. "His defiance of money and the money interests," historian Frank Lockwood noted, "his detestation of snobbery and pretension, whether social or intellectual; his big-hearted humanity and his extraordinary intellectual shrewdness and political foresight, have made him the trust champion and advocate of the people and the scourge of the unjust, the dishonest, and the autocratic." Seemingly incorruptible, Hunt professed a brand of "enlightened industrialism" that sought to control but not derail the railroad and mining interests in Arizona. In an essay that would resonate a century later, he drew the dividing line over democracy:

> The same spirit of ruthless aggression which has crushed life and hope out of millions of lives in the factories, mills and mines of unhappier states, is gradually invading Arizona, calling upon the courage and determination of every citizen for the defence of human rights. It is, regrettably, a fact that the same small, but powerful, coterie of capitalists, which has wrought havoc among the workers of certain other states, which greedily forced wages downward to a minimum far below the point of subsistence, and which—not content with doing that—thrust several millions of children into unsanitary mills and factories—all for the glory of the almighty dollar—is undoubtedly laying its plans to gain control of every function of government in the state of Arizona.

It is right and just for every citizen, be he wealthy or be he poor, to take an active interest in public affairs, but the bounds of justice are transcended, and the rights of a free people are seriously menaced when corporations, as such, become compactly organized into political alliances for the influencing of legislation and the election of officials.

The Labor Party didn't hesitate in drawing up its laundry list of constitutional requirements: Among its twenty-seven main demands, the party ranked an eight-hour workday, women's suffrage, workmen's compensation, anti-corruption and fair banking practices (including the publishing of campaign contributions prior to elections), an industrial commission of inspectors, compulsory education, state-backed industries, an end to the abuse of injunctions (against labor strikes), and the outlawing of blacklists at the top of its progressive platform.

Topping the list, of course, was the right to hold an initiative, referendum, and recall of public officials. On the heels of its passing in the state constitutions of Oregon and Oklahoma—and being fiercely debated in state capitols across the country—the recall was seen as the benchmark for political accountability, especially among industry-friendly judges and politicians who had interfered in labor disputes.

In short, the recall provision stated: "Every public officer in the State of Arizona, holding an elective office, either by election or appointment, is subject to recall from such office by the qualified electors of the electoral district from which candidates are elected to such office. Such electoral district may include the whole State. Such number of said electors as shall equal twenty-five per centum of the number of votes cast at the last preceding general election for all of the candidates for the office held by such officer, may by petition, which shall be known as a Recall Petition, demand his recall."

"The working class, if it utilizes it, has the power to make this constitution to its own liking," declared a mining union representative from Bisbee. "And if it is properly drafted, our economic struggles of the future will be greatly simplified and our opportunities of bettering our conditions rendered much easier."

In an unprecedented campaign of union hall meetings, rallies, and effective pamphleteering, the Labor Party advocates framed the narrative of the constitutional debate in the largest mining towns—the de facto capitals of labor—and managed to get Democratic candidates to pledge to their platform. More than 80 percent of the delegates heading to the convention joined Hunt, a rotund and bald politician nicknamed "The Walrus" for his imposing mustache, in the pro-labor camp.

Not that the copper kings and their territorial sycophants planned to accept this takeover lightly. Hailing the "radical" and "socialist" agenda, the conservative *Arizona Republic* singled out the recall provision as "another nail, the longest and strongest of all," in the coffin of statehood.

Women's suffrage was one of the first planks to be discarded. An attempt to limit foreign-born workers to 20 percent of the workforce in hazardous (mining) occupations—a reminder of a brewing conflict between Anglo and Mexican and immigrant workers, despite joint ethnic labor gains in the mining camps—was also narrowly defeated. An English literacy test for voters—a holdover from the territorial legislature in 1909, even though the former governor had protested that the measure amounted to a "wholesale disenfranchisement of the respectable element of our Mexican population"—would eventually be deferred but made into law in 1912. Such a move, as Arizona historian Thomas Sheridan noted, "severely limited Mexican political power in Arizona."

Represented by a single Mexican American merchant from Tucson and not a labor representative, Mexican Americans and immigrant workers in the copper camps became a political casualty in the fallout over labor's bitter ethnic divide. "At the state constitutional convention in Phoenix on October 10, 1910," Acuña noted, "labor organizers exposed their true colors," winning Hunt over to their demand that "alien labor offers unfavorable competition."

But first the convention debate raged "with all the fury vested interests could carry against the progressives," Hunt recounted. Some Democrats joined the Republicans in denouncing the constitution as the foul play of a band of radicals.

William Jennings Bryan arrived in Tucson the night before the ratification vote and sought to ease concerns over the recall plank. "The Great Commoner" told Arizonans that the recall would be employed only in "extreme" and very select cases; one unjust removal, Bryan argued, "would result in the repeal of the provision." In an extraordinary outreach campaign, copies of the constitution were distributed across the territory, and each provision was explained to gatherings led by labor advocates.

On February 9, 1911, the convention ratified arguably the most progressive (and shortest) state constitution at the time by a three-to-one margin. "These things should commend it," the Labor Party declared, referring to the unabashedly radical planks, "to all those who believe with Lincoln that labor is superior to capital and that people are more important than property."

In light of the looming national battle over ratification, including the controversial recall amendment, Gompers placed Arizona within the historical legacy of the nation's forefathers:

> People who regard Arizona as excessively "radical" and look upon her new constitution as "a zoological garden of legislative freaks," as did President Taft, and then extol the courage and wisdom of the revolutionary fathers, either have no historic sense or lack the saving grace of humor. The fight in Arizona for a form of government to meet the needs of the twentieth century, and that of the fathers to gain economic and political freedom from Great Britain is, in essence, one and the same thing. If you have a picture of "Signing the Declaration" on your library walls, you should have a copy of the Arizona constitution on the shelves.

Indeed, one of Arizona's delegates declared their work "the greatest and grandest document since the Declaration of Independence." Unfortunately, President Taft and the US Congress did not agree with that assessment. "Washington sneered at the Initiative, sniffed at the Referendum, and had spasms over the Recall," wrote historian James Wright.

Featured again in the national headlines, Arizona's constitution and its recall provision highlighted the clash of interests between labor and industry within Congress and the nation. One Southern representative charged that Arizona's constitution was "socialism gone mad."

While Owen's emotional filibuster termed it the "progressive vs. the regressive" debate, the senator from Oklahoma placed statehood as a test of sovereign rights: "The people of Arizona have adopted a constitution which is intended to restore to the people of that State all of the powers of government and to put it out of the power of special interests."

Even former President Theodore Roosevelt was invoked; although he was reticent in his approval of the controversial provision, he had explained to an audience in Chicago that the "State of Massachusetts put into its constitution precisely that provision for the recall," in 1780.

The showdown over Arizona's statehood had reached an impasse in Congress. The debate endured over several months. President Taft's veto admonition remained a shadow of doubt. Hunt agreed to head a "Recall or Nothing" movement in Arizona, which threatened to give up statehood if the recall plank was removed. In the eyes of labor, the recall was the workingman's "declaration of independence" from the control of industry. In a defiant expression of the progressive forces in Congress, the "floor resolution" on behalf of Arizona was finally passed.

Taft called their bluff and vetoed the proposed resolution. In no uncertain terms, he lambasted the "pernicious" provision of the recall, "so destructive of independence in the judiciary, so likely to subject the rights of the individual to the possible tyranny of a popular majority."

Not all was lost. A new amendment was offered that removed the recall from the constitution but allowed for a subsequent special vote to reconsider the provision in a state election. In essence: Taft could sign Arizona's constitution without the recall, and then Arizonans could simply vote it back in. The amendment was rammed through the Senate and then the House. In a circuitous maneuver, both sides were able to claim victory.

"Once we are admitted to statehood," Hunt confirmed with his labor advocates, "we are free to amend the constitution and enact a recall." Such a situation, of course, was predicated on Hunt's election as the first governor in the state of Arizona. At the opening rally of his campaign, he declared, "If I am elected governor, I shall see to it that there will be no delay in invoking the recall." Hunt and his progressive Democrats swept the elections. The governor-elect declared that the recall amendment would be the legislature's first order of business.

On Valentine's Day in 1912, with the "moving pictures" camera rolling for the first time in American history in the White House, President Taft proclaimed the conditions had been met to accept Arizona as a "state into the Union on an equal footing." An official telegram from Washington, DC, arrived in Arizona at 10 a.m.; forty-eight sticks of dynamite were detonated for a celebration in the hills outside the new state's largest city, the copper mining town of Bisbee and nearby settlements.

Inaugurated as governor, Hunt oversaw a mile-long parade that marched along with patriotic tunes and ragtime airs. "Arizona is progressive," he told the crowd, "and Arizona is Democratic." He quickly outlined his plan for business, telling his listeners that "the dollar bill will not be placed above manhood, nor wealth above humanity." In a symbolic presence of the "progressive" movement, William Jennings Bryan stood nearby at Hunt's inauguration as the nation's representative.

Two months later, Senate Bill No. 1—an act to amend the state constitution, "as Adopted under Coercion," and return the right to recall public officials—passed without delay by both houses. It was approved by the Arizona voters in the fall election.

"Many statehood campaigns," noted the *Arizona Daily Star* in Tucson, "seemed hopeless," but in the end, Arizona had contributed to the education of "our neighbors of the East, regarding the resources of Arizona and the character of its people."

The definition of Arizona's character was about to be tested, as the hard-fought right to a recall—and its implications for Mexican American and immigrant laborers—would now apply in Arizona.

"MAN'S WIT IS NO MATCH FOR WOMAN'S IN POINT OF KEENNESS"

The role of women in the progressive movement in Arizona was inextricably linked to politics over labor and immigrant rights. To be sure, Governor Hunt framed suffrage as a "dangerous and radical thing" in the constitution proceedings, even if he personally supported its passage. It was not Arizona's lack of support for the women's plank, Hunt explained, but the political reality that Congress would not accept a state constitution that granted women voting rights.

Although women were forced to wait until after statehood, the agitation of the suffrage movement, not unlike the subsequent civil rights and Chicano movements, ensured their rightful place in society and placed Arizona in the vanguard of the struggle for women's rights. Indeed, four of the past five governors in Arizona have been women.

As Governor Hunt noted when he signed the bill granting women the right to vote, eight years before their female counterparts east of the Mississippi, his act was "a vindication of woman's struggle for enfranchisement." That enfranchisement fell short of being included in Arizona's constitution, but like the recall plank, it would be added to the state's law books within a year of the vote for statehood.

In a dramatic account of her work as head of the Arizona Women Suffrage Organization, Frances Willard Munds wagered that the campaign for suffrage in her state was "probably the most unique in history."

Munds, standing five feet tall, did not suffer literary fools gladly. The educated daughter of ranchers, the staunchly progressive wife of the Yavapai County sheriff, and the state's representative to the 1913 International Woman Suffrage Alliance in Budapest, Hungary, she confronted equivocating politicians and threatening police in her campaigns and chastised the East Coast magazines and novelists who depicted her beloved state as a backwater of civilization.

In fact, the territory of Arizona first considered a bill for women's voting rights in 1883, before Munds even headed up the suffrage movement. The bill provided that "every female person shall be entitled to vote at all elections, in the same manner in all respects, as made [male] persons are, or shall be, entitled to vote by the laws of the Territory." (Though it is undocumented, some historians suggest that there was an even earlier bill in 1881.) Introduced by Prescott legislator and business magnate Murat Masterson, the 1883 bill didn't fail because of conservative dismissal of women's rights but because of a far greater concern that the electoral demographics would shift dramatically to include the growing number of Mormon women (and plural wives).

With Munds at the helm, the largely Protestant suffrage campaign joined ranks with Mormon communities and managed to get a bill passed in 1903. Again fearing the potential impact of the Mormon vote on the still-emerging territory, Governor Alexander Brodie vetoed the bill—though he publicly justified his actions as a matter of constitutional concern.

Realizing that "the Labor Party would become the dominant Party in Arizona" and the "Democratic Party trimmed it sails to catch the breeze of popular sentiment," Munds fashioned an alliance with the copper miners' union, among other labor interests, but still failed to win a majority at the constitutional convention in 1911. They lost the vote 30–19.

The women's campaign did win a compromise with Hunt, forcing him to commit to a constitutional amendment, much like the recall plank, once statehood passed. "We commenced bombarding the governor with petitions and letters," Munds recalled. As one of his first acts as governor, Hunt introduced an amendment to give all citizens "of certain qualifications" the right to vote, regardless of sex. It failed by a single vote in the Senate.

Undeterred, Munds launched a campaign in the summer of 1912 to get suffrage on the ballot for a referendum vote. Women advocates were sent to the mining camps, where the older alliances with labor and Mexican rights groups were renewed, and suffrage speakers also addressed issues of education and living conditions; others campaigned in the Mormon settlements. Recognizing that women's rights transcended any political party, Munds also made the brilliant tactical move of playing the parties off each other for support, asking the Democrats and the Republicans—as well as the Socialist and Labor parties—to adopt a suffrage plank on their own platforms. She later wrote of her efforts to "beat the reactionaries who had gained control of the machinery."

"We had a battle royal," Munds declared, "but we won by the simple play of wit, which taught me that man's wit is no match for woman's in point of keenness."

When the votes were tallied on the fall day of the 1912 election, suffrage passed by a three-to-one margin across the state. More than 95 percent of labor, according to Munds, supported the suffragists' cause, including the largely Mexican copper camps; some of the largest voting blocs came in the Mormon communities. The suffrage movement had secured the support of much of the Mexican American community decades earlier; an 1893 editorial in the Tucson-based *El Fronterizo* newspaper championed the right of women to vote.

Nearly a decade before women would celebrate the Nineteenth Amendment, Munds praised Arizona's victory on the state's "noble and progressive manhood." Within two years, she was elected to the Arizona state legislature. Munds wrote:

> Arizona is still the Mecca toward which a certain class of writers of fiction turn their eyes, for her very history is interwoven with romantic

tales of Aztecs and Montezuma. The ambitious story-teller who longs
to write impossible stories of wild and woolly cowboys feels there is
still a land in which he can lay scenes conjured up by the morbid fan-
cies of his disordered brain, tales which are eagerly sought after by
many lovers of fiction. Few indeed are the writers who have come
among us and studied the people and the country and given a correct
amount of conditions.

As a rooted Arizonan, Munds simply dismissed the media depictions as
acts of ignorance. At her signing of SB 1070, Governor Jan Brewer exhibited
the same distrust of "outside" observers. Unlike Munds, Brewer forever reminded the media of her "twenty-eight years in public service," and expressed
thinly veiled paranoia about her critics' motives. She warned: "Some of those
people from outside our state have an interest in seeing us fail. They will wait
for a single slip-up, one mistake, and then they will work day and night to create headlines and get the face time they so desperately covet."

Munds traveled the state—and the world—to get some of those headlines
and face time. Failure was not an option to her.

THE FIRST RECALL

It took less than three years for Arizona to launch the first recall campaign of
a public official, and in the strange fate of politics, it targeted none other than
Governor Hunt. In 1915, the Phelps Dodge mining empire mounted a recall
drive in retaliation for Hunt's support for a mining strike that united Mexican, Anglo, and immigrant miners in the labor hotbed of Clifton-Morenci.
But in an even more twisted episode revealing the racial mores of the day—
something that exposed the contradictions that abounded in Arizona's mining
camps—the Copper King also took out its wrath on Hunt's earlier support
for a discriminatory 1914 law that cracked down on the company's reliance
on contract labor from Mexico.

With its own newspapers on the company payroll, the copper industry justified the recall effort because of Hunt's "wanton and reckless extravagance,"
condemning his involvement in a strike compromise that could have cooled
off a situation that looked like it was going to explode into unimaginable vi-

olence. In September 1915, miners in Clifton-Morenci called for a strike. Without the support of the Western Federation of Miners, which claimed to lack funds, thousands of mostly Mexican American, immigrant, and Yaqui workers walked out of the pits of the Phelps Dodge subsidiary. They demanded better working conditions and uniform pay for Mexicans and immigrants, who typically received half the wages of Anglo workers. In a nearby mining camp, for example, Anglo miners earned a minimum of $3.50 underground, while the Clifton-Morenci miners pulled in as little as $1.62 a day.

"Everyone knows that the Mexican situation as it affects this country is economic as well as military," *The Survey* magazine wrote in 1916.

> It is not so widely known that the economic question relates to Mexican labor in the United States as well as to American capital in Mexico. There were 382,000 Mexicans on this side of border in 1910, the overwhelming majority of whom were in the Southwest, and most of whom were laborers, everywhere they have been willing to work for less than that which the American would accept. It was a matter of more than ordinary interest, therefore, when the copper miners in the Clifton-Morenci district of southern Arizona went on strike last fall, for most of them were Mexicans, who had for years been working for a lower wage than that paid in the other sections of the state.

Despite his earlier support for the anti-immigrant Alien Labor Act, Hunt appeared sympathetic to the plight of the immigrant laborer: "The poor Mexican" was "working for a pittance" in a state of feudalism. He declared that "no self-respecting" miner would "submit to such humiliating conditions." Yet less than a year before, Hunt had sided with the overwhelming majority of Arizona voters in resurrecting an old bill that called for limiting immigrant labor to 20 percent of the mining workforce. It was one of the more ignoble moments in his long political career. Yielding to the initiative cherished by the Anglo miners from his town of Globe, Hunt kowtowed to the so-called "80 percent law" as "the will of the people of this state," and even instructed his attorney general to fight its appeal all the way to the Supreme Court. The law was quickly struck down by the federal courts in 1915 as a violation of the Fourteenth Amendment: "The right to work for a living in the common occupations of the community is of the very essence of the personal freedom and opportunity that it was the purpose of the [14th] Amendment to secure."

Hunt fared better on the side of the striking miners in Clifton-Morenci, albeit with another twist. With the nation watching his moves, fearful of a repeat of the massacre in a Ludlow, Colorado, coal camp by National Guardsmen in 1914, Hunt sent in the state militia to protect the strikers. In an extraordinary reversal of state policy in that period, Hunt ordered his soldiers to prevent anyone from breaking the strike.

The governor justified his move as preventing the company's "invitation to violence," which "almost surely presages bloodshed and other disastrous consequences." When the company representatives fled the state in a fit of feigned terror, Hunt dismissed their efforts as theatrics and demanded that the company negotiate in good faith.

Within a few months, Hunt and a federal mediator had hammered out a compromise that overruled any union organizing, but met the demands of the strikers:

> The elimination so far as possible of all racial distinctions: a minimum wage equal to that paid in the best mining camps of Arizona; a general advance of fully 20 per cent in wages to about 80 per cent of the workmen; the withdrawal of the companies' objections to union organization; the re-employment of former strikers without discrimination, except in a few isolated cases of an unusual nature; the payment of better wages to all skilled workmen; the perfecting of an arrangement whereby differences arising between employers and employees will be discussed in conference monthly by representatives of both sides.

The national press championed Hunt's middle-road endeavor. *The New Republic* commended Hunt for reversing the towering demands of "a handful of owners in New York, Boston and Edinburgh," who "can impose upon ten or fifteen thousand men or women the choice between surrendering their liberties or starving." Labor leaders supported his unprecedented embargo on strikebreakers. Even Mother Jones, the legendary socialist and miner's angel, couldn't resist naming it one of the "most remarkable strikes in the history of the American labor movement."

She also drew a parallel between the state's recent battle to become part of the Union and its laborers' drive for their own union in the mining camps: "I know that every man and woman here is a loyal member of the union. I refer to the United States, the union of all states. I ask then; if in union, there is strength for our nation, would there not be for labor?"

In an address to labor advocates, Hunt insisted his action had "no parallel in the industrial history of the United States," and didn't hesitate to praise his achievement, as the "eyes of a whole nation were witnessing" this "championship of human rights." He added: "It is doubtful whether you fully realize the magnitude and far-reaching importance of the precedent which you have set for the workers of the world's greatest country."

Phelps Dodge dismissed the accolades as "half-baked philosophy from the highbrows" and was incensed by the precedence. Hunt's "greatest offense," as one labor magazine wrote, was refusing "to help the mine owners crush the strike by the use of the 'army of defense.'"

Citing his utter "incompetence" and actions of "class hatred and divisions," which had brought the town to "near anarchy," the copper company representatives pursued their recall campaign with the fervor of true believers. As part of their "education" campaign on Hunt's motives, *Collier's Weekly* noted, "Incidents harmless in themselves were made to appear grave. Lying half-truths were told. Facts were distorted. False statements were printed—in short, the Governor's prison policy was not only reviewed critically, but its results were so misrepresented that many of the sincere and well-meaning people of Arizona, reading these horrible tales and having no means of knowing their falsity, could not but be of the opinion that the Governor was the soft-hearted sentimentalist his critics made him out to be."

It didn't work. The new Arizonan electorate refused to buy the corporate propaganda. The recall petitions remained blank. Within a couple of months, when the recall campaign failed to collect enough signatures, the industry barons shifted to a "big drive" against Hunt's reelection in 1916. "Rockefeller and other interests are doing in Arizona what was their practice in Colorado, New Mexico and other States in the West," wrote the *Locomotive Firemen's* magazine. "It was understood that the 'Wall Street' of the mining interests were dumping vast amounts of money into the State of Arizona with which to corrupt the election and, as usual, in addition to hiring henchmen the newspapers were pressed into service through means that are nothing less than bribery. A certain detective agency took up a news dispensing feature, and letters were sent to the newspapers in the State asking for their advertising rates as will be shown in the following correspondence reproduced from a Phoenix paper."

Concerned about Hunt's election campaign, Mother Jones returned the favor and came to Arizona to campaign for the "greatest governor that the country has ever produced."

Her profanity-laced influence, though, came up short—out of fifty-five thousand votes cast in the 1916 gubernatorial election, Hunt lost by thirty votes in an election marred by apparent fraud and voter manipulation. Thrown out of office by the copper industry, the labor champion had to wait more than a year before a proper recount of the ballots restored his seat.

In the meantime, the combined forces of corporate power and anti-immigrant fervor set in motion a power play that irremediably altered the progressive state—and remains a cautionary reminder that SB 1070 was not the first time Arizonans took punitive immigration laws and extreme measures into their own hands. In the copper town of Bisbee, a critical hub in the nation's soon-to-be war effort, Arizona would once again serve as the front line in a larger American showdown over commerce, immigration hysteria, and civil rights.

BISBEE DEPORTATION: A HOAX PURE AND SIMPLE

In the spring of 1917, Cochise County Sheriff Harry Wheeler desperately wanted to be sent to the front lines of World War I. He wired the governor; he wrote to the president of the United States. But an old cavalry injury kept him from passing a medical exam.

Wheeler got his war—except the front line was on the US-Mexico border, in the biggest city of Arizona at the time: Bisbee and surrounding areas.

At dawn on July 17, 1917, Wheeler and his squadron of two thousand deputized vigilantes launched one of the most audacious captures of "enemy forces" on American soil. Going door-to-door in the hillside neighborhoods of Bisbee, Wheeler instructed his armed troops to ask a single question: "Are you an American, or are you not?" The sheriff carried out his roundup under

the guise of defending the nation from an impending attack by German sympathizers and their so-called Mexican allies during World War I.

Among the many waves of immigrant crackdowns and punitive deportation measures over the past century, the hysteria behind the deportation of
striking copper miners in Bisbee might be one of the most chillingly similar
events to today's anti-immigrant measures.

"In 1917," wrote historian Katherine Benton-Cohen, author of *Borderline
Americans: Racial Division and Labor War in the Arizona Borderlands*, "concerns over revolutionary violence and contempt for immigrant workers, combined with anti-union sentiments, resulted in one of the largest violations of
civil liberties in American history—the Bisbee Deportation." In an essay on
historical comparisons, she noted:

> Three weeks into a copper mining strike in the town of Bisbee, Ari-
> zona, just eight miles from the border, over one thousand temporary,
> shotgun-wielding "deputies" swarmed the streets. They rounded up
> 1,200 suspected strikers—ninety percent of them immigrants from
> three dozen countries. Two men, one on each side, were killed. The
> rest of the captives were loaded into the boxcars of a mining-company
> railroad and shipped nearly 200 miles into the New Mexico desert,
> where they were rescued by a nearby army camp. The incident—like
> Arizona's recent immigration law—made front-page news across the
> country and prompted national debates about civil liberties and federal
> vs. local police power.

Phelps Dodge engineered the Bisbee deportation as a clear response to the
triumph of Mexican laborers in Clifton-Morenci, and as a brazen affront to
Hunt's dethroned governorship and general law and order in Arizona. Not
only in Bisbee. Days before Wheeler's roundup, Phelps Dodge had orchestrated a similar deportation of striking miners in Jerome, in northern Arizona.
Appointed by President Woodrow Wilson to serve as a mediator, Hunt was
dealing with another strike in Globe at the same time, fending off Phelps
Dodge–generated rumors that his compromising ways marked him as a supporter of the radical International Workers of the World.

Once again challenging the dual-wage system, Mexican miners had joined the Wobbly strike in Bisbee during the great copper rush fueling the needs of World War I. The rest of the Wobbly demands dealt with increasing workplace safety, abolishing the physical examination, and incorporating a flat daily wage. For the first two weeks, the strike drew out nearly 80 percent of the workforce, dealing a blow to copper production.

By July, the copper bosses, refusing to negotiate with "rattlesnakes," had taken measures to halt the strike into their own hands. They singled out immigrants, Mexican Americans, and radicals. The copper industry boosters were unequivocal in their need to protect copper production—and profits. In a later meeting with President Wilson, whose college roommate was the vice president of Phelps Dodge, members of the Citizens Protective League from Bisbee first discussed "the subject of the price of copper and its relation to our scale of wages in force," before the subject ever "drifted" toward the deportation.

When Hunt was informed that the deportation would affect his negotiations in Globe, he approached the commander of the National Guard and demonstrated his "credentials" as a representative of President Wilson. Hunt threw down the gauntlet and sent the Guard colonel a stinging message for the three copper company representatives in Globe: "There will be no deportation from this community."

Within days, Hunt traveled to Columbus, New Mexico, to make a report to the president on the Bisbee deportation. He was outraged, even scandalized. As news of the deportation eventually filtered into the national media, the brutal act by the loose-cannon sheriff and the copper company's henchmen rattled Hunt's belief in democracy in Arizona. He telegraphed Wilson to say that the deportation had been "so un-American, so autocratic," that he felt compelled to insist on the "constitutional rights and a resumption of American justice in this State."

After spending five days in the miners' refugee camp, Hunt concluded that "there was not to be found the slightest evidence of German influence or the work of German money. . . . That charge, emanating from the defenders of the deportation, I am satisfied, was a hoax pure and simple."

Although Wilson failed to follow through on Hunt's request to repatriate the deportees, he ordered troops to tend to deportees' needs in the New Mexico camp, and then he sent the Harvard law professor and future Supreme Court justice Felix Frankfurter to Bisbee to conduct an investigation.

Bullied by the company representatives, Frankfurter noted that the deportation was "so shallow and so pathetic, as well as brutal. These old bags, who have fought labor and unions as poison for decades, now wrapped themselves in a flag and are confirmed in their old biases . . . and obscurantism by a passionate patriotism. Gee—but it's awful."

It was more than awful for Hunt. The aftermath of the strike-breaking and deportation left his state in ruins. He wrote in his diary: "It is a Shame that the big interest can pull off such a stunt."

"The counteroffensive by management grew to include the control of every aspect of Arizona life—economic, political, social, even religious," noted historian James Byrkit in *Forging the Copper Collar*. "The mining men intimidated editors, threatened ministers, bought sheriffs, seduced lawmakers and bullied union leaders. They rigged elections and manipulated the legislature. . . . Between 1915 and 1918, the companies, led by Walter Douglas (Phelps Dodge), completely reversed the direction of Arizona politics and destroyed the liberal influence in the state."

Nearly a century later, Bisbee's enduring legacy raised the question: what were the underlying corporate interests behind Arizona's anti-immigration and radical Tea Party agenda, and would they push the state over a modern-day abyss of deportation or "attrition through enforcement" like in Bisbee?

SB 1070 protest, Arizona.
(Photo courtesy of Chris Summitt, Summitt Photography.)

CHAPTER THREE

MANUFACTURING THE CRISIS

*The Arizona Desert has been used as a testing ground for all
sorts of measures that are spreading around the country. Most
of us, however, sit on the sidelines silent. I feel as though I'm
now living the future of the United States. Where legalized
criminality and attendant impunity have become the accepted
and acceptable norm.*

DR. LINDA GREEN, DIRECTOR OF THE CENTER FOR
LATIN AMERICAN STUDIES AT THE UNIVERSITY OF
ARIZONA, FEBRUARY 2011

THE FAILED STATE

"We face a state fiscal crisis of unparalleled dimensions," Governor Jan Brewer
declared in the spring of 2010, "one that is going to sweep over every single
person in this state as well as every business and every family."

Now holding the governor's reins she had inherited from former Governor
Janet Napolitano in 2009, whose departure to head up the Department of
Homeland Security allowed for the Republican secretary of state to gain office

regardless of party affiliation, the sixty-five-year-old self-professed fiscal conservative stood at the crossroads of her political future. As a state legislator and county supervisor, she had watched Arizona swell with real estate speculation and reckless development—an acre an hour, the construction industry claimed—during the housing boom of the 1980s and '90s.

Those were the golden years of Arizona unbound; now the state housing market and house-of-cards economy had collapsed to the bottom of the Grand Canyon, and Brewer found her state ranked aside Mississippi as the poorest in the nation. With one of the most entrenched debt problems in the country, the fiscally tight conservative legislature—which typically ranked at the bottom for per capita expenditures in education, health care, and social services—had whittled its budget to the bone.

"Opposition to big government and the Obama administration plays well at the State Capitol," longtime Southwestern observer Tom Barry wrote in the Boston Review. "Conveniently missing from this narrative is the back-story of federal subsidies and contracts. At last count, Arizona received $1.19 in federal spending for every dollar sent to Washington, which makes it a beneficiary state."

In essence, Arizona received more federal money per tax dollar ushered off to Washington's coffers than neighboring California or Nevada. While Arizona touted itself as anti-Washington and opposed to big-government handouts, the open secret was that the state had always been one of the great welfare queens of federal aid—from huge subsides for agriculture, water, and irrigation projects (and now Homeland Security and Immigration and Customs Enforcement monies), to a $4.3 billion check from President Obama's American Recovery and Reinvestment Act, which had kept the state afloat. While characterized as a rogue state, Barry noted, Arizona may have been better described as a "failed state."

None of this dismal news was going to help Brewer's election chances in the fall of 2010. Worse, her ratings were plummeting in the polls, as challengers in the Republican primary surged ahead of her. On March 23, 2010, Brewer received the bad news: State Treasurer Dean Martin was now the front-runner in the latest Rasmussen poll, which also showed Brewer lagging far behind her potential Democratic opponent. More important, the poll noted that 85 percent of Arizona voters were concerned about drug-related violence in Mexico "spilling over into the United States."

Brewer's flagging campaign—and her career—had a reckoning with history.

Four days after that disastrous poll, borderlands rancher Robert Krentz was murdered, setting off a frenetic news media crush and legislative maneuver by Tea Party leader Russell Pearce that culminated with Brewer's newfound support and signing of the SB 1070 bill within a month. Her ratings soared. So did her rhetoric, which had suddenly let loose the hounds of anti-immigrant fervor.

In her impassioned memoir, *Scorpions for Breakfast: My Fight Against Special Interests, Liberal Media, and Cynical Politics to Secure America's Borders,* Brewer frames her conversion to SB 1070 and her political motivations in a different way. "We are under siege," she writes. "And we have been totally disrespected by the federal government."

Brewer makes it clear from the first line that it is not really "we," as in the collective Arizona populace, but *she* who has been unfairly treated by the "liberal" media and President Obama, in particular, in the aftermath of Arizona's defiant legislative act. She so identifies herself with the state that she writes at one point, "Kind of like me. Kind of like Arizona." The substantial portion of the state that is *not* like Brewer is what torments her.

In the witching hours before she signed the controversial bill in the spring of 2010, with protesters outside her office and a nation divided over immigration policy, Brewer set the scene as a drama of her own victimization: "The best comparison I could think of was: This must be what it's like to be waterboarded."

In *Scorpions for Breakfast,* reportedly written with the help of ghostwriter Jessica Gavora (who also penned Sarah Palin's memoir), Brewer wants readers to know she lives on the Arizona front lines: "I was involved in a war with a deeper and more entrenched set of political interests than I had realized." In an attempt to make her own "war" more real, Brewer dedicates a chapter to the unsolved murder of Krentz and mentions his name more than thirty times throughout the book, while referring only once to SB 1070 architect Pearce.

Brewer argues that the Obama administration has intentionally allowed an immigration crisis to spiral out of control on the US-Mexico border, and even spill over into international controversy. When Mexican President Felipe Calderón addressed a joint session of Congress and criticized Arizona for SB 1070, Brewer could not believe that a foreign leader was actually allowed to criticize the United States.

"I had to wonder where our country was going under Obama," she writes. "It started to dawn on me that this president and his liberal allies in Congress don't really understand what America is all about and what our fundamental principles are." Depicting her state as a victim in a campaign of recrimination and blame, she writes again, "It was then that I knew that we were in a war."

Throughout the book, in fact, the Arizona governor constantly reminds readers that her state "didn't cause this crisis," but acted only when the federal government refused to do its job. "And what did we get for our effort?" she asks. "We were demonized and called racists. We were sued and treated like subjects instead of citizens. . . . We were slapped down like wayward children."

Brewer's war is not limited to the US-Mexico border in Arizona, where an "invasion" of "drug dealers, human smugglers, generic criminals, and the sheer volume of people pouring over our unsecured border" has given her state no other option but to "lead when their representatives in Washington failed to do so." Her "war" is with President Obama. And for the governor of Arizona, it gets personal.

Attempting to speak with the president during his commencement address at Arizona State University in Tempe, only weeks after signing SB 1070, Brewer claims Obama "blew me off." Finally, at a long-awaited meeting in the Oval Office, Brewer writes, "He proceeded to lecture me about everything he was doing to promote 'comprehensive immigration reform,' which was code for encouraging more illegal immigration by letting those already in the country illegally jump the line."

Brewer's account of Obama's remark ignored the fact that the Obama administration had deported a record number of immigrants—more than his Republican predecessor—and ramped up Border Patrol and border security funds to unprecedented levels. Instead, Brewer had an epiphany: "He's treating me like the cop he had over for a beer after he had badmouthed the Cambridge police, I thought."

This level of self-obsession and victimization overrides the discussion of virtually every policy decision and event in Brewer's eyes, and frames much of her leadership in Arizona's rebellion. Take her rendition of the legislative process leading up to the signing of SB 1070, one of the biggest media events in recent memory for the state. A Tucson station even broke into the soap opera *One Life to Live* to cover the press conference, she crows.

"I steeled myself and whispered, 'Jesus, hold my hand. I'm going to do this for the people of Arizona,'" the governor recounts, as if the closely watched election polls had no bearing on her decision. "If it affects my reelection and political reputation, it doesn't matter. This isn't about Jan Brewer's political future. It's about Arizona's future."

Brewer's version of Arizona's future covered the front pages of newspapers around the world in a bizarre incident in the spring of 2012, when the governor made sure President Obama got his comeuppance for mistreating her. Pointing her index finger at the president's nose as he crossed the tarmac at the Phoenix airport, Brewer lectured Obama about their disagreements. The photo of the finger-wielding governor nudged aside the saguaros and sunsets as the iconic image of the state's defiance; it was immortalized on a hot-selling T-shirt. And *Scorpions for Breakfast* shot to the bestseller list on Amazon.

"As I write, I have almost 500,000 friends on Facebook," Brewer concludes in her memoir, "and every day I take time to read the comments people leave on my wall."

THE FIRST SAGEBRUSH REBELLION

"This only happens when there's a Democrat in the White House," Peter Goudinoff said, reaching under the control panel of his Lancair Legacy airplane. "We spent half our time fighting off these crazy ideas when Bruce Babbitt was governor, and he spent half his time vetoing the craziest of ideas."

Goudinoff looked back, his crown of bushy white hair framed by large glasses. After two decades as one of the lonely liberal voices in the Arizona state legislature, the University of Arizona political science professor retired to pursue his passion for airplanes. He had built his experimental aircraft from a kit. He haunted the hangar with other "old white guys." He spent his days reflecting on his public service from above, taking off from Ryan Airfield, outside Tucson, and roaming across the corridors of commerce between the US and Mexico, the massive open-pit copper mines, and the sprawling cluster subdivisions that now define the region.

Retirement didn't keep him out of trouble. When the so-called "illegal alien" fires roared across southern Arizona in the summer of 2011, Goudinoff and a friend piled into his single-engine plane and headed toward the "monument fire," near the border in Cochise County. After losing contact with the Libby Army Airfield outside Sierra Vista, Goudinoff soon found himself being escorted by two F-16 fighter jets, whose pilots forced his plane to land at an airstrip in Tucson. Officials from the North American Aerospace Defense Command grilled Goudinoff; their jobs had increasingly shifted to monitoring the traffic of drug smugglers.

"I didn't know I had penetrated Mexican airspace," he said. "But I guess I had."

Even at ten thousand feet, the border had its virtual wall. Although Goudinoff never got near the fire, he recalled the media sensation that hovered over the question of immigration and state versus federal jurisdiction.

"It wasn't like that back in the 1970s," he said, picking up a screwdriver that sat on one of his wings.

Another rebellion over states' rights in Goudinoff's era, though, underlined an antifederal streak among Arizona hard-liners who finally found an ally in the state capitol with the ascension of Brewer. And indeed it took place, as Goudinoff noted, during the liberal Democratic administration of President Jimmy Carter.

"Just boilerplate, just like today," Goudinoff said, "making noise to generate political turmoil. There's always been a wing of the Republican Party that pushes this rhetoric."

In the late 1970s, the right-wing Republicans in Arizona took that rhetoric to the next stage, joining a Western movement they called the Sagebrush Rebellion. Senator Orrin Hatch from Utah referred to it as "the Second American Revolution." Goudinoff called it "theft."

Manufacturing a constitutional crisis in a similar fashion as today, conservative legislators from several Western states sought to take "sovereign control" over the public lands administered by the Bureau of Land Management (BLM) under the guise of constitutional rights and federal mismanagement. "This was land that no one originally wanted," Goudinoff scoffed. "That's why it ended up in the hands of the feds."

In 1912, Arizona's state constitution legally relinquished "forever . . . all right and title to the unappropriated and ungranted public lands lying within the boundaries thereof." "Thereof" notwithstanding, states' rights had been the mantra of a cadre of pioneering lawmakers long before Tea Partiers like

Russell Pearce. The *Tucson Citizen* noted that the rebellion's main sponsor in 1979, Representative Joe Lane, a rancher from Cochise County, was a "state's-righter from Day One."

But what did states' rights really mean for the majority of residents who did not dwell or work or roam across those precious and remote public hinterlands in the clutches of the federal government?

Within a few months, the Sagebrush Rebellion's adherence to such sacred sovereignty would quickly dissipate to a thinly veiled front for private landowners. An amendment sought to obtain the land from the federal government and put it up for sale in a state lottery within five years. As one Sagebrush senator declared, the "land is best left to private ownership." Calling the action a "landmark" for the West, one Arizona lawmaker reminded his colleagues that the land grab could result in "more than $1 billion in land value because of the energy and land resources."

In a region where oil and mining interests and real estate companies encircled counties for cheap deals, and huge ranching operations sought to expand unfettered grazing on public lands, the states' rights parade was a bandwagon to support.

"If the state was going to get the land," one critic surmised, "they'd [the developers] spring out of the desert like wildflowers."

The rebellion spread across the West for a reason: most of the BLM land, such as the estimated 11.6–12.5 million acres in Arizona, sat to the west of the 100th meridian. In its attempt to seize on this "abuse" by the "dictates" of the federal government and "eastern environmentalists," the Western movement ramped up its rhetoric to Civil War terms. "The Mason-Dixon line has shifted," declared one Alaskan legislator, "and runs north-south now, separating the Eastern states from an increasingly isolated, angry West."

Such outrageous statements tended to undercut the seriousness of the rebellion. Like the Tea Party today, the movement showcased a distant and deep-seated anti-Washington distrust, pitting itself against a liberal Democratic administration in an ideological battle to provoke a judicial showdown over constitutional issues. The movement coincided, as well, with the revival of conservative rebels in the Republican Party that had emerged during Barry Goldwater's brief reign in 1964 and would spike again with the insurgent presidential campaign of California Governor Ronald Reagan in 1980.

As Lane told his fellow Arizona supporters, the rebellion was really about bringing this constitutional crisis to the courts. In other words, can a state claim sovereignty over federal land and jurisdiction if it passes a law that gives it the right to do so?

Despite the interpretations peddled by the League for the Advancement of States' Equal Rights, which fronted as the lobby for the Sagebrush Rebellion, court decisions over the past 150 years had clearly sided on behalf of federal domain. The *Wall Street Journal* reminded its readers: "Most experts believe the federal government will prevail in any court challenge to its land ownership." In Arizona, as scholar John Keane noted, virtually all of the state's lands were originally "acquired by national force of arms in the War with Mexico and by a payment to Mexico of millions of dollars from the Federal treasury in the Treaty of Guadalupe Hidalgo and in the Gadsden Purchase. When Sagebrush supporters call for the land to be 'returned' to the states or individuals, Sagebrush opponents are quick to point out that the land never did belong to the states or to anyone but the nation as a whole."

Much like the Tea Party rebellion in Arizona, the Sagebrush Rebellion refused to allow a bit of historical reality to block its path.

The rebellion even halted Governor Bruce Babbitt's record of twenty-eight vetoes. Voting 46–8 to override his veto, the Sagebrush renegades passed the measure and donated $60,000 toward the legal battle with fellow legislators in Nevada and Utah. One of the dissenting Democrats referred to the bill as the "Stagecoach Rebellion, because we're all being taken for a ride."

That ride didn't go too far, and not because of a federal crackdown or judicial decision. Conservative Republican hero and self-proclaimed Sagebrush rebel Ronald Reagan was elected president in the fall of 1980, and as the cowboy rode into town and quickly sought to gut federal oversight and legislation for wilderness and environmental management, the Sagebrush Rebellion dissipated for the next decade.

Back in Arizona, the Cochise County rancher and legislator Lane and other states' rights advocates knew the party would never end. "It won't be resolved today," he declared, "and many of us here won't live to see it, but our children and grandchildren can be proud that we started the fight."

Lane was right. That fight over states' rights never ended. Brewer joined the state legislature two years later as part of a new wave of powerful "Republican wives" in politics. In the spring of 2012, more than three decades after the last "sagebrush rebellion," the state legislature revived the campaign and passed a bill to reclaim control over an estimated forty-eight thousand square miles of federal land, including national forests, monuments, and wildlife areas. The lawmakers' intentions were unabashedly clear; the bill included measures to sell off the public lands to private interests.

"The Tea Party's taken over," Arizona House minority leader Chad Campbell told the *Arizona Republic*. "This entire Capitol is run by conspiracy theorists and the Tea Party."

Brewer's surprising veto of the "sagebrush" bill fell on deaf ears, however; in an added gesture of bravado, the state legislature had already passed HCR 2004, the "state sovereignty" resolution, which placed a proposition to amend the state's constitution before the voters in the fall 2012 elections. The bill read in part: "The state of Arizona declares its sovereign and exclusive authority and jurisdiction over the air, land, public lands, minerals, wildlife and other natural resources within its boundaries."

THAT WAS AN ERROR, IF I SAID IT

For any student of history, Brewer followed a fairly typical path of election-time fear-mongering that had been part of Arizona politics since its inception. But as Brewer and Pearce understood, just like the infamous Sheriff Wheeler in Cochise County knew a century ago, it wasn't always convenient to report the truth.

Although Brewer may have eaten "scorpions for breakfast," a series of gaffes and outright lies often made her eat crow for lunch. "Jan Brewer has serious issues with the truth," Three Sonorans wrote in the summer of 2010, just as she was ramping up her nativist credentials. "Everyone lies at one point or another," the blog admitted, "but she has a special knack for choosing lies that are extra-sensational, using Nazis, terrorism and immigration as her subjects."

In what she described as her "lightbulb moment" in politics, Brewer traced her career back to her stint as a "young wife and mother" so detached from the community that she had to ask her husband about the strange huddle of people sitting at the front of the room at a school board meeting in Glendale,

Arizona, in the early 1980s. (The Brewers, contrary to the *Scorpion* book jacket, were California transplants in 1970, not "lifelong Arizona residents.")

"And he said, 'Well, they're the school board.' So I said, 'How did they get there?' He answered, 'They were elected by the people in the school district.' And I said, 'Well, I could do at least as good a job as they are, if not better.'"

Skipping any school board race, Brewer decided to make the leap straight to the state legislature. She recalled that she hand-addressed her campaign announcements from "my beach house in Rocky Point, Mexico." In the state legislature, she picked up the nickname "Janbo" for her effort to halt a "monument to Vietnam war protests." Her proudest legislative effort, even though the bill never passed, was an attempt to require labels for "obscene" lyrics on record albums.

Emboldened by the SB 1070 notoriety in her revived gubernatorial race, Brewer uttered some fairly obscene whoppers of her own in the course of a single month in the summer of 2010. In response to criticism that SB 1070 had the overtones of Nazi-era police enforcement, the Arizona governor had attempted to flip the accusations and nearly broke down in tears, claiming she had lost her father at the age of eleven, "knowing my father died fighting the Nazi regime in Germany." Brewer had shaken her head. "It hurts," she went on. "It's ugliness beyond anything I've ever experienced."

Not that factual experience had much to do with her claim. When a follow-up investigation found that her father had actually died ten years after the end of the war, and had not served on the European front lines but as a civilian supervisor in a naval munitions factory in Nevada, she quickly admitted that she had taken some liberties with the truth.

That little white lie vanished in the lure of dark mistruth a few days later, when Brewer charged that "the majority of illegal trespassers" from Mexico were "drug mules" and criminally involved in the drug wars. Without much evidence to support her charge, the sneer of racist association even raised the eyebrows of the most convinced Tea Partiers. But Brewer refused to back off her offensive portrayal of the hundreds of thousands in Arizona's workforce who had kept afloat the state's building, tourist, and service industries, and toiled in its fields. The stance scored her more national coverage.

The allegation was so ludicrous, of course, that even the conservative *Arizona Republic* newspaper in Phoenix ran an editorial rebuking the governor for making "the state look foolish." Senator John McCain, who had joined the chorus of SB 1070 advocates and made his fair share of unfounded gaffes—telling Fox News host Bill O'Reilly, for example, that "drivers of cars with illegals in it" *intentionally* caused the lion's share of car accidents in Arizona—called out Brewer's fact-challenged comment. The head of the Border Patrol labor union countered that the "majority of the people continue to come across in search of work, not to smuggle drugs."

Brewer went for the jugular with her third tall tale in the summer of the brown scare. She made national news again when she claimed on Fox News that the Arizona deserts were littered with "bodies that had been beheaded" as part of the Mexican drug cartels' reign of terror, which had allegedly spilled over the border. (Earlier that spring, Brewer had told a Fox News interviewer: "Arizona has been under terrorist attacks, if you will, with all of this illegal immigration that has been taking place on our very porous border.")

Brewer's tale even took the breath of Cochise County Sheriff Larry Dever, the conservative border sheriff who had railed against the Obama administration on the TV circuit. "We're not seeing the multiple killings, beheadings and shootouts that are going on, on the other side," he told the *Arizona Republic*. His county's crime rate had been flat for nearly a decade.

After other law enforcement officials threw up their hands at the absurdity of the comment and immigrants' rights groups and local and national media demanded to see evidence, Brewer dodged press encounters for nearly two months until she finally uttered a halfhearted clarification. "That was an error, if I said it," she admitted.

Brewer got the last laugh, of course. The image of beheadings, real or delusional, was now a permanent part of Arizona's immigration debate. Never one to run away from a fight, Russell Pearce covered Brewer's back. "I can tell you there's been 300 to 500 beheadings and dismemberments along that border," he told the AP. "It is a national security concern, yet we're worried about this game playing, this word-smithing."

On election night in the fall of 2010, when the Republicans swept every statewide race and Brewer celebrated her own victory, Pearce basked in his role as a new kingpin in Arizona and national politics. "I think, out of fairness, the governor would have to admit that if it wasn't for 1070, she wouldn't be elected," Pearce boasted to a Phoenix TV news reporter. "I know other folks ran on 1070. Nationally, folks ran on 1070. I had three governor candidates call me to do calls for them and support them, not because I'm Russell Pearce, but I'm the face of 1070."

Pearce was right, of course. The long road to Brewer's victory had been foretold in an extraordinary script of a manufactured crisis. And far from Arizona's volatile borders, it wasn't only true-believer nativists and opportunist politicians peddling its message.

ARIZONA WAS MELTING DOWN

Or, at least, that was the viewpoint of former Fox News broadcaster Glenn Beck on the eve of the signing of SB 1070. He wagered that Brewer didn't have the courage to sign the bill. Beck mused, "It would be amazing if she did. I just can't believe I live in a country where we have to pass a law to make it illegal to be illegal." The guffaws abounded.

Although Brewer trumped Beck on this supposed act of bravery, no one would minimize the broadcaster's role in shaping and inflaming the right-wing narrative in the country over the past several years. His role was crucial in the fertile and ever-growing debate on Arizona's immigration and border security policies.

And that role largely served to disseminate incorrect or misconstrued information. On February 13, 2009, Beck attempted to one-up news outlets like ABC News, blasting the urban legend of Phoenix as the "number-two city in the world for kidnapping." Feigning disbelief, he railed, "That is staggering. I love Phoenix, Arizona. I used to live in Phoenix. I was just in Phoenix. Here's what you're not getting. You're not getting in the news the truth on Mexico. I am—God bless them, man. You're not going to find this story in the AP. You're not going to find this story anyplace else."

In truth, the story was everywhere, especially on Fox News—even though it wasn't based on fact. Nearly a year before Beck's revelation, on June 23, 2008, Sean Hannity brought Phoenix Police Sergeant Phil Roberts onto his *Hannity's America* program. Hannity told listeners, "Bloodshed south of the border is spiraling out of control and the effect is being felt, right here in America. . . . Mexican drug cartels are waging an increasingly bloody battle for control of smuggling routes into the United States. . . . The violence does not stay south of the border. Two hundred miles north of the Sonora. . . . It's a scene that plays out over and over again in Phoenix, where the kidnapping problem is exploding." Roberts filled in the numbers, claiming, "Ninety-nine percent of all the kidnappings we are investigating are in some way related to illegal border activity."

Despite Beck's staggering disbelief, in the summer of 2010 the PolitiFact news service ran a check on its "Truth-O-Meter" about the assertion. It came to a resounding thump of falsehood. The fact-checkers noted: "Neither the FBI nor the U.S. National Central Bureau of Interpol, an arm of the U.S. Department of Justice that serves as the United States' representative to Interpol, could confirm that Phoenix has the second-highest frequency of kidnapping cases worldwide.

"Scott Stewart, vice president of tactical intelligence for Stratford, an Austin-based global intelligence company, separately chimed in: 'According to our analysts, there is no way that Phoenix is the No. 2 city in the world for kidnapping.'"

Phoenix Police spokesperson Sergeant Tommy Thompson told PolitiFact that kidnapping statistics have "no reliable empirical data" and are "inherently under-reported, anyway." Thompson placed such unreliable data and terms into context. "Unless you're involved in the dope trade," he told PolitiFact, "there's a very very slim chance that you'll be kidnapped."

Nonetheless, thanks to Beck's following, the kidnapping legend continued to swell. It became a staple in the stomp speeches of pundits, talk-show hosts, Republican and Tea Party candidates, and presidential wannabes. Interviewed at a Tea Party meeting in Los Angeles right after the signing of SB 1070, Representative Michele Bachmann justified her support for the draconian bill by claiming "innocent Americans being killed on their ranches and in their homes . . . when you have Phoenix the kidnap capital of the United States, I applaud Arizona, what they have to do to keep their people safe."

Accepting his Annie Taylor Award on November 18, 2010, at right-wing darling David Horowitz's "Restoration Weekend" in Palm Springs, Florida, Pearce dramatically reminded the audience that Phoenix was "second in the world in kidnapping," adding in disgust: "Apparently that's just collateral damage to some folks, for cheap labor and cheap votes."

For former Arkansas governor and Republican presidential candidate Mike Huckabee, it wasn't enough for Phoenix to be ranked as number two in the sphere of kidnapping. Speaking with Fox News *On the Record* host Greta Van

Susteren in the wake of the SB 1070 signing, he amplified the legend with his own version of facts along the "doggone borders." Huckabee charged: "People in Arizona were just frustrated. They're the number-one kidnapping capital in the world. They've seen people murdered who were simply trying to take care of their farms and families. And in exasperation because of the complete ineptness of this federal government, they took action."

Beck's initial barrage didn't stop with the "ineptness" of the federal response. He held McCain, one of his favorite Republican targets, accountable for an apparent conspiracy of a news blackout. Despite Beck's blessing, right-wing former Representative J. D. Hayworth failed as a Tea Party insurgency candidate to dethrone McCain in the 2010 Republican primary.

Beck roared: "How did John McCain go an entire two years or not [sic] campaign trail without America showing that the second-most dangerous city to have your kids or somebody in your family kidnapped is Phoenix, Arizona?"

More than a year after Beck repeated the legend, McCain embraced the issue as his own. Appearing on NBC's Meet the Press on June 27, McCain issued his own outrage: "By the way, on that issue, why is it that Phoenix, Arizona, is the number-two kidnapping capital of the world? Does that mean our border's safe? Of course not."

Neither Beck nor McCain seemed to notice that Phoenix Mayor Phil Gordon had already appeared before the House Subcommittee on Commerce, Justice, and Science in the spring of 2009 and painted a less-than-romantic picture of the American West. "Almost every night, Phoenix police will get one or more calls," the Phoenix New Times newspaper reported, "about an immigrant smuggled into the country being held for ransom and tortured. And for each one of the calls, Gordon said, the police department has to divert as many as 60 officers to find, rescue, and protect those kidnap victims."

Ramping up the volume, Beck continued his crusade: "Our republic is at stake."

In the summer of 2010, fifteen months after Beck's first kidnap-mania broadcast, he insisted that Phoenix "has become the kidnapping capital of America, with more incidents than any other city in the world outside of Mexico City. . . . Do you think we've got a problem in our country?"

Arizona indeed had a kidnapping problem, but it was not the one Beck obsessed over. The truth had been kidnapped.

First, kidnapping rates in Phoenix were actually falling, though they still remained significant. Thompson, from the Phoenix police department, told PolitiFact in the summer of 2010: "There were 358 reported kidnappings in 2008 (10 fewer than reported by the *LA Times*, due to later reclassification of the crimes), 318 in 2009 and there were 105 from January through May 2010, he said, putting the city on track to sustain less than 300 this year."

In the spring of 2011, the *New Times* fact-checked the numbers that the Phoenix police department and politicians were circulating. More important, it checked the origins of the crimes. Analyzing 264 of those 358 reported kidnappings, the *New Times* found that "only about one of every four incidents labeled as kidnappings in 2008 appeared connected to border-related crimes."

End result: "Phoenix was dealing with Mexican-style kidnap-for-ransom cases an average of once a week, not daily." Mark Spencer, president of the Phoenix Law Enforcement Association, told the *New Times*: "One a week still indicates a crisis. Those figures didn't need to be inflated. Either the police management team was . . . disingenuous or grossly incompetent."

Disingenuous or grossly incompetent. Or unabashedly dipping in the federal coffers. In her book *Illegal: Life and Death in Arizona's Immigration War Zone*, Phoenix-based journalist Terry Greene Sterling recounted the difficulty in getting any clarity on the situation. "It was clear to me," she wrote, "that Thompson faced a public relations quandary. On one hand, his job was to spin Phoenix as a safe city. On the other hand, he had to confirm that Phoenix was the Kidnapping Capital of the United States. (At the same time, Police Chief Jack Harris was seeking federal stimulus funds by milking the Kidnapping Capital theme.)"

"Not long after Harris and Gordon's testimonies," Monica Alonzo wrote in the *New Times*, "the Phoenix Police Department applied for and received $2.45 million in federal grants, in part to combat the kidnappings." In a subsequent "Project Eagle Eye" grant, the city scored another $750,000 by directly linking a majority of the kidnappings "to border issues of drugs and human smuggling." Another $1.7 million poured in for "Operation Home Defense," once again to combat "daily" kidnappings.

By the summer of 2011, Alonzo had gone straight to the root of the federal pillorying. Police Sergeant Phil Roberts, the very spokesperson who rang the bell of kidnapping lore on *Hannity's America* in 2008, and who subsequently briefed every major news outlet over the next year, suddenly decided to come clean. He accused the Phoenix police of exaggerating kidnapping cases as a "golden ticket" for detectives to "build their résumés." Alonzo noted that Roberts "started downplaying the figures he'd been touting. In his voluminous memos, Roberts claimed that Phoenix kidnapping statistics were bogus and intentionally inflated by police officials to defraud the federal government of grant money. He claimed that Phoenix had only 20 to 30 border-related kidnap cases a year, instead of the 300-plus logged in 2008."

A federal investigation of the Phoenix police department was eventually opened and remains in progress. The police chief left. Whistleblower or hero or accomplice, Roberts underscored the gullibility of shock broadcasters like Beck and mainstream news outlets, and their willingness to hype fear over reason and raise the terror alert in our collective minds with little truth and grave consequences.

A STATE OF CONFUSION

For all their inaccuracies and panic-inducing accusations, Brewer and Pearce and their media allies successfully reframed the discussion over immigration in Arizona and the United States. They deflected any criticism with ease. When an Immigration Policy Center report chastised Arizona's new immigration law for setting off "a state of confusion" that would unravel into a patchwork of interpretations by police officers, Pearce invoked his tenure as a former chief deputy sheriff who had been shot in the line of duty.

Yet buried in an informative overview of the political posturing over borderland security and the real line of fire, an *Arizona Republic* article published a week after SB 1070 passed noted one important detail. For all of the "brown scare" tactics that had been unleashed, and the outcry over the potential for violent spillover from Mexico, the drug cartels, and deviant immigrants without papers, this fact remained: "According to the Border Patrol, Krentz is the only American murdered by a suspected illegal immigrant in at least a decade within the agency's Tucson sector, the busiest smuggling route among the Border Patrol's nine coverage regions along the U.S.-Mexican border."

"This is a media-created event," Pima County Sheriff Clarence Dupnik noted in the spring media fever over SB 1070 in 2010. Unlike frequent Fox

News media commentators and so-called "border" law enforcement experts, including Maricopa County Sheriff Joe Arpaio and Pinal County Sheriff Paul Babeu, Dupnik's jurisdiction actually covered the US-Mexico border. "I hear politicians on TV saying the border has gotten worse. Well, the fact of the matter is that the border has never been more secure."

But there had been other murders.

Few Arizonans—few Americans, for that matter—knew that the first post–9/11 hate crime in the United States took place in Pearce's own town of Mesa, when Frank Silva Roque set out to "shoot some towel-heads" and gunned down Balbir Singh Sodhi, a turban-clad immigrant Sikh from India, at his gas station on September 15, 2001.

The Three Sonorans blog reminded its readers of another murder that should have changed the nation, as well. Thirteen days after Brewer signed SB 1070 into law, a reportedly drunk Phoenix man approached his neighbor Juan Varela to chat about the new immigration rules; he called the man a "wet-back" and told him to "hurry up and go back to Mexico, or you're going to die." Varela's family traced their Arizona heritage back several generations—not that it should have mattered. After a brief argument, Varela was gunned down in cold blood.

"You know Arizona has been under terrorist attacks, if you will, with all of this illegal immigration that has been taking place on our very porous border," Brewer argued on Fox News when asked about the criticism she had received over SB 1070. "The whole issue comes back, that we do not and will not tolerate illegal immigration bringing with it, very much so, the implications of crime and terrorism into our state."

But would she tolerate terrorism among her own citizens? By the time Varela's gunman was sentenced to twenty-seven years in prison for the murder of a US citizen—by comparison, the undocumented Mexican immigrant who shot and injured Russell Pearce's son in the line of duty in 2004 received a fifty-one-year prison sentence—the hate-crime charges had been dropped by an all-white jury. When *New Times* reporter Stephen Lemons looked at the latest figures from the FBI's Uniform Crime Reports, he found that the outlook was dismal: "Hate crimes have been increasing steadily since 2006, when there were 60 hate crimes reported by the PPD [Phoenix Police Department] to the FBI. In 2007, there were 80. This means that from 2006 to 2010, the numbers have more than doubled, a whopping 125 percent increase."

Lemons didn't pull any punches: "The Grand Canyon State has a well-deserved reputation for being the 'state of hate,' what with its demonizing of the undocumented (who are mostly Latino) and the blanket atmosphere of intolerance that pervades Sand Land, a.k.a., 'the white man's last stand.' We can thank such politicos as state Senator Russell Pearce, Governor Jan Brewer, and Attorney General Tom Horne for helping to encourage this climate of bigotry. But they are not responsible for it. They have merely capitalized on it. And it existed prior to the noxious rise in nativism here."

Was it fair to blame incendiary rhetoric for the rise in hate crimes? Was it fair to point the finger at political and media figures who had openly incited violence?

Arizona, of course, hadn't cornered the market on radio rage or political assassinations.

As the fear-mongering in Arizona against Mexican immigrants reached absurd levels (with "terrorist attacks" and "drug mule" accusations), a deranged man in Oakland acted on Glenn Beck's inflammatory rhetoric against the liberal Tides Foundation and attempted an armed assault on the organization. Thankfully, his attempt was foiled.

Yet the episode, like the Varela murder that same summer, raised the question of complicity, especially when it came to the backlash against immigrants. History reminded us that Arizona was hardly a pioneer in immigration violence or rank discrimination to serve political means.

Beck's German ancestors could have lectured the TV host on what had happened in a similarly long summer more than a century and a half ago in Louisville, Kentucky, when a nationally prominent newspaper editor repeatedly fomented what became the worst anti-immigrant massacre in US history—the murder of German and Irish Catholics on "Bloody Monday," August 6, 1855. Beck, ironically, had launched his first political radio rant in Louisville in 1986, when American war planes rocked the compound of Libya's Muammar el-Qaddafi; as a morning shock jock, he played patriotic country tunes and banged the drums for more bombardment.

A Connecticut Yankee turned Louisville *Journal* editor, George Prentice was considered the best-known commentator in the nation, according to the *New York Times,* which described him as a "bitter, unrelenting political foe [who] several times had street fights." As the great editorial voice of the anti-immigrant Know-Nothing Party, Prentice relished attacking the "foreign hordes" of Germans and Irish that poured into the Midwest. Fearful of an election upset, he penned a series of editorials that unleashed the wrath of hired thugs on Louisville's darkest and bloodiest day.

On the eve of the riots, Prentice declared, "Let the foreigners keep their elbows to themselves to-day at the polls. Americans are you all ready? We think we hear you shout 'ready,' 'well fire!' and may heaven have mercy on the foe."

Fueled by rumors and booze, drunken mobs roamed the German and Irish wards that August day with rifles and muskets and pitchforks and torches, and left behind the smoldering remains of destruction, strewn and burned bodies, and at least twenty-two dead (most historians place the death toll much higher). In the process, hundreds if not thousands of immigrants and sympathizers fled Louisville.

Writing in the *Washington Post* after the Tides Foundation episode, columnist Dana Milbank called out Beck's verbal warning that "it is only a matter of time before an actual crazy person really does something stupid":

> Most every broadcast has some violent imagery: "The clock is ticking. . . . The war is just beginning. . . . Shoot me in the head if you try to change our government. . . . You have to be prepared to take rocks to the head. . . . The other side is attacking. . . . There is a coup going on. . . . Grab a torch! . . . Drive a stake through the heart of the bloodsuckers. . . . They are taking you to a place to be slaughtered. . . . They are putting a gun to America's head. . . . Hold these people responsible."
>
> Beck has prophesied darkly to his millions of followers that we are reaching "a point where the people will have exhausted all their options. When that happens, look out."

In Louisville back in 1855, the opposing *Courier* newspaper similarly called out Prentice's violence-inciting words for disgracing the great city: "We fully agree with the *Journal* that there is a terrible responsibility somewhere, and that no language is too strong for its condemnation. And the *Journal* knows full well where this responsibility belongs. To its incendiary articles continued day after day before the election, and its violent appeals on the morning of the election, articles and appeals calculated to bring into active exercise all bad passions of the human heart."

Toward the end of his life, the famed Prentice spoke publicly about his regret in stirring anti-immigrant violence. Within a decade of the riot, Louisville had elected a German-American mayor.

WHY WE NEED SB 1070: HOW LONG WILL IT BE BEFORE WE WILL BE JUST LIKE MEXICO?

Violence had always been part of Russell Pearce's career on the front lines. His campaign website began, as in all Pearce pronouncements, with the fact that he had been shot in the line of duty. Then it reminded its readers—Dear Patriots—of Pearce's vision of his vanguard role in the nation's battle for freedom and secure borders against illegal immigration: "Leadership, practiced at its best, is the art and science of calling to the hearts and minds of others. It is engaging others in an enterprise of sound strategic focus, where they can experience a sense of ownership, of making a difference, of being valued and adding value."

Beautiful words, of course, but a closer examination revealed that Pearce had plagiarized them from well-known motivational speaker and author Robert Staub's book *The Heart of Leadership*.

Earlier that summer, as President Obama and congressional leaders wrangled over the debt ceiling, Pearce had turned to Facebook to express his personal outrage. "Folks," he wrote, "if there was ever an argument for NO to raising the debt limit and YES to stop the reckless socialist spending in this Gangster Government in DC. Watch this video."

The video showed an "elaborate welfare housing project" built for "illegal immigrants" and funded through alleged "refugee pay." Just one problem: the five-month-old viral video—created by a far-right gadfly from Tacoma, Washington—had already been thoroughly debunked by the Tacoma *News Tribune*. By Sunday morning, Pearce had deleted the post from his Facebook page. In truth, he had lifted the video and comments from anti-immigrant crusader Tom Tancredo, a former US Representative and perennial right-wing candidate.

Even with the election heating up, Pearce didn't seem concerned about associating himself with the work of fringe characters. In 2006 he had been caught circulating an article from the Holocaust-denying National Alliance, a West Virginia–based white supremacist group. In issuing an apology, Pearce claimed not to have known about the group's views. Dismissing him as a relic, then Arizona Governor Janet Napolitano had told the Associated Press in 2006 that Pearce's antics proved that "he's so far to the right that his contribution to public discourse is limited."

An examination of Pearce's website and public statements showed that the self-proclaimed architect of Arizona's "papers please" immigration law had regularly borrowed and presented as his own significant portions of text from the writings of hard-line white nationalists, fringe anti-immigrant activists, and others whose views fell far outside the mainstream.

Even his authorship of SB 1070 seemed to be in question.

Pearce was particularly fond of the right-wing American Constitution Party, which championed "sovereign" states' rights and opposed immigration. In an August 31, 2010, press release that chastised the Obama administration for including SB 1070 in a United Nations report on human rights, Pearce borrowed whole paragraphs from an essay that had been written in 2009 by Tim Baldwin, a prominent Constitution Party activist (and the son of radical activist Chuck Baldwin, who previously ran for president under the party's banner). Pearce lectured Obama with Baldwin's work, without attribution: "Particular to the United States, the U.S. Constitution was voluntarily formed as a compact by existing sovereign states with existing state constitutions. Despite the deceptive proposition that the States were created by Congress, the States existed prior to and independent of any Congress, as confirmed by the Treaty of Paris in 1783 (which, by the way, was not overturned by any subsequent legal action of the states). The state's authority is not delegated; it is inherent authority and has inherent responsibility to its citizens. The State governments, by their original constitutions, are invested with complete sovereignty."

Those last phrases had been part of Pearce's stump speech for the past two years.

Pearce did the same thing on his personal website. Under the tab for his three main constitutional issues—"Birth Right," "14th Amendment," and

"Supreme Court Decisions"—he borrowed wholesale from the website writings of Fred Elbel, an anti-immigrant extremist who had been linked to various fringe nativist organizations.

According to a Southern Poverty Law Center report from 2007, Elbel "is, in effect, the house webmaster for the anti-immigration movement." The SPLC added, "Elbel displayed his temperament during the debate over the Sierra Club's future in 2004, when he wrote an E-mail that read: 'Damned right. I hate 'em all—negroes, wasps, spics, eskimos, jews, honkies, krauts, ruskies, ethopans, pakis, hunkies, pollocks and marxists; there are way too many of them.'"

Called out on a number of other plagiarized texts, Pearce took down all of his borrowed work and revamped his campaign website.

More evidence then emerged that Pearce had possibly plagiarized significant parts of an outrageously inaccurate email on immigration from one of his state's fringe lawmakers, State Senator Sylvia Allen, for an important article on the origins of SB 1070 he had supposedly written in the *Social Contract Press,* run by the shadowy Federation for American Immigration Reform (FAIR) founder and board member John Tanton. *The Social Contact Press,* the Center for American Progress noted in a report, "publishes the views of white nationalists such as John Vinson, including a gem about how God prefers racial separation."

Despite being called the "mastermind behind the organized anti-immigration movement" by the Southern Poverty Law Center, Tanton tended to fly under the radar of most mainstream news outlets. While FAIR was "more nuanced in its use of language than other anti-immigrant groups," the Anti-Defamation League concluded, "a close look reveals a pattern of extremist affiliations and a strategy of founding and empowering smaller groups that promote xenophobia."

Such as in Arizona. In a special report on the "racist roots of Arizona's immigration law" in the spring of 2010, MSNBC host Rachel Maddow examined the state's link with FAIR, as well as Tanton's infamous "WITAN Memo" from 1986, in which he declared, "'To govern is to populate' . . . In this society where the majority rules, does this hold? Will the present majority peaceably hand over its political power to a group that is simply more fertile?" Seven years later, Tanton wrote to a colleague, "I've come to the point of view that for European-American society and culture to persist requires a European-American majority and a clear one at that."

In the 2010 summer issue of the *Social Contract Press,* Pearce's name appeared as the author of the article "Arizona Takes the Lead on Illegal Immigration Enforcement." In the article, Pearce opines on "why we need SB 1070" and on the need to follow the rule of law. He rails against "leftists here and in DC" and asks, "How long will it be before we will be just like Mexico? We have already lost our language; everything must be printed in Spanish. We have already lost our history since it is no longer taught in our schools. And we have lost our borders."

To support his argument, Pearce reports unsubstantiated evidence from a recent State Senate hearing he had sponsored, including testimony from one rancher who had found "17 dead bodies and two Qur'an bibles" on his property and the unverified claim that "in the last few years, 80 percent of our law enforcement personnel who have been killed or wounded were done by an illegal alien."

However, earlier that summer, on May 3, Sylvia Allen—who made national news in 2009 for her comment that uranium mining was safe because "the earth was 6,000 years old"—had sent out a very public email explaining her views on SB 1070. The email was so ridden with factual errors that one Democratic state senator published a response in an attempt to clarify Allen's wild claims.

In her email, Allen also reported that "17 dead bodies and two Koran bibles" had been found on a rancher's property, and also stated without any factual evidence that "in the last few years 80% of our law enforcement that have been killed or wounded have been by an illegal." In the spring of 2012, Allen would introduce a state Senate bill to fund an armed volunteer militia on the US-Mexico border, in order to stem the tide of Hezbollah insurgents pressing at Arizona's gates.

In fact, Allen's email and Pearce's most important article on the backstory of his support for SB 1070 were nearly identical. Did she plagiarize from Pearce, or did he borrow again from her work? Or perhaps neither Tea Party legislator actually had a hand in drafting the document? That question also applied to Pearce's self-professed "authorship" of SB 1070.

The day after Governor Brewer signed SB 1070 into law, an op-ed appeared in the *New York Times* by Kris Kobach, a former adviser to Bush-era Attorney General John Ashcroft and a well-known anti-immigrant advocate who would eventually be elected secretary of state in Kansas. Kobach was no stranger to Arizona. In 2006, he had served as legal counsel for the state law that made immigrant smuggling a crime. Five years later, Kobach signed on to Republican presidential candidate Mitt Romney's campaign as the top immigration adviser.

As Stephen Lemons noted in the *Phoenix New Times,* Kobach was also "the proponent of a near-mystical legal concept; that local cops have the inherent authority to enforce all federal statutes." Lemons mused, "Most legal scholars find this idea laughable, but folks like [Maricopa County Sheriff Joe] Arpaio and Arizona state senator Russell Pearce cling to it like a life preserver in choppy waters." Kobach, in fact, had trained Arpaio's officers in immigration law.

At a rally later that summer for Kobach's successful campaign for secretary of state in Kansas, Arpaio made a special appearance and hailed Kobach's role as one of the authors of SB 1070.

In keeping with Pearce's other favorite authors to plagiarize, Kobach had also represented FAIR and its Immigration Reform Law Institute in various court challenges.

"Arizona is the ground zero of illegal immigration," Kobach wrote in the *New York Times.* "Phoenix is the hub of human smuggling and the kidnapping capital of America." In a final jab at the president, he added, "President Obama and the Beltway crowd feel these problems can be taken care of with 'comprehensive immigration reform'—meaning amnesty and a few other new laws. But we already have plenty of federal immigration laws on the books, and the typical alien is guilty of breaking many of them. . . . Is it any wonder the Arizona legislature, at the front line of the immigration issue, sees things differently?"

"As a senator in a state on the front lines of the illegal invasion, I see firsthand the damage being done to our state and our country," Pearce had concluded in the *Social Contract* essay. "It is clear we cannot wait for the feds to secure the border or to enforce the laws that are already on the books even as the violence and cost continue to soar for our citizens."

The time had come, as Kobach wrote, for Arizona to draw the line. The nation—and Arizona voters—didn't know, however, that another lobbyist had already made the first draft.

ALMOST WORD FOR WORD, ARIZONA'S IMMIGRATION LAW

National Public Radio broke the story in the fall of 2010. Combing hundreds of pages of "campaign finance reports, lobbying documents and corporate records," NPR reporters discovered the paper trail of a private prison lobby effort to draft and pass SB 1070.

"The law could send hundreds of thousands of illegal immigrants to prison in a way never done before," NPR reported. "And it could mean hundreds of millions of dollars in profits to private prison companies responsible for housing them."

Within days, noting that Brewer's campaign chair and former deputy chief of staff were former or present lobbyists for the Corrections Corporation of America (CCA), a report from Phoenix CBS News questioned whether the Arizona governor had signed the bill with "ulterior motives." With the exclusive hold on the federal contracts for prison detainment in Arizona, CCA had raked in $11 million a month from the state of Arizona, according to the report, "and that, if SB-1070 is successfully implemented, its profits would be significantly padded as it would take responsibility for imprisoning immigrants arrested by Arizona police." According to other reports, "a significant portion" of CCA revenues came from the Immigration and Customs Enforcement, an agency under Homeland Security Chief Janet Napolitano.

The NPR investigation found that it had been Pearce, not Brewer, who shepherded the idea to a hotel room in Washington, DC, during a special meeting with the American Legislative Exchange Council (ALEC), the shadowy lobby front of various multinational corporations and conservative legislators. CCA lobbyists took the hotel elevator ride to SB 1070 glory, as well.

"I did a presentation," Pearce said on NPR. "I went through the facts. I went through the impacts and they said, 'Yeah.'"

With the assistance of the ALEC lobbyists, including the prison representatives, Pearce watched as the language for SB 1070 took shape.

"Four months later," NPR reported, "that model legislation became, almost word for word, Arizona's immigration law. They even named it. They called it the 'Support Our Law Enforcement and Safe Neighborhoods Act.'"

"Maybe it is too late to save America," Pearce had concluded in his essay on SB 1070 for the *Social Contract Press*. "Maybe we are not worthy of freedom anymore. But as an elected official I must try to do what I can to protect our Constitutional Republic. Living in America is not a right just because you can walk across the border. Being an American is a responsibility, and it comes through respecting and upholding the Constitution, the law of our land which says what you must do to be a citizen of this country. Freedom is not free."

IT'S NOT WE THE PEOPLE OF THE UNITED STATES

With the border fence in the background, Russell Pearce stood in his blue jeans and tucked-in red shirt, microphone in hand, giving his stump speech at a Tea Party rally. American flags dangled from the rust-color fence. The makeshift stage sat on the ranch property of Glenn Spencer, a California transplant who had created the shadowy American Border Patrol, a conspiratorial vigilante front. It was a hot day in August, but something else had set Pearce ablaze in the summer of 2010.

"Enough is enough is enough," he told the crowd, perhaps as many as a thousand Tea Partiers, border watchers, and an assortment of gun-toting militiamen and -women from around the region. "We'll take back our country, and it's one state at a time, and it starts here in Arizona."

It also started with President Obama. With former Representative J. D. Hayworth, a Tea Party challenger of Senator John McCain, lurking on the stage, Pearce delivered his verdict on the White House: "This is the first time in the history of the United States that a president of the United States has sided with a foreign government to sue the citizens of the United States for enforcing our laws. Never has it happened before. I believe it's impeachable."

Pearce sucked in his barrel chest with the cheers. He delivered his jokes. He choked on the emotional parts—he had a finger shot off, he reminded the crowd, and he had been shot through the chest. He had been in the immigration battle for twenty-five years, and he couldn't rest yet. The country was on its last legs because illegal immigrants were "going to destroy the republic." Arizona needed to protect itself against an "invasion coming across the border."

With a nod to his Tenth Amendment revisionists, Pearce repeated his states' rights mantra: "Again, it's not we the people of the United States. It's we the people of the sovereign states. These rights that belong to the states are inherent in the Constitution. We have an inherent right to enforce these laws. . . . That's exactly what 1070 is about."

In fact, he told the crowd, SB 1070 was Arizona's and America's success, and thanks to their efforts it was being talked about from coast to coast. Then Pearce quieted and dropped his voice into that crusty baritone of a prophet readying to deliver the message. He set the stage of those dark moments in the American Revolution when only a "ragtag army, mostly made of up congregations, led by ministers," had any faith in America. His words made the crowd look around and embrace their prophetic role as border guardians.

"Nobody could have expected them to prevail and win that war," Pearce continued, dramatically. "Nobody. But they did. And I'm here to tell you I believe because we had divine intervention. God had a hand in the making of this republic, the making of this America."

The crowd roared. "What's it gonna take to wake people up?" Pearce asked.

Much to Pearce's surprise, the answer to that question would take a decidedly different twist.

Arizona pioneers. (Photo courtesy of the Arizona Historical Society.)

CHAPTER FOUR

FEAR AND LOATHING IN A LAND OF CARPETBAGGERS

The question was: What was to be the real Arizona? Another California, an economic colony like Nevada, or Spanish-American like New Mexico? Was it to be predominantly a ranching, mining, or farming state? Would its culture be Northern, Southern, Southwestern, Indian, Mormon, Mexican, or what? These were real issues, for virtually every economic pursuit and cultural group to be found in the whole Southwest was represented in Arizona by the 1880's. What would come out of this desert melting pot?

HOWARD R. LAMAR, "CARPETBAGGERS FULL OF DREAMS: A FUNCTIONAL VIEW OF THE ARIZONA PIONEER POLITICIAN"

THE BROWN SCARE

The newspaper headlines on the glorious Valentine's Day in 1912, when Arizona "assumed its place among states of nation," couldn't have been more foreboding: "Rebellion in Mexico Spreads Fast." Within days, the celebratory forty-eight-gun salute of statehood a distant memory, even more ominous signs of sombrero-capped trouble were at the Arizona-Mexico border, waiting to spill over into the new state at any minute. "Rebels Carry the War into All Sections."

On the front lines of an international crisis, the gunslinging former Arizona Ranger and sheriff of Cochise County, Harry Wheeler, sent a much-publicized telegram to Arizona Governor George Hunt ten days later, asking for the troops from "cavalry to protect Arizona citizens against the ravages of Mexican bandits."

In a haunting foretelling of the tragic murder of Cochise County rancher Robert Krentz in the spring of 2010, Wheeler claimed that Mexican bandits had raided an American ranch (in the same county where Krentz lived) and killed a man named Elias.

Arizona and the entire US-Mexico borderlands dominated the headlines the next day: "American Troops Are Ready to Cross the Line into Mexico." President Robert Taft declared, "No more American lives can be sacrificed." The newspapers reported that orders had been issued for "all commanders of the United States [to] hold their men ready to move at an instant notice."

Not everyone was buying the brown scare or the imminent Mexican invasion in 1912. The *Arizona Daily Star,* in fact, questioned how "Mexican news finds its way out and into the world," and reported that "order prevails" on the border. "Even in the days of the revolution," the Tucson paper noted in an editorial, Arizona's neighboring state of Sonora "was less disturbed than any other Mexican state."

Mocking other news agencies, especially in El Paso, the newspaper declared that certain interests were exaggerating border concerns to garner more federal funds or even to sell more newspapers. The *Star* called on the media not to take the political bait: "The people of Tucson and especially the merchants—and the same may said of the people of all American towns not far removed from the border—are naturally desirous that the truth and only the truth, be reported about Mexico. If the situation is a bad one or should become a bad one, of course, we could have no interest in suppressing that fact, but we have a great and material interest in letting the world know that conditions are not bad when they are not so."

The *Star* had reason to be suspect. "Complaint has been justly made that now and then news agencies have been imposed upon and have been induced to represent a situation in Mexican affairs which has no existence," the newspaper concluded less than a week after the celebration of statehood.

"The Maligning of Mexico," as the Tucson newspaper headlined, was not simply rooted in fear, but cultivated for opportunity in the new state. Half a century before statehood, in fact, the pioneers who had ventured into the territory learned quickly how to exploit such dispatches of borderland security to prime their lucrative businesses.

The carpetbaggers: Charles Poston, the colorful "father of Arizona," called them "the curse of the country." He reserved his greatest contempt for Richard C. McCormick, the *Tucson Citizen* newspaperman, mining promoter, and second territorial governor of Arizona. In Poston's view, "Little Mac" was the "prince of the carpetbaggers."

Poston wasn't alone. Even the Arizona delegate in 1902 lamented in congressional hearings that a "miserable carpetbag government" had afflicted his territory since its inception. Every governor appointed to Arizona had been affiliated with the railroad or mining industries, land speculators, or irrigation and agricultural projects.

Little did Poston know that a 150-year parade of carpetbagging politicians, including "Big Mac," would follow in their footsteps.

To be sure, Poston was only a twenty-seven-year-old Kentucky adventurer and mining entrepreneur "full of Samian wine" when he set sail for Mexico's Sea of Cortez to "take possession of the newly acquired territory of Arizona" before the Gadsden Purchase was signed in December 1853. As fate would have it, he arrived two weeks after the business deal between the US and Mexico was officially sealed, handing over nearly thirty thousand square miles and effectively cordoning off southern Arizona's border. (Final ratification took effect on June 8, 1854.) A storm with "Neptune's pitchfork" pushed Poston and his crew off course and toward shipwreck, then detainment by the Mexican authorities for lack of proper documents and permits. Poston finally dragged himself across the new border in search of the legendary Spanish silver mines.

Setting up camp in the Spanish-era presidio of Tubac, south of Tucson— the northernmost settlement to be sold by Mexico's infamously corrupt dictator

Antonio López de Santa Anna in the Gadsden agreement—Poston managed to strike silver in the nearby Santa Rita Mountains. His Sonora Mining and Exploration Company, underwritten by investors from San Francisco and the East Coast, soon established a thriving mining town composed mainly of Mexican and Native American laborers and European and American engineers.

Poston, who dabbled in Middle Eastern mysticism and wrote operas and poetry, depicted Arizona's first "American" settlement as a quasi-utopian society in his diary entries, where he played the role of a benevolent overseer and even conducted marriage ceremonies that intentionally attracted elopers from Mexico: "We had no law but love, and no occupation but labor. No government, no taxes, no public debt, no politics. It was a community in a perfect state of nature."

With the outbreak of the Civil War in 1861, Tubac lost its Army protection and quickly fell to ruin from Apache attacks. Strangely enough, it rested on the shoulders of a single Mexican immigrant—and not the carpetbagging Anglo pioneers and mining chiefs—to hold up the American flag in the face of the Confederate occupation of Arizona.

A MEXICAN IMMIGRANT'S ACT OF HONOR

Although the brief skirmish at Picacho Peak between the Texas-led Confederates and Union soldiers from California was taken out of the mothballed chests for annual celebration, one Mexican immigrant's courageous act in the face of the Confederate occupation of Tucson remains an enduring story of honor during the Civil War.

Impeccably dressed, Estevan Ochoa strolled the streets of Tucson like a benevolent don over the territorial version of Tammany Hall. One of the Southwest's most enterprising businessmen in the pre– and post–Civil War era, the five-foot-four merchant amassed a small fortune from his shipping business and pioneering ventures in cotton, livestock, and mining.

Contemporaries, journalists, and historians alike always proffered the honorific title of "Don Estevan," perhaps to justify Ochoa's influential role in an increasingly Anglo-dominated gentry. Born in 1831 in Chihuahua, Mexico, his family held huge land grants and claimed that their coat of arms dated back to the historic sixteenth-century Cortés expedition from Spain.

Mild-mannered, famously courteous and generous, he liked to roll his tobacco cigarettes in corn husks. He didn't marry until the age of forty, and then he showered his young bride with the best linens, silks, and elegant clothes imported from Mexico's great markets.

Adorned with bamboo bird cages and meandering pheasants and peacocks, Ochoa's hacienda in Tucson served as the watering hole for the town's most prominent families and visitors and enlightened schemes.

Military chronicler John Bourke, who served on the Apache war campaigns with General George Crook, described Ochoa as "one of the coolest and bravest men in all the southwestern country." Bourke quotes a fellow pioneer's tribute: "He was a typical frontiersman, bold, aggressive, and fertile in resource, laughing danger to scorn, rarely daunted by any obstacle, and in brief, possessing just those qualities which are essential in the foundation of a new state."

Although statehood in Arizona would be delayed for more than half a century after the Civil War, in 1859 Ochoa served with mining pioneer Sylvester Mowry on a special committee at a convention in Las Cruces, New Mexico, that called for the organization of Arizona as a separate territory. At the age of twenty-eight, having immigrated to the United States only two years before, Ochoa was noticed as a leader in the emerging territory by the *Weekly Arizonan* newspaper for his "beautiful and happy style peculiar to himself requesting every member of the meeting to labor diligently and energetically in the good cause in which they had embarked."

It took the Civil War to bring such long-sought territorial recognition, which came with competing claims and declarations. As Congress dallied, Confederate sympathizers gathered in Mesilla, New Mexico, on March 16, 1861, and hastily claimed that the greater Arizona territory would not "recognize the present Black Republican administration." A subsequent convention in Tucson elected a delegate to the Confederate Congress.

As Jefferson Davis signed southern Arizona—below the thirty-fourth parallel—into the rebel states as their westernmost capital on Valentine's Day in 1862, Mowry sided with the Confederate forces and offered to provide lead from his mines for their ammunition. The Johnny Rebs were joined by Mark Aldrich, a recent migrant from western Illinois who had been indicted but not convicted for the murder of Mormon founder Joseph Smith (and who had also served as an informal mayor in Tucson).

When the Confederate flag rose from the mesquite poles in Tucson's depopulated main plaza, Ochoa refused to follow Mowry's expedient profiteering. The Mexican American merchant could have made a tidy little wartime fortune meeting Confederate demands as the conduit of the main wagon supply trains. With the Texan Confederates occupying his town, Ochoa had to make a choice. Historian Frank Lockwood narrates the dramatic moment from the perspective of the rebel captain:

> Mr. Ochoa, you realize, of course, that the United States no longer exists. I trust, therefore, that you will yield to the new order, and take the oath of allegiance to the Confederacy and thereby relieve the necessity of confiscating your property in the name of the new government and of expelling you from the city.
>
> Politely and unflinchingly Don Estevan replied: Captain Hunter, it is out of the question for me to swear allegiance to any party or power hostile to the United States government; for to that government I owe my prosperity and happiness. When, Sir, do you wish me to leave?

Ochoa, who was allowed to take his favorite horse, twenty rounds of ammunition, and some rations, set off across Apache country alone.

In truth, a third army held more sway in Arizona than the ragtag remnants of Union troops and the occupying force of the Texas Confederates: the famed Apaches, the Athabaskan tribes that had dominated sections of southern Arizona and the trade corridors into Mexico for the last two centuries. Their threat worried the self-appointed governor of the Confederate territory of Arizona, Texas Lieutenant Colonel John Baylor, as he raised his army across the Southwest.

In the spring of 1862, Baylor took the barbarism of slavery one step further for the Native Americans as part of a calculated strategy of extermination. In a letter to his commander in Tucson, he wrote, "The Congress of the Confederate States has passed a law declaring the extermination of all hostile Indians. Use all means to persuade the Apaches of any tribe to come in for the purpose of making peace, and when you get them all together, kill all the grown Indians and take the children prisoners and sell them to defray the expense of killing Indians." (That declaration cost Baylor his Arizona governorship, though he managed to remain in the Confederate Congress.)

The Confederates' stay was shorter than that of modern-day snowbird tourists. By the summer of 1862, Union forces from California had sent them fleeing from Tucson. Mowry was arrested as a "Confederate sympathizer, spy and traitor" and imprisoned briefly in Yuma.

Some claimed that Ochoa foretold the state's destiny upon his heroic departure—"I will yet live to see you drive out of here in a worse condition than you are now sending me." But he would eventually return and lose his business empire to a new invader: the railroad. Indeed, President Abraham Lincoln finally signed Arizona into existence as its own territory on February 24, 1863.

THE RED SCARE

The Apache threat, or the perceived threat, did not end with the Civil War or the coming of the railroad.

"The Arizona pioneers owed much to the Apache," historian C. L. Sonnichsen noted. "Without him, there would have been none of those dangers and vicissitudes they loved to talk about, none of the bloody revenges they defended, no contracts for beef and flour for the reservations, no Washington Ring pulling strings in the nation's capital, no Tucson Ring accused of profiteering at the expense of the Army and the Indians in Arizona. Without the Apache, there probably would have been no pioneer society to claim credit for bringing civilization to the savages."

In the volatile period of the 1870s and '80s, Arizona's pioneers and their carpetbagging representatives informed the federal government that "nothing short of removal" of the Indians "shall be deemed satisfactory." Extermination, in truth, was preferable. "Attrition by enforcement" would come at a certain price.

Operating on a healthy dose of Manifest Destiny, the stalwarts continued to dismiss Washington's distant foibles and fashioned their territory amid the "hostile Indians, formidable deserts, suspicious Mormons, and alien Mexicans." Their theme, historian Howard Lamar suggested, had been staked out in the first territorial governor's address to the Arizona legislature: "The Aztec has been here, the Spaniard has retreated. The Anglo-Saxon stands secure. The tide of our civilization has no refluent wave, but rolls steadily over ocean and continent."

Arizona's territorial capital, Prescott, had been named after the celebrated historian and author of the classic text *The Conquest of Mexico*, William H. Prescott, if only as a reminder of the region's momentous destiny. (In a bitter fight over the trough of territorial dividends in 1885, Prescott kept the capital, Tucson received the University of Arizona, Phoenix got the "insane asylum," and Yuma retained the prison.) In his 1908 chronicle *The White Conquest of Arizona*, Orick Jackson dismissed the Mexican influence in Tucson and praised Prescott and Yavapai County as "the cradle of Arizona," laying out a cultural division between southern Arizona and its more conservative central and northern parts that still exists today.

But as Poston and other Arizona pioneers knew, there was nothing like a fight with Washington over border security to raise one's political profile, as well as a lot of capital for your district. In Poston's time, of course, that meant the territory's war with the borderless bands of Apaches. Yet with the laying of the railroads and the emergence of mining commerce and growing towns, Poston claimed that both the Apache terror and the right to be hailed as "pioneer" had come to an end in a new era for the territory of Arizona.

Carpetbagging politicians didn't agree. Over the past twenty years, they had "run Arizona as a rotten borough," Poston claimed, "dispensing the federal patronage from Washington among a ring of immaculate patriots." Much of the patronage came in the form of federal troops and funds to combat the elusive Apache bands.

The "Tucson ring" of political power in the territory, which essentially united merchants and mining interests, effectively doled out federal monies to make Indian policy "the key to the business economy of the territory," according to Lamar. "With some reason outsiders began to complain that the

Apache hostilities were a business and not a war. Indeed, a member of the ring stated wittily and cynically: 'Our policy is to punish those who will not accept the generosity of the government.'" The security outlays became so large that one general called the territory "a vortex" for federal coffers. Another Army general mused that the "hostilities in Arizona are kept up with a view of protecting the inhabitants most of whom are supported by the hostilities."

Arizonans were not amused by any criticism from Washington or outside the territory. When President Grant announced his peace plan for the Indians in March 1871 and sent out a representative to set up reservations, the *Arizona Miner* newspaper simply dismissed the effort as a pacifist folly and suggested they "dump the old devil down a mine shaft and pile rocks on him."

While the newspapers "kept the fear alive," Arizonan politicians and sheriffs chastised Washington for its lack of action, and demanded "of the government that protection which we are guaranteed by the constitution of the United States," a sentiment at the very heart of today's debate over SB 1070.

Indeed, taking action against the Apaches was the one issue that allied carpetbagging interests with Anglo pioneers and their Mexican American and O'odham counterparts, unifying all Arizonans under the banner of benighted patriotism. "These native volunteers," Governor McCormick declared in a tribute to former Mexican soldiers who had suddenly found themselves enveloped by the Gadsden Purchase into the new territory, "who are at home in the country, are the men to hunt the Apache." When it came to killing Indians, the Anglos considered a Mexican "one of us."

As historian Karl Jacoby noted in *Shadows at Dawn: A Borderlands Massacre and the Violence of History*, one of Arizona's first appointed territorial judges was astounded by the ethnic hatred of the Apaches in the region: "It is difficult to convey . . . an adequate idea of the intensity of this feeling."

The largely fabricated hysteria and fear-mongering over the Apaches by the local newspaper proved to be a lethal mix with the spiraling vigilante sentiment over federal control, which had the tacit approval of the territory's leadership. It led to one of the worst tragedies in Arizona history.

After weeks of preparation, a posse of more than 150 Anglo, O'odham, and Mexican Americans—led by Tucson rancher Jesus Elias and former Confederate soldier William Oury, among others—launched an attack at dawn on

April 30, 1871, on a federally established camp for Apaches in Aravaipa Canyon in today's Pinal County, approximately fifty miles northeast of Tucson. The attack was ostensibly retaliation for an Apache raid on some of Elias's livestock. With most of the Apache men away on a hunting trip, the posse faced little resistance in surrounding and then unleashing their firepower on the makeshift Camp Grant village. In the end, the posse massacred 144 Apaches, mainly women, the elderly, and children, and rounded up twenty-seven children and sold them into slavery (the 1863 Proclamation of Emancipation notwithstanding).

If Arizona vigilantes had wanted to send a message of defiance over any peace treaty between belligerent Apache and federal officials, their actions backfired completely in the eyes of the nation.

Oury commanded the posse forces to keep their attack a secret, but within days versions of the massacre had been filed in the local newspapers, and soon the story spread across the nation. After receiving a report from the commander at the camp, the *San Francisco Examiner* opined: "It seems that this was but another massacre, in cold blood, of inoffensive and peaceable Indians who were living on the Reservation under the protection of the Government."

"Arizona at the best is a sort of borderland between barbarism and civilization," the *Every Saturday* commented. "But even for Arizona," the massacre at Camp Grant was "of unparalleled ferocity and malignity."

Arizona may have lost in the court of public opinion, but it took only a few minutes for a Tucson jury to find the defendants not guilty.

In Jacoby's masterful chronicle of the Camp Grant massacre, he reminds us that "history is thus seldom about past violence alone, but violence in the present and future as well." The historical significance of the Arizona tragedy, he suggests, forces us to widen our perspective of the American West and view it also "as an extension of the Mexican north and as the homeland of a complex array of Indian communities."

A decade after the massacre, invoking the efforts of a Confederate posse that had launched attacks on Indians in eastern Arizona, a group of vigilantes was revived as the "Minute Men" in Tucson—a similar organization called the Phoenix Guards emerged in that city—when another round of the "Indian scare" spread across the territory.

"While their mettle never was tested in battle and they were disbanded without ever hearing a blood-curling war cry of an Apache foe," according to a newspaper report, the Minute Men were a reminder of the enduring resolve of Arizonans to take security matters into their own hands.

More than a century later, a new generation of carpetbaggers, vigilantes, and "Minute Men" operations would clamor in their own tragedies.

The Border Patrol, 1928. (Photo courtesy of *Popular Mechanics*.)

CHAPTER FIVE

THE DANGED FENCE

Arizona is trying to be like an independent country. Arizona is not a sovereign nation. It's part of the United States of America.

FORMER GOVERNOR RAÚL CASTRO,
EAST VALLEY TRIBUNE, MAY 7, 2010

ONE OF US

One hundred fifty-six years after Charles Poston's entry, Senator John McCain and Pinal County Sheriff Paul Babeu walked that same border with cameras rolling for a TV commercial. Faced with a surprisingly serious primary challenge from Tea Party candidate and former US Representative J. D. Hayworth, McCain refers to "drug and human smuggling, home invasions, murder." Babeu confirms: "We're outmanned. Of all the illegals in America, more than half come through Arizona." He asks McCain to "bring troops, state, county, and local law enforcement together" (presumably in a federally bankrolled plan). McCain chimes in with his salty sailor's language: "And complete the danged fence."

Babeu concludes with the Rambo kicker: "It'll work this time, Senator. You're one of us."

One of us? Most longtime Arizonans probably wondered: Who was Paul Babeu? Most listeners of Fox News and conservative talk shows already knew; the overnight sensation had appeared on the network twenty-nine times in 2010.

In the tradition of the nineteenth-century "Tucson ring" carpetbaggers, every one of Arizona's most vociferous "nativists"—including Governor Jan Brewer, Maricopa County Sheriff Joe Arpaio, Attorney General Tom Horne, State Superintendent John Huppenthal, various state legislators, Babeu, and McCain—was a transplant from out of state. Horne, who led the legislative effort to end Mexican American Studies, was a Canadian, whose Jewish parents had fled wartime Poland. The only exception was State Senate President Russell Pearce, whose shadowy ancestry would later haunt his recall campaign.

In many respects, the political power of these new nativists had also been gained at the expense of generating fear of the borderlands and fomenting a battle over who would control the state's natural resources—including its laborers.

With the aging Sheriff Arpaio and his barbed-wire ripostes saturating the airwaves, news producers had plucked the baby-faced and lanky Babeu from anonymity in his rural county and placed him in a new role as the TV darling of right-wing border defenders. With searing blue eyes and a shaved head, always clad in his decorative uniform or a cowboy hat and boots, the forty-one-year-old Babeu swaggered with the air of a veteran frontier sheriff and had the tough-guy language to match it.

But he couldn't quite claim Pearce's status as a fifth-generation Arizonan. Like Arpaio, Babeu could hardly hide his New England upbringing, despite his attempts at a complete Western makeover; he came from North Adams, an ailing mill town in Massachusetts, where he had been an upstart in the Republican Party and won a seat on his small town council as a teenager. In subsequent elections, he reportedly dressed up in his National Guard uniform to campaign, a habit that would remain in Arizona. When North Adams snubbed Babeu in an embarrassing mayoral race loss in 2001, he did what any deeply rooted and committed citizen would do: he pulled up anchor and followed his parents to Arizona, where he became a cop in the sprawling Phoenix suburb of Chandler.

Babeu was hardly a slacker, though: by 2008, he had managed to get elected as sheriff of Pinal County, a semirural area of cotton farms and cluster suburban housing subdivisions connected to the umbilical cord of Phoenix highways.

He was one of us now.

When the controversy over SB 1070 ignited in 2010, Babeu stationed himself at Fox News and other outlets as if on assignment. He echoed McCain's fear-mongering ad on various tours of the border, telling CBS News about "assaults against police officers, officer-involved shootings, home invasions, carjackings, violent crimes. And you ask why is that? We can clearly point to the flow of illegal immigrants." Huppenthal, who later campaigned for the state superintendent position with the promise that he would "Stop La Raza" (effectively translated as "stop the Mexican or Chicano people") and the slogan that he was "One of Us," had presented a more dramatic picture when he represented Chandler in the state legislature: he railed on the Senate floor that undocumented immigrants had "nuclear-bombed" neighborhoods in his district.

In the spring of 2011, Fox News featured a report on Babeu's refusal to tone down his rhetoric, and noted in an interview that "Babeu said he has recently increased enforcement near the border with 'constant patrols' by SWAT team officers armed with AR-15s and night vision goggles. 'I'm sending out deputies to meet these armed cartel members,' Babeu said Wednesday. 'And we will not use less than lethal force.'"

Just one thing Fox News and many news outlets forgot to note: although Pinal County supped at the federal trough for large-scale law enforcement funds, Babeu's jurisdiction ended more than ninety miles from the border, blocked by Pima and Cochise counties. In essence: Babeu was all hat and no border.

That little detail didn't seem to bother anyone when he appeared on the openly white supremacist and Holocaust-denying radio show *Political Cesspool* in the summer of 2010. On its website, the show championed "a philosophy that is pro-White. . . . We wish to revive the White birthrate above replacement level fertility and beyond to grow the percentage of Whites in the world relative to other races."

Babeu encouraged listeners to apply for his "posse" program in order to combat a nation "sprinting down the path to socialism." (That socialism presumably didn't include millions of dollars in federal funds for immigration law enforcement in Pinal County.) He also gave a plug for political donations. Though the prime-time sheriff gig must have been gratifying, Babeu clearly had his sights set on Congress. Nonetheless, a posse of white supremacists conjured up all sorts of scenarios gone awry.

In the summer of 2011, Babeu sent an open letter to President Obama, charging that he "has failed to fulfill his core constitutional duty to protect America." "We need focus on the solution to secure our border, not on a path to citizenship or amnesty for 12 million," Babeu lectured the president. He threw down the gauntlet of terrorism and ramped up his rhetoric to include a threat to an American way of life: "If the majority of regular illegal immigrants can sneak into America, what does this say about the ability of terrorist sleeper cells? The porous US/Mexican border is the gravest national security threat facing America. This is no longer just a political fight to stop Barack Obama from giving amnesty to over 12 million illegals, it's also about protecting our nation from terrorist threats. Thousands of illegal entrants hail from State Department countries of interest—Iraq, Iran, Afghanistan, Somalia, Saudi Arabia, Yemen, and others. In some cases, we have confirmed their troubling ties to terrorism."

Not that everyone in Arizona agreed with Babeu. On February 9, 2011, the mayors from the three main border towns wrote Babeu a letter and urged him not to "cultivate a culture of fear." "While your misstatements about efforts to keep communities along the U.S.-Mexico border may keep national media coming to Arizona," the letter noted, "at the same time your consistent inaccuracies hurt cities and towns like ours by causing those who live and travel to the border to fear for their safety when in our communities. . . . The facts show that violent crime is down or remains flat in our border region as we are sure it is in your area as well. In 2002, it peaked at 742 per 100,000 residents, but has since drastically dropped to 219 per 100,000 in 2009 (per the FBI Uniform Crime Reports Program)."

A retired Mesa police officer who had worked on the border for the Drug Enforcement Agency told a Tucson newspaper during the SB 1070 debate that "Babeu's claims of soaring violence have more to do with his own political aspirations than reality." The retired officer, Bill Richardson, likened Babeu to a "college freshman pre-med student who's had one anatomy class telling a veteran pathologist how to do an autopsy."

"What he's very skillfully doing, much like (Joe) Arpaio and (State Sen. Russell) Pearce," Richardson told the *Arizona Daily Star*, "is he's creating fear or fanning the flames of fear, that the undocumented are the root cause of crime in Arizona. In fact, they are not."

"They want us to sit and shut up," Babeu responded. "Well, that's not going to happen. This isn't a time to sit on our hands and ignore the issue. It's a time for action."

In the spring of 2012, Babeu's soaring political career and front-runner status in a campaign for a seat representing Arizona's Fourth District in Congress crashed when the *Phoenix New Times* broke the story that the sheriff had allegedly threatened to seek deportation measures against his former gay lover, a Mexican citizen whose visa status remained in doubt. Dogged by investigations over abuse of power and his office's destruction of public records by the US Office of Special Counsel, the Arizona Solicitor General, and the Pima County Attorney's Office, he officially abandoned his campaign on May 11 in a bid to salvage his sheriff's position.

McCain's career had been far more enduring.

ARIZONA IS BURNING

The venerable senator and onetime presidential candidate should have joined a celebratory summer-day gathering in 2011 at the Grand Canyon National Park when Interior Secretary Ken Salazar upheld a moratorium on a million-acre zone of uranium mining claims, assuring federal protection for Arizona's singular natural heritage. Yet as Salazar stood beside Havasupai tribal elders and Congressman Raúl Grijalva for the historic announcement, Republicans across Arizona were scurrying to create their own roadside attraction about the state's other iconic obsession—undocumented immigrants.

Much of Arizona was burning that summer. The Wallow Fire raging across the eastern part of state was the largest forest fire in Arizona history. More than 530,000 acres of ponderosa pines burned in the Apache and Sitgreaves National Forest areas, forcing thousands of people to temporarily relocate and costing nearly $80 million in damages. Two other fires in southeastern Arizona blazed near the US-Mexico border.

Amid such destruction, it might have seemed ironic that Salazar, Grijalva, and the tribal elders were gathered at the Grand Canyon in an act of preservation. "The announcement today begins to reverse the poisonous legacy of uranium mining and its devastating contamination to our region's people, water, and land," said Roger Clark, the air and energy director for the Grand Canyon Trust.

Instead of joining his colleagues at the Grand Canyon, McCain was falling over himself to trump Alabama's new immigration crackdown and reclaim Arizona's reputation as the xenophobic stalwart of the nation. A day before, he had unleashed his own firestorm on a Saturday TV news program, declaring he had "substantial evidence" that undocumented immigrants or smugglers were responsible for the Wallow Fire and other blazes across the state. McCain tried to clarify that his statement was intended as a general overview on border security, but he didn't seem to notice that national forest rangers had already dismissed these types of rumors.

Quoted in the *New York Times*, one ranger "cited four other southern Arizona fires, all of them in known smuggling areas, that were found to have been caused by American citizens." Far from any illegal alien activity, a rancher's careless welding near dry underbrush, the sparks of target shooters, and training exercises by military jets accounted for the fires.

Not to be outdone, Fox News took McCain's rumors one step further the next day. An interview with Cochise County Sheriff Larry Dever carried this dramatic headline: "Arizona Sheriff: Wildfires Likely Started by Mexican Drug Traffickers, Smugglers." Without any hard evidence, though, Dever had to admit toward the end of his interview, "there's no way to know" who was responsible.

That little nugget was buried in the Fox News interview. And it didn't prevent the newsroom from citing data linked to the nefarious activities of undocumented immigrants that had been collected by Glenn Spencer, an infamous anti-immigrant extremist and militia activist. To back up Dever's claims and the screaming headlines, Fox News featured "an aerial photograph purportedly taken on June 12 of the area by American Border Patrol, an independent organization that monitors the border [which] claims the blaze actually started in Mexico and traveled upwind into the United States. Dever said that was an 'accurate picture' of what occurred." Hardly an "independent organization," the American Border Patrol was hailed by the civil rights watchdog Southern Poverty Law Center as a "virulent" magnet group for a motley crew of vigilantes on the border.

"When you have this much lunacy running rampant," US Customs Service agent Lee Morgan II wrote in his memoir, *The Reaper's Line*, "a government agent needs to figure out the single worst threat and deal with it first. To me, the vigilantism was the most dangerous."

With decades of experience on the border, Morgan had written about the fire blame-game in 2006: "But it seemed to me that a conspiracy to blame the aliens for everything wrong in America was starting to form in Cochise County. I even overheard rednecks in a San Pedro bar planning to start a prairie fire and blame it on the aliens so their 'cause' would have more gunpowder with the politicians in Washington."

Their gunpowder was certainly kept dry by McCain. Not everyone was impressed. "This level of intolerance has reached a new low," Grijalva fumed.

Sure enough, two months after McCain's comments, the US Attorney's office hauled a pair of campers into court, charging them with the fire. The two cousins had inadvertently left their campfire ablaze one morning as they went on a hike with their dogs. They assumed the fire was out "because David threw a candy wrapper into the fire" and it didn't melt. The two twentysomething Arizona residents now faced a possible six-month prison sentence. McCain never issued a retraction, or even a response.

What had happened to John McCain? Was he a casualty of the politics of SB 1070, as well? With Florida overbooked with transplanted politicians, the Vietnam War hero and celebrated POW had come to Arizona in 1981 in search of a congressional district. He was elected to the House a year later, deflecting the carpetbagger charges with his famous retort on his military family's legacy: "The place I lived longest in my life is the Hanoi Hilton." By 1986, McCain had joined the Senate.

McCain's track record on immigration followed Senator Barry Goldwater's fairly moderate views on keeping the borders open for guest-work permits. But McCain went further in representing the views of his Latino constituents.

The National Council of La Raza honored McCain in 1988 for his outspoken criticism of English-only legislation. According to journalist Geraldo Rivera, McCain told a La Raza gathering in Washington, "The building of our great nation is not the work of immigrants from one or two countries. . . . Our nation and the English language have done quite well with Chinese spoken in California, German in Pennsylvania, Italian in New York, Swedish in Minnesota, and Spanish throughout the Southwest. I fail to see the cause for alarm now."

In 2003, McCain even used the loaded word "amnesty" in a special press conference in Tucson on guest-worker provisions. "I think we can set up a program where amnesty is extended to a certain number of people," McCain declared. "Amnesty has to be an important part because there are people who have lived in this country for twenty, thirty, or forty years, who have raised children here and pay taxes here and are not citizens."

When McCain teamed up with liberal icon Ted Kennedy in 2006 for the introduction of their Comprehensive Immigration Reform Act, the Arizona senator went as far out on a limb for immigration reform as any Democrat. In a speech on the Senate floor that summer, he attempted to fashion a compromise: "Without enactment of comprehensive immigration reform as provided for under this bill, our nation's security will remain vulnerable.... The new policies as provided for under this legislation will increase border security and provide for a new, temporary worker program to enable foreign workers to work legally in this country when there are jobs that American workers won't fill. And it will acknowledge and address in a humanitarian and compassionate way the current undocumented population."

Despite President Bush's support, the bill never made it through Congress. And McCain recoiled. Admitting defeat, he shifted his focus to border security in his 2008 presidential campaign.

McCain explained: "Many Americans, with good cause, did not believe us when we said we would secure our borders, and so we failed in our efforts. We must prove to them that we can and will secure our borders first, while respecting the dignity and rights of citizens and legal residents. But we must not make the mistake of thinking that our responsibility to meet this challenge will end with that accomplishment."

The retreat became a full reversal in 2010, when J. D. Hayworth's insurgent Tea Party candidacy suddenly appeared to make inroads during the fallout over SB 1070. McCain completely threw his record of tolerance to the wind and fell into line behind Governor Brewer's assertion that the federal government had failed to secure the border. "The border is broken," McCain told CBS News a few days after the bill was signed. "The cartels are in an existential struggle with the government of Mexico, the violence is at an all-time high, and the federal government has a responsibility to secure the borders."

"He risked his political career for immigration reform, and now he is compromising his principles to fight for his political life," Frank Sharry, executive director of America's Voice, told the Politico.com news site.

The onetime champion of immigration reform finally embraced the reality of Republican politics in Arizona's post–SB 1070 moment when his campaign aired the now infamous TV ad with Babeu along the US-Mexico border in Arizona: "Complete the danged fence!"

ONE OF THOSE LITTLE BAREFOOTED MEXICAN KIDS

Raúl Castro clutched at the railing on his back porch and stared across the valley to Mexico. His balcony looked down the final seventy-yard stretch on the American gridiron of Nogales, Arizona. Once *ambos,* or conjoined—now divided by rusted iron bars.

"They just don't understand the border or our history," Castro said. At the age of ninety-five, Castro had experienced nearly a century of his state's history. After he retired from his legal practice in Phoenix, Castro and his wife left the affluent Paradise Valley in Scottsdale and purchased a historic home on Nogales's hillside border neighborhood. "I've lived along this border all of my life. I even spent time in San Diego and Tijuana. I worked in Mexico in Aqua Prieta. I used to walk across the border. I'd go to Juarez, El Paso."

The son of a pearl diver from Baja, Mexico, Castro was born in the historic mining camp of Cananea in 1916, when his father crossed the Sea of Cortez and found work in Colonel William Greene's former copper mine. A onetime business partner with newspaper magnate William Randolph Hearst, Greene had built a ranching and mining empire in Sonora and Chihuahua that underscored the vast American corporate interests in Mexico's economy during the thirty-year dictatorship of Porfirio Díaz. Many historians consider the brutal crackdown on a strike at Greene's mine in 1906, which resulted in the "massacre" of twenty-three miners, as the opening salvo in the Mexican Revolution. A huge posse of mercenaries, led by the government-funded Arizona Rangers, crossed the border on Greene's orders to suppress the strike.

For Arizona mining barons like Greene, whose Cananea Consolidated Copper Company headquarters was based in Nogales, the concept of "national interests" and "protecting border security" applied only to the northern route. Americans had a right to plunder Mexico. In his study "Southern Arizona and the Mexican Revolution," historian Paul Schlegel showed how the low taxes and concessions granted by the Porfiriato dictatorship to mostly

American companies led to the "push-pull" relationship that characterized labor conditions along the border and in Arizona. "Peasants lost their land and were forced to seek employment with foreign firms," which eventually led to large-scale migration to the United States or urban centers.

Castro's family fell victim to the new rapacious mine operations. As a union leader, his father was targeted by owners as a rabble-rouser and thrown in prison for leading a wildcat strike in Cananea in 1918. Six months later, he was released as part of a special asylum deal that sent Castro and his family across the border to a small community near Douglas, Arizona.

In effect, perhaps as a precursor to Greene's misfortune during the Mexican Revolution, the copper baron's repression of miners inadvertently gifted Arizona with one of Mexico's best and brightest native sons.

Castro grew up in Douglas, where a smelter treated the ore from Bisbee's copper mines. His father ensured Castro's international and border-crossing upbringing; he would read aloud from Spanish-language newspapers from Mexico and Texas in the parlor room. He died, though, when Castro was ten, leaving behind his wife and ten children in the hardscrabble mining region. Castro's mother became a *partera,* or midwife. His brothers found work in the mines or smelter. Notably studious, Castro was the first child in the family to finish high school, and he earned a football scholarship to the Arizona State Teacher's College in Flagstaff.

This was no free ride. Over the next decade, Castro went through a series of achievements and setbacks from racial discrimination that would have derailed most people. As a child, he had walked four miles to school while Anglo children in the same area were picked up by a school bus. During his school breaks, Castro earned half the salary of his Anglo counterparts at the smelter.

Despite a number of honors, Castro couldn't find a teaching job after he graduated from the university in the 1930s. Not that his problem was a secret: "The community would never hire a Mexican American," he told me in his Nogales living room. Forced to hit the road as a migrant worker and bantamweight boxer, Castro roved across the country at the height of the Great Depression.

If anything, he learned that Mexican Americans were not unique in ethnic discrimination. In the ring in Pennsylvania, catcalls to kill his "dago" and "bohunk" rivals stunned the Arizona boxer.

When his younger brother turned down a chance to attend college, citing the futility of the job market, Castro returned home and found a job across the border at the US consulate in Agua Prieta. With impeccable bilingual skills, Castro was hired to handle the protective services for Americans in Mexico. He spent the next five years carving out an impressive niche in borderland diplomacy. His work didn't go unnoticed. His main supervisor praised Castro's level of diplomatic skills and then suggested he look elsewhere for work: no Mexican-born alien would ever have a future in the American foreign service.

The experience both devastated and challenged Castro; he headed to Tucson to pursue a law degree at the University of Arizona, only managing to enter the program by talking his way into a job as a Spanish teacher. Unable to read in English, Castro's mother failed to open his successful results on the Arizona bar exam, fearing it might be a brush with the law, until he arrived home. Within months, Castro opened his attorney's office in downtown Tucson.

In the 1950s, sitting in a barbershop in the Tucson barrio, Castro overheard customers complaining about racism and discrimination. "What are you going to do about it?" he asked. He criticized their retreat into Mexican American and immigrant enclaves, and the fear or timidity that prevented them from confronting Anglos in their political games. "I'm going to run for county attorney," he announced, if only to prove that Mexican Americans should be part of the law enforcement field, not its victims. People thought he was nuts. Active in the Red Cross, the YMCA, and other civic groups—"I joined everything I could join, including the Tuberculosis Association"—Castro was the first Mexican American in Arizona to be elected county attorney. Within a few years, he ran and won another historic election as a Superior Court judge.

Hailed by the Latin American press as the "Yanqui" Castro, not to be confused with Fidel's younger brother, he was appointed as ambassador to El Salvador and then Bolivia by President Lyndon Johnson. (At one point, incredible as it may seem, the Texan had asked Castro to consider changing his surname. He didn't.) His timing in the mountainous South American country in 1967 was chilling; revolutionary hero Ernesto "Che" Guevara was murdered by the military on the same day Castro arrived for his appointment. With the country in an upheaval, he spent the rest of his term dodging assassination threats.

The most trying episode occurred in 1969, when New York Governor Nelson Rockefeller and his wife wired to announce their impending arrival in Bolivia as part of a special twenty-country fact-finding mission on Latin American affairs for the Nixon White House. At first, Castro turned them down. Rockefeller's Standard Oil family legacy in Bolivia was nothing less than a match in search of petrol; Castro imagined such a visit would set off violent protests. When Rockefeller insisted on landing, Castro finally relented, setting up a brief press conference at the airport. Within an hour, Rockefeller was gone, but the political clash had long-term repercussions for Castro. He soon received a cable from Nixon "accepting" a resignation he had never tendered. The IRS began an investigation of his tax filings.

For most diplomats, this would have been the end of the road. For Castro, who had overcome unthinkable odds to become an ambassador and elected official in Arizona, this was simply one more hurdle in his extraordinary mission to prove that Mexican Americans belonged in leadership positions. The dismissal sent him back to Tucson. When Castro stepped off the plane, an arrival party of Democrats had plans for his future.

His international stature placed him in the forefront of other Democratic candidates for governor in 1970. Agreeing to challenge Jack Williams, the conservative radio announcer and longtime Phoenix politician, Castro ran a campaign on a shoestring budget that stressed his law-and-order background and placed an emphasis on environmental and criminal justice issues. He rejected any doubts that a Mexican immigrant could become governor of Arizona.

"I've been lots of places for a guy who didn't have a chance," he declared. In a speech in Yuma, he referred to his naturalized status as an "asset" for a governor in the borderlands.

The *Arizona Republic* had other thoughts. The Phoenix newspaper endorsed Williams, and even printed a photo of Cuban leader Fidel Castro with the headline: "Running for Governor of Arizona."

Castro lost the race to Williams by a hair—less than 1 percent, or 7,400 votes.

Thanks to the fieldwork of Cesar Chavez and a failed recall campaign against Williams by the United Farm Workers in 1972, which added more than 150,000 new voters to the state ranks, Castro had the infrastructure to launch a statewide campaign in 1974 against Goldwater-backed businessman

Russ Williams (no relation to Jack Williams). Emphasizing his law enforcement background, Castro did not embrace the Chicano movement but ran as a conservative Democrat in an admittedly conservative state.

With one of the highest turnout rates in the state's election history, Castro became the first and only Mexican American governor in Arizona on November 6, 1974, once again by a hair. The late-night results from the Navajo Nation pushed Castro over the victory hump by a little more than four thousand votes.

Such a legacy was foretold, perhaps, by Arizona's first state governor, the progressive Democrat George W. P. Hunt in the 1920s. For, in 2002, Castro returned to his hometown of Douglas for the renaming of a park in his honor. On the same bandstand platform, Hunt had made an incredibly prescient speech that had always remained in Castro's memory. The rotund and bald politician, dressed impeccably in his white linen suit, pointed to the crowd and announced: "In this great state of ours, anyone can be governor. Why, even one of those little barefooted Mexican kids sitting over there could one day be governor."

THE WALL TO NOWHERE

Nearly a decade later, with the Tea Party in control of his state, Castro took to his back veranda to contemplate his state's regression in view of the border wall. In 2011, as the state's failing schools languished at the bottom of national rankings for funding (rivaling Mississippi for last place) and the legislature cut an estimated $450 million from the education budget, Arizona's Tea Party–led politicos launched a $50 million online fundraising campaign to build an additional border wall. The price tag seemed a bit low—the George W. Bush and Obama administrations had already invested $1.1 billion on the scrapped high-tech "virtual border fence," and most estimates (including from the non-partisan Government Accountability Office) typically price a mile of border fence at between $3 million and $6 million. Borrowing a page from nineteenth-century convict leasing policies, the state's new border law *required* state prisoners to build this illusory border wall. Supporters hoped that suppliers from the war in Iraq would chip in surplus materials for free.

To kick off the campaign, Arizona's extremist legislators threw a party with then State Senate President Russell Pearce as its headline speaker.

"What a media stunt," Castro muttered. For Castro, it should not be a crime to cross the border for vacant jobs. "If people are willing to do jobs Americans won't do, we should come up with some sort of temporary labor permit."

For the state's most experienced diplomat, the border "problem" was a diplomacy problem. "We have abandoned Latin America," he told one newspaper after the signing of SB 1070. "We spend all our time in the Middle East. We need more diplomacy."

More than four decades ago, Castro had invoked his diplomatic experience and made the same charges against Republican Governor Jack Williams in their gubernatorial race. "Thirty years ago," Castro told reporters at a news conference in Yuma in the summer of 1970, "I was holding conferences with Mexico on drug control. So the problem is not new to me. Has the governor of Arizona been invited to Mexico for anything?"

Unlike former Arizona governor and current Department of Homeland Security Chief Janet Napolitano—and every other governor in the past half-century, for that matter—Governor Jan Brewer never consulted with Castro. Then again, Brewer's staff didn't even bother to inform her about one of Napolitano's much-publicized visits and policy updates on the Arizona border during the summer of 2011.

In fact, flanked by a detachment of border and immigration commissioners in Brewer's absence, Napolitano issued an update in Nogales, Arizona, on July 7, 2011, on the Obama administration's border security policy, which included a record number of deportations and the deployment of 21,000 Border Patrol agents and unmanned aerial drones along the US-Mexico border.

Not that Brewer and Castro had failed to meet. A week before Brewer signed SB 1070, she appeared for a photo-op at a Hispanic Chamber of Commerce awards banquet in Phoenix, where Castro was being honored.

"Some woman approached, put her arms around me, asked for a photo, and then introduced herself," Castro recalled. "She signed the bill a week later." Castro told Brewer he considered the new law unjust and wrong. "Immigration is a national problem," he continued. "A federal problem. Can you imagine every state in the union having its own immigration policy?"

In an extensive review of crime data from 1,600 local and federal law enforcement agencies along the border by a team of *USA Today* reporters, law enforcement experts echoed Castro's sentiments. Tucson Police Chief Roberto Villaseñor told the reporters: "Everything looks really good, which is why it's so distressing and frustrating to read about these reports about crime going up everywhere along the border, when I know for a fact that the numbers don't support those allegations." According to a *USA Today* analysis that week, "rates of violent crime along the U.S.-Mexico border have been falling for years—even before the U.S. security buildup that has included thousands of law enforcement officers and expansion of a massive fence along the border." The newspaper report concluded:

> The murder rate for cities within 50 miles of the border was lower in nearly every year from 1998 to 2009, compared with the respective state average. For example, California had its lowest murder rate during that time period in 2009, when 5.3 people were murdered per 100,000 residents. In cities within 50 miles of the border, the highest murder rate over that time period occurred in 2003, when 4.6 people were murdered per 100,000 residents.
>
> The robbery rate for cities within 50 miles of the border was lower each year compared with the state average. In Texas over that time span, the robbery rate ranged from 145 to 173 per 100,000 people in the state, while the robbery rate throughout Texas' border region never rose above 100 per 100,000.
>
> Kidnapping cases investigated by the FBI along the border are on the decline. The bureau's Southwestern offices identified 62 cartel-related kidnapping cases on U.S. soil that involved cartels or illegal immigrants in 2009. That fell to 25 in 2010 and 10 so far in 2011.

In the spring of 2012, the nonpartisan Pew Hispanic Center released a new report stating that undocumented entries by Mexican immigrants had plunged in the past year. "The historic wave" of Mexican migration, according to center director Paul Taylor, "seemed to have come to a standstill."

"This is the difficulty with Arizona," Castro explained, describing the issues surrounding SB 1070 as cyclical. "When times are good, the economy is good and sound, you won't find a single person who wants to work in the cotton fields or pick fruit. Then the immigrants, even illegals, are welcome. No one squawks. When times are bad, and the economy is in the condition it is today, people don't want them around. They're criminals. I've been through three recessions, I know."

Declaring that SB 1070 was a step backward—"at least forty years, maybe seventy, eighty years"—Castro reminded every reporter that racial profiling by immigration authorities was not a new issue.

"I once had a home in San Diego. One day my daughter and I returned and were stopped by Border Patrol. 'Hey, where were you born, *donde nació?*' I wasn't about to lie. I was born in Mexico, I said. The guard starts questioning me. 'What about that young lady?' She was born in Japan, I said, during the Korean War. He thought we were being smart. In the meantime, someone came by and recognized me. Governor, how are you?"

A similar incident had occurred in Tucson at his horse farm in the 1960s. Working on the front fence in his farm clothes, Castro was stopped by a passing Border Patrol car. The agents asked if he had his work card. Castro said no. When they asked whom he worked for, Castro referred to "the señorita inside." The agents nearly arrested Castro until he showed them the sign by his farm entrance: "Judge Castro."

Such stories would be meaningless to State Senator Steve Smith, who introduced the bill to build a new wall to keep out undocumented immigrants.

A first-term senator, Smith represented the suburban sprawl zone of Maricopa, where Sarah Palin's daughter Bristol had purchased a home. A Midwestern transplant and the director of a talent agency, he had lived in Maricopa for less than ten years. During the month of the signing of SB 1070, his town had one of the highest foreclosure rates in the country.

Unfair as it may seem, comparing Smith to Castro underscores a demographic shift in Arizona's politics.

"I just loved coming out here because—well, first, it was new," he gushed to a public radio reporter at the kickoff event for the new border wall. "And my wife likes new. I mean, new buildings and new restaurants. I mean, nothing was sixty years old. It was all built in the last seven to eight years. Yet much like Maricopa itself, underneath the newness is a deep affinity for the traditional."

He told the reporter he was "horrified by the phenomenon he refers to as 'Press Two For Spanish.' Don't make me change my country for where you come from. If you don't like this country with you, you wanna bring your language with you, your gangfare with you, stay where you were! Or face the consequences. But don't make me change because you don't want to."

Smith singled out Pearce as his inspiration for entering politics. "When I had this idea of running," he said, "I looked through the whole legislature and I said, 'Well, who do I identify with? Who do I want to talk to, who do I want advice from?' I asked one person. I asked Russell Pearce."

Looking across the valley into his native Mexico, Castro was speechless, shaking his head at Smith's inane media circus and his new law, which failed to take into account the exorbitant costs or the fact that much of the unfenced border areas crossed federal and private lands.

Within six months, despite a full-press publicity effort by numerous Fox News TV reports, Smith had raised less than $300,000—not quite enough money to build and maintain a fence the size of a few football fields, according to GAO estimates. Smith was undaunted.

"I call this *Extreme Home Makeover: Border Edition*," he told the Fox Business show *Follow the Money*. With inmate labor to dig the ditches and trenches, since "we are paying for them anyways," Smith still held out hope of getting the job done.

LAGGIÙ NELL'ARIZONA

Maricopa County Sheriff Joe Arpaio went beyond a mere wall to divide the United States and Mexico and prevent illegal entries.

"And I wasn't kidding, or speaking off the cuff, when I talked to Lou Dobbs about putting up tents near the border," he wrote in his best-selling memoir, *Joe's Law: America's Toughest Sheriff Takes on Illegal Immigration, Drugs, and Everything Else That Threatens America*. "That's what I wanted the federal government to do, to gather together as many old army tents as they could find, erect those tents along the border, arraign and try the illegals in courts set up close to those tents, and put those people convicted of illegally crossing the border into the United States into these tents for six months."

First, though, Arpaio had more pressing issues. In the somber days of the tenth anniversary of the 9/11 attacks, long after Donald Trump had thrown in the towel and Rush Limbaugh and Glenn Beck had exhausted their diatribes,

Arpaio met with Tea Party activists from Surprise, Arizona, and agreed to assign his "Cold Case Posse" to reopen an investigation on the authenticity of President Barack Obama's Hawaiian birth certificate.

"The individuals on this posse have been sworn in by me, and I have granted them the authority required to conduct this investigation," Arpaio told the media. "But the results of their investigation ultimately come to me, and I will then decide how best to proceed from there."

It was breaking news: Arpaio graced the cover of the venerable supermarket tabloid *Globe* magazine.

Many critics tended to describe Arpaio as the modern-day embodiment of civil rights scourge Eugene "Bull" Connor, the onetime Klansman and commissioner of public safety in Birmingham, Alabama, who presided over a reign of terror against African Americans for more than twenty years. Connor famously unleashed police dogs and fire hoses on activists, including children, and harassed, arrested, and imprisoned religious and civil rights leaders during some of the bloodiest episodes in that period. His most egregious work, perhaps, was his complete indifference (if not tacit approval) of violent attacks, including bombings, against African Americans and white supporters by racist elements in his state.

The comparison with Arpaio ends there, though. Marketed as "America's toughest sheriff," Arpaio drew national attention for his use of chain gangs and the cruel deprivation tactics of his "Tent City," which had been subjecting prisoners to 120-degree summer weather conditions since 1993. Arpaio was also under investigation by the Civil Rights Division of the Justice Department for racial profiling and abuses, and even deaths during detention in his facility. And he has become the poster image of ruthlessness in the immigrant debate as a result of his choreographed crime sweeps, which have targeted and shattered the lives of untold thousands of immigrants and their families.

But once Connor's bigotry and brutal tactics appeared on the evening news, it affected the conscience of enough people in the nation to shift the discussion on civil rights laws and instigate federal intervention. Connor himself was out of a job within a year of the bloody summer of 1963 in Birmingham.

The nearly eighty-year-old Sheriff Arpaio, with his Italian American crooning and Massachusetts-accented folksiness, on the other hand, became an ever more popular TV celebrity with virtually every sordid allegation over two decades. Few interviews ended without the sheriff belting out a bar of "My Way" by his beloved *paisano* Frank Sinatra. He became "Sheriff Joe."

Had Arpaio manipulated the media for his own gains on behalf of punitive law enforcement, or, in the profitable and competitive business of media entertainment, had he been coddled as the nasty caricature of a frontier sheriff to meet the insatiable appetite of true-crime chronicles for a national viewership?

According to the watchdog group Media Matters, Fox News hosted Arpaio eight times in the immediate aftermath of the SB 1070 debate, "with virtually no criticism of his controversial statements and enforcement tactics."

In the fall of 2007, Arpaio quipped on CNN's *Lou Dobbs Tonight* that he thought it was "an honor" to be compared by his critics to the Ku Klux Klan—an obnoxious gaffe that would have cost any sheriff in the South his job. Sheriff Joe got away with a few shrugs and a "clarification" of his comments.

One thing was certain: although the mainstream media had no problem holding Southern racists accountable in the days of black-and-white television, the verdict was still out on folksy Italian American attacks on Latinos in living color.

If anything, Arpaio borrowed more from the media-savvy antics of gunman Wyatt Earp, the legendary Tombstone marshal who embellished his exploits in the shootout at the OK Corral for fame and fortune, and from Earp's Hollywood pal Tom Mix, the gunslinging cowboy hero of silent movies, than from any of Bull Connor's vicious devices. Mix wept as a pallbearer at Earp's funeral in California in 1929; it should have marked an end to the mythic six-shooter approach to law enforcement that had made Arizona so famous, but Arpaio was doing his best to keep Arizona on the big screen.

In 2008, Phoenix Mayor Phil Gordon wasn't so entertained by what he deemed Arpaio's "made-for-TV" raids. He asked the FBI to investigate the sheriff for civil rights abuses. When the Major League Baseball All-Star game came to Chase Field in the summer of 2011, Arpaio, undaunted by the seeming slap on the wrist by the Justice Department, announced his intentions to parade his clean-up chain gang of immigrants and women in front of the nationally televised event. He opted out at the last minute, thanks to pressure from Gordon and city law enforcement officials.

It probably didn't matter to Arpaio; the national media, including National Public Radio, had already covered his plans. In effect, if the intent was to showcase Arizona's punitive stripes to the world, it didn't really matter if it happened. He had made his point.

Nonetheless, the blur between tall tale and reality, history and Hollywood, and right and wrong didn't die with the passing of Arpaio's beloved Western icons. Their version of Arizona justice defined the great American myth of the lawless frontier and its heroes and villains for a century of blockbuster movies and best-selling books.

"Let me tell you something and I'm not bragging," Arpaio gushed to reporter Terry Greene Sterling in 2009. "I'm so high profile I went from 98 percent to probably 99 percent on name identification. . . . You know, sometimes I understand how a movie star feels, or a celebrity."

Case in point: on the day Arpaio appeared on Comedy Central's *The Colbert Report* in 2008, peddling a ghostwritten memoir he would later admit he hadn't even read thoroughly, two reporters from the *East Valley Tribune* won the Pulitzer Prize for their damning five-part exposé on how Arpaio's obsession with hunting down nonviolent undocumented immigrants shifted limited resources and law enforcement efforts from violent crime investigations. Pointing out that more than forty thousand felony warrants remained on Arpaio's desk, Mayor Gordon chastised the sheriff for fashioning a "sanctuary" for felons.

"Let them blast me," Arpaio boasted in *Illegal: Life and Death in Arizona's Immigration War Zone*, as Sterling reported. "I ought to pay them for blasting me, since it makes me go up in the polls."

In fact, much of Arpaio's book is a rehash of self-promotional appearances on TV and criticism he has received in major newspapers and magazines. In the chapter "Media Matters," he mocks TV talk-show host Phil Donahue for comparing him to a character in a Charles Dickens story. He also cites all his big ideas—such as erecting a tent city on the border—from interviews on TV, including multiple appearances with former CNN host Lou Dobbs.

Arpaio, of course, is hardly an original. In some respects, he follows in the tradition of the first city marshal in Phoenix, Mexican immigrant Henry Garfias. Elected for the first time in the newly incorporated town in 1881, Garfias won six elections as a no-nonsense law-and-order enforcer. Unlike

Arpaio, Garfias also edited a Spanish-language newspaper and meted out his forms of "lightning-fast gunfighter" justice in every neighborhood. The *Gazette* newspaper praised Garfias most of all for his "good work" with "his chain gang." In fact, he earned an extra two dollars a day for his chain-gang initiatives.

Like Garfias, Arpaio is the son of an immigrant; his father slipped into the country from the volatile southern Italy region of Campania only months before the restrictive quotas from the Immigration Act of 1924 clamped down on Italian immigration. A popular Italian song of the period, *Laggiù nell'Arizona,* waxed romantically about Arpaio's future land (though it was joyously populated by guitar-playing *bandoleros*).

In *Joe's Law,* Arpaio juxtaposes the experience of his Italian family of immigrants and those of Mexicans. Dismissing the legacy of his predecessor Garfias, who was praised by the *Republican* newspaper in Phoenix "as one of the bravest men who ever was known," Arpaio makes a startling one-liner of racist revisionism that would have made Bull Connor blush: "My parents, like all other immigrants *exclusive* of those from Mexico, held to certain hopes and truths."

Among various points, Arpaio doubts Mexican allegiance to the United States and claims that Mexican immigrants and "some Mexican-Americans" cling to the belief in the "*reconquista* of these lands, returning to them to Mexico." And while Italians congregated in their "Little Italy" communities, this was in "stark contrast to the exceptional concentration of Mexicans in the Southwest."

For all of his nearly eight decades of wisdom, Arpaio's chronicle demonstrates a select memory of recent American history. Among the estimated 4.5–5.5 million Italian immigrants who poured into the United States in the decades around the turn of the twentieth century, 90 percent congregated in urban areas in eleven states. The great majority of Italian immigrants in that period originated from Arpaio's impoverished and politically disenfranchised southern provinces. In a haunting resonance with today, the "racial threat" of his ancestors underscored the most egregious planks in setting quotas on Italians, among others, in 1924. A congressional report set out the scenario that loomed if the "invasion" of Arpaio's people wasn't slowed:

> With full recognition of the material progress which we owe to the
> races from southern and eastern Europe, we are conscious that the

continued arrival of great numbers tends to upset our balance of population, to depress our standard of living, and to unduly charge our institutions for the care of the socially inadequate.

If immigration from southern and eastern Europe may enter the United States on a basis of substantial equality with that admitted from the older sources of supply, it is clear that if any appreciable number of immigrants are to be allowed to land upon our shores the balance of racial preponderance must in time pass to those elements of the population who reproduce more rapidly on a lower standard of living than those possessing other ideals.

While more than six hundred thousand of Arpaio's Italian kinfolk were obliged to tote "resident alien" identity cards during World War II, the loyalty of Mexican Americans and Mexican immigrants was never questioned. An estimated three hundred fifty thousand Mexican Americans served in World War II, bringing home seventeen Medals of Honor. In a different form of discrimination than that against many Italians in the period, Mexican American soldiers returned to wage their own battles for veterans' benefits and civil rights in Arizona and across the nation. In Arpaio's adopted city of Phoenix, in fact, the American Legion Post 41 was founded by returning Mexican American vets who had to struggle for fair housing benefits. Even access to certain city swimming pools had been cut off to returning vets because of segregation.

Without any documentation, Arpaio asserts in his book that "no other group except the Mexicans, and other Hispanics as well, has broken the immigration laws in such astonishing numbers." The statement helps explain Arpaio's quip on *Larry King Live* in the spring of 2010 that his forces admittedly arrest "very few" suspects who are not Latino. Such a blanket pardon for other immigrant groups—not only Italians but also the Irish, whose ranks reportedly included more than thirty thousand undocumented immigrants in New York City alone in the year Arpaio published his book—might be the most telling reminder of his select view on who has the right to the American Dream.

Nonetheless, the bizarre investigation of President Obama's birth certificate obsessed Sheriff Joe, with his posse and a handful of "birther" extremists flanking his showdown.

Arpaio's sense of timing was impeccable. On the anniversary of Cesar Chavez's celebrated birthday in March 2011, he unveiled a new media stunt, invoking wartime with Operation Desert Sky—a thirty-plane air posse of armed volunteers tracking Mexican immigrants. Only days before, Arpaio had rolled his department's private tank into a quiet west Phoenix neighborhood to apprehend a flock of chickens and their unarmed cockfighting enthusiast.

While Arpaio's reality show on Fox, *Smile . . . You're Under Arrest,* went the route of Sarah Palin's hopeless reality show in Alaska, he didn't hesitate to place his Maricopa County Sheriff's Office at the disposal of Steven Seagal's reality show *Lawman.*

One spring morning, as Phoenix resident Debra Ross told KPHO-TV, she thought an earthquake was rocking her West Valley neighborhood. It was Seagal and his posse, decked out in Arpaio's celebrated Army tank in search of a suspected cockfighting operation. The thunder of the operation blew out windows in the area. SWAT members took up defensive positions around armored vehicles and a bomb robot. "When the tank came in and pushed the wall over and you see what's in there, and all it is, is a bunch of chickens," Ross told KPHO. In the end, Seagal and Arpaio busted an unarmed and solitary homeowner, 115 chickens, and a puppy. The animals didn't fare as well as the alleged cockfighter, who later sued Arpaio for killing his dog.

While many would question the logic of Arpaio's extremist follies, or the cost to taxpayers (Arpaio was quick to point out that donations and RICO [Racketeer Influenced and Corrupt Organizations Act] funds underwrote his armory), he was under investigation for the mismanagement of nearly $100 million—at the same time the state of Arizona was witnessing the deaths of denied transplant patients and dealing with draconian cuts to education.

But such questions had been asked in vain in Arizona. The real question might be: who represented Arizona in the media's eyes—episodes from reality TV spotlighting the anti-immigrant antics of a Massachusetts-transplanted DEA agent-turned-sheriff who ran a travel agency with his wife in Phoenix until boredom set in, or the towering legacy of Arizona native and labor leader Cesar Chavez, who devoted his life to the pursuit of environmental justice and democratic reform? On the other hand, if the travel industry had been lucrative for Arpaio, would America ever have placed Phoenix on the road map to penal perdition?

French pop star Manu Chao framed the question for the national media over who truly represented Arizona in the fall of 2011. Appearing at a protest in front of Arpaio's office at the downtown Phoenix Wells Fargo Bank building before his benefit concert for the Alto Arizona human rights group, Chao pulled out his guitar and played a few verses from his song "Clandestino": "*Mano Negra, clandestino, Mexicano, clandestino, Boliviano, clandestino*, Joe Arpaio, illegal."

Informed of the growing crowd and large media pool, Arpaio had come out to confront the internationally renowned recording artist, crowing that he might belt out a version of "My Way" to join the fun. Hardly anyone noticed the sheriff. Especially not Chao, who worked the media and discussed his hopes for a new generation of activists. "That's not poetry, that's a reality," he told *New Times*, referring to Arizona's demographic shift.

The media converged on Chao. Upstaged by the French singer, Arpaio stormed off.

THE MOST EGREGIOUS RACIAL PROFILING IN THE UNITED STATES

The bell finally tolled at 1,095 days and eleven hours for Sheriff Arpaio—at least according to the ticking icon on the *Phoenix New Times* home page that had asked readers for years: "How long has Sheriff Joe been under investigation by the feds?"

That investigation culminated in the winter of 2011 when the Civil Rights Division of the Justice Department released a long-awaited report that found a "chronic culture of disregard for basic legal and constitutional obligations" in Arpaio's office. Drawing from tens of thousands of documents and more than four hundred interviews with sheriff's department personnel, inmates, and experts, the report documented "a widespread pattern or practice of law enforcement and jail activities that discriminate against Latinos," resulting in gross violations of constitutional rights.

Assistant Attorney General Thomas Perez threw down the gauntlet for Arpaio, giving him until January 4, 2012, to accept the Justice Department's measures and start taking "clear steps toward reaching an agreement with the Division to correct these violations in the next 60 days," or face a lawsuit. Perez expressed the department's willingness "to roll up our sleeves and build a comprehensive blueprint for reform" of the Maricopa County Sheriff's Office, adding, "if the will exists" on Arpaio's end.

One federal department was not even waiting: within hours of the announcement, the Department of Homeland Security had terminated Maricopa County's access to immigration status data under the federal Secure Communities program.

The announcement came amid growing calls for Arpaio's resignation, in the aftermath of allegations that his department had mishandled hundreds of sex crime reports in the Phoenix area township of El Mirage.

Representative Raúl Grijalva was the first to call for Arpaio to step down. "Mr. Arpaio might love headline-grabbing crackdowns and theatrical media appearances," the Tucson Democrat said, "but when it comes to the everyday work of keeping people safe, he seems to have lost interest some time ago."

A few days later Representative Ed Pastor, who represents Maricopa County in Congress, endorsed a call for Arpaio's resignation. So did nine state legislators. Even Cafe Con Leche Republicans, a national organization, released a statement saying that "Arpaio has disgraced his office and the Republican Party."

"This is a very important day for Maricopa County," County Supervisor Mary Rose Wilcox, a critic of Arpaio, told supporters following the release of the report. "It's a day many of us have been awaiting. Let this be the end of Arpaio. Give us a better criminal justice system."

Arpaio acted unimpressed. The sheriff expressed his disdain for federal oversight, especially from the Obama administration—earlier in the week, Arpaio couldn't resist tweeting his glee about a dubious report in the *Globe* tabloid newspaper that his Cold Case Posse's investigation of Obama's birth certificate had the first lady "in a panic."

Two years earlier, after Janet Napolitano announced her intentions to terminate the Department of Homeland Security's cooperation with Arpaio's office, Sheriff Joe appeared on Glenn Beck's show and openly mocked federal authority. Arpaio claimed that local and state laws allowed him to target "some people who have an erratic, scared . . . whatever . . . if they have their speech, what they look like, if they look like they come from another country, we can take care of that situation."

The Justice Department's report concluded that Arpaio was engaged in racial profiling. "Our investigation uncovered substantial evidence of the kind identified by the Supreme Court in *Arlington Heights*," the report noted, "showing that Sheriff Arpaio has intentionally decided to implement his immigration program in a manner that discriminates against Latinos."

The report added a telling detail about Arpaio's effectiveness as a law enforcement officer. While his operations involved "the most egregious racial profiling in the United States," according to one expert, "enforcement actions rarely result in human smuggling arrests."

Another law enforcement officer levied a similar charge against Arpaio on the botched sex crimes investigations. Bill Louis, former assistant police chief in El Mirage, wrote an op-ed in the *Arizona Republic* declaring, "Sheriff Joe Arpaio failed these victims. At this point there is little that can be done to undo the harm they have endured."

Would Arpaio comply with the Justice Department's demands? "I've seen police chiefs, DAs and others who have been able to reform the system," Perez said at his press conference. But "reform" and "Arpaio" were two words rarely seen together. In the spring of 2012, as if in defiance of the Justice Department, Arpaio released the results of his Cold Case Posse investigation of the president's birth certificate: it was a "forgery," worthy of a criminal investigation.

The media attention this time, however, was sparse in comparison to his earlier stunts. Within days, the sheriff shifted his attention to his reelection campaign, which suddenly seemed in doubt. For the first time in his career, he faced serious opposition. The Phoenix-based human rights group Puente, whose leader, Sal Reza, and other activists had long been targeted by Arpaio's department, had launched the "Arrest Arpaio, Not the People" campaign.

"When they passed SB 1070, its authors declared a war of attrition on immigrants where 'undocumented people are treated as criminals and Latinos are treated as suspects,'" Puente director Carlos Garcia said in Phoenix. "But as the Department of Justice concluded in their investigation into Arpaio, that was already the reality we lived in the state."

On April 4, 2012, chastising his office's "refusal to engage in good faith negotiations," the Justice Department announced its decision to sue Arpaio. The sheriff remained defiant. "Appointment of an outside monitor essentially usurps the powers and duties of an elected Sheriff and transfers them to a person or group of persons selected by the federal government," he said in a statement. "And so to the Obama administration, who is attempting to strong arm me into submission only for its political gain, I say, 'This will not happen, not on my watch!'"

One month later, Arpaio received a thirty-two-page letter detailing the Justice Department's "notice of intent to file civil action": *United States v. Joseph M. Arpaio*. Assistant Attorney General Thomas Perez called the sheriff's bluff. The federal government would see Arpaio in court "to remedy the serious Constitutional and federal law violations."

OPEN SEASON

On June 12, 2009, little over a year before Sheriff Arpaio and Russell Pearce headlined a "United We Stand" Tea Party rally on Glenn Spencer's ranch property in 2010, a battalion of sheriff deputies, FBI agents, and SWAT team members in armored vehicles blocked off the entrance to Spencer's nearby home. Earlier that day, a leader of a renegade faction of an anti-immigrant border group called the Minutemen American Defense (MAD) had dropped into Spencer's home and sent an email. Within hours, MAD leader Shawna Forde was in custody for the murder of American citizen Raul Flores and his nine-year-old daughter, Brisenia.

Earlier that spring, *Phoenix New Times* reporter Stephen Lemons had uncovered a blog message that Forde, a transplant from the state of Washington, had written after she attended a Tea Party rally in Phoenix. "This is the time for all Americans to join organizations and REVOLT!!!" The message went on: "Refuse to be part of a system only designed to enslave you and your children. Times will be worse before they get worse. *Say no to illegal immigration* Lock and Load, Shawna Forde."

Brisenia was the same age as Christine Taylor Green, who was murdered in the tragic Gabrielle Giffords shooting. When Forde and another partner threatened their way into the Flores household in the town of Arivaca, Arizona, less than an hour south of Tucson, Brisenia had begged for her life after her father was shot. She was shot in the face and died. Her mother managed to call 911 before exchanging shots. Pima County Sheriff Clarence Dupnik, who also handled Giffords shooter Jeremy Loughner, summed up his thoughts on Forde: "She's, at best, a psychopath."

Despite the fact that he had allowed Forde to encamp on his ranch, Spencer immediately denied any connection to her rampage—an apparent bungled robbery attempt to fund her militia group. Within recent years, though, Forde had become a well-known character in the vigilante sphere, both online and on the ground, and had split with the Minuteman Civil Defense Corps to form her own group. In fact, with the rise and fall and changing of names of groups on the border vigilante circuit, it could be difficult to keep up. Not that their mission of stopping the "invasion" of Mexicans ever faltered.

All border-patrolling militia, vigilante, and white supremacist groups did share one trait: as a magnet for out-of-state extremists, they sported some of the slickest websites, with updates and photos of their activities.

There were some local exceptions. The Hannigan family in Cochise County made national headlines in the late 1970s for the level of depravity they meted out against undocumented Mexicans on their property. "After being robbed and burglarized a few times by Mexican bandits," customs agent Lee Morgan wrote in his memoir of life on the border, "the Hannigans had taken it upon themselves to administer Wild West justice to the next aliens who ventured across the ranch."

> They caught a couple or three Mexican fellers one day crossing their property and strung them up by ropes in a tree. Now, it didn't matter to the Hannigans that these boys were innocent "looking for work" fellers and not border bandits. . . . So the salty old son of a bitch started a fire on the desert floor, much like the one a rancher would use for the branding of cattle. When the irons were hot, the Hannigans' Beast was exposed to the world. After the sadistic bastards were done burning and torturing the Mexicans, the redneck vigilantes unleashed a volley of shotgun blasts that ripped apart the flesh of their defenseless victims.

The elder Hannigan died before the trial in which an all-white jury found the sons not guilty in 1977. "The outcome incensed Mexican Americans and Mexicans alike," reported *Time* magazine. "Racist, frontier justice," charged Raúl Grijalva, then a Tucson school district board member. When a second trial ended in a hung jury, more protests erupted and the US prosecutor warned about a "chilling effect" among ethnic divisions in the state. According to a local poll in 1980, "100 percent of the Hispanics and 64 percent of the Anglos surveyed expressed the opinion that the brothers were guilty." In the third round in federal court, one brother was found guilty by a jury and sentenced to three years in prison, while the other walked free. Not entirely free—he was soon convicted on marijuana smuggling, reenforcing the hypocrisy of the supposedly antidrug border patrols.

While the fallout over the Hannigan case continued to overshadow public debate on immigration and border security, the Barnett brothers emerged in Cochise County as the next *cause célèbre* for the extremist right wing in the 1990s. In large part because of a tremendous amount of media coverage, according to Mark Potok, legal director of the Southern Poverty Law Center, the Barnetts were "probably more than any people in this country . . . responsible for the vigilante movement as it now exists." In a 2000 *Time* magazine feature, Roger Barnett toted an M-16 automatic rifle and bragged about knocking an undocumented migrant to the ground after being challenged for his credentials. "So I slammed him back down and took his photo," he recounted. "'Why'd you do that?' the illegal says, all surprised. 'Because we want you to go home with a before picture and an after picture—that is, after we beat the s____ outta you.' You can bet he started behavin' then." (In 2011, the Ninth Circuit Court of Appeals upheld a lower court ruling that Roger Barnett had to pay $87,000 for holding four unarmed undocumented immigrants at gunpoint. The Arizona Supreme Court had upheld a similar judgment for a different case in 2008.)

Described as ranchers, the Barnetts seemingly had more in mind for their vast grazing lands. After a period of "hunting" with mercenaries in South Africa, agent Morgan claimed, the Barnetts approached him as a US customs agent to see if they could be named "informants," which would have granted them "a legal license to hunt Mexican dope mules and illegal aliens." Morgan said no, but that didn't stop him from encountering "a baker's dozen of the armed dickheads riding in pickup trucks up and down Highway 80" in search of migrants. The "ranch-hand" vigilantes dressed in camouflage tagged with patches that read "US Patriot Patrol," almost indistinguishable from a Border Patrol patch; one of them told Morgan of the Barnetts' big plans to build a hunting lodge. Morgan added, "You guessed it. These crazy sons of bitches were going to have safari adventures for people who wanted to track down il-legal aliens!" A 2006 *New York Times* profile of Roger Barnett that depicted him with a "pistol to his hip" and "an assault rifle in his truck" described his hunts: "Hunt illegal immigrants, that is, often chronicled in the news."

An even more outrageous episode nearly took place in the same county in 1929, when a cadre of local entrepreneurs in Cochise County had formed the Fimbres Apache Expedition as a "gentlemen's club" to carry out another kind of big-game hunt; for $200, participants would have the opportunity to shoot Apache Indians in the Mexican outback in Chihuahua. "I have hunted big game in many parts of America," one applicant wrote, "but I am sure shooting at an Apache Indian would give me a greater thrill than any I have heretofore shot at." Thanks to the Mexican government and the intervention of the sec-retary of state, that applicant didn't get the chance. The operation was shut down.

For Phoenix playwright James Garcia, who organized a series of plays in the aftermath of SB 1070 on immigration issues, the measure effectively opened a new season of police hunting of anyone of Mexican, Latino, or in-digenous heritage. "You felt like you had a target on your back now," he said as he prepared for a new show, *Amexica: Tales of the Fourth World*, which ran at the Mesa Arts Center in the heart of Russell Pearce's district.

On February 22, 2011, two weeks before Pearce would have his final show-down over his omnibus immigration legislation, including a special bill that would prevent undocumented immigrants from obtaining any legal damages in court from attacks, the forty-three-year-old Forde was convicted and sen-tenced to the death penalty. Another death on Sonora's death row.

By taking the stage at Spencer's ranch after Forde's murder spree—along with J. D. Hayworth and Arpaio—Pearce openly flaunted his associations with other vigilantes and extremists. His own son Sean, in fact, had partici-pated in the Minuteman Project, "a month-long action in which revolving casts of 150 to 200 anti-immigration militants wearing cheap plastic 'Undoc-umented Border Patrol Agent' badges mobilized in southeastern Arizona," according to a Southern Poverty Law Center report in 2005. The project's stated goal was to "protect America" from the "tens of millions of invading il-legal aliens who are devouring and plundering our nation."

Despite being denounced by President George W. Bush, the Minuteman Project captured the fancy of the news media, which reportedly outnumbered the gallant force that assembled in Tombstone that spring. Once again an invention of outsiders—in this case Jim Gilchrist, a California-based Vietnam veteran, and Chris Simcox, a California-transplant to Arizona—that movement eventually faltered and splintered into various factions.

In Pearce's Mesa district, neo-Nazi enthusiast J. T. Ready had formed his own US Border Guard, which not only led armed excursions along the border but embraced Sheriff Paul Babeu's challenge across the white supremacist radio airwaves to conduct patrols for undocumented immigrants in Pinal County's Vekol Valley. Forever on their trail, Lemons posted a *New Times* blog about Ready's announcement in the summer of 2010 on his "white supremacist New Saxon site, inviting participants to 'bring plenty of firearms and ammo.'" Ready admonished, "Camouflage or earth tone clothing [is] preferred. . . . Bandanas, balaclavas, or other identity concealing items are permissible and encouraged." He declared, "This is the Minuteman Project on steroids! THE INVASION STOPS HERE!"

As delusional as Ready's patrol might have been, Pearce couldn't stay away from the militia leader's media parade. The more he attempted to distance himself from Mesa's most notorious white supremacist, the deeper his connection seemed to grow. Ready had been court-marshaled twice from the military, yet he still managed to invoke the veteran tag until he was stripped of his role as master of ceremonies for a Veteran's Day parade in Mesa. That didn't stop him from making a failed bid for the Mesa City Council, or from gaining a spot as a precinct committeeman for the Republican Party in 2008. Lemons's indefatigable muckraking at *New Times* over several years exposed Ready's involvement with the National Socialist Movement and his crossover exploits with border groups. But none of these revelations seemed to upset his relationship with Pearce, who had taken part in Ready's baptism in the Mormon Church and ordained him as an elder in the Melchizedek priesthood.

Despite the mounting evidence, Pearce denied any association with Ready beyond casual contact at public events. But in a stunning discovery, legendary videographer Dennis Gilman uncovered footage from 2006 of Pearce commenting on Ready's Mesa City Council candidacy: "He's a true patriot, to the real purpose, the limited purpose, to the Republican platform that we have."

Pearce emailed Lemons in response to the video in the winter of 2011: "No one could have known or guessed he [Ready] would later become involved with radical hate groups."

However, the Anti-Defamation League in Phoenix had already warned Pearce about Ready's Nazi activities in 2006. A year later, after a legislative hearing, local media began to report on Ready's white supremacist affiliations. At an anti-immigrant rally in Phoenix in the summer of 2007, Pearce watched admiringly as Ready wooed the crowd.

In the end, it was Ready who felt betrayed by Pearce's political maneuvers. "He's supposed to be a lawman," Ready charged after Pearce closed the door on their relationship in response to all the media attention, "but he has a pattern of criminality."

"He is the worst kind of racist," Ready said of Pearce in a *New Times* interview in the fall of 2010. "One who will do anything to achieve power, then trample on our rights like a tyrant when he gets that power."

Ready added, "I christen him Grand Wizard of the AZ Senate!"

On May 2, 2012, two weeks after armed militia activists in camouflage ambushed and killed two undocumented migrants in a Pinal County incident that remains unsolved, Ready drew a borderline inside his own home in the neighboring suburb of Gilbert and gunned down his girlfriend, along with her daughter, her daughter's boyfriend, and their eighteen-month-old toddler, and then turned the gun on himself in an apparent mass murder/suicide. Investigators found an enormous stockpile of weapons, including anti-tank grenades.

Hounded by the media, Russell Pearce released a statement on his association with the murderous neo-Nazi. "I knew JT Ready, I did, as did many of us who have been involved in Mesa politics for a long time. When we first met JT he was fresh out of the Marine Corp and seemed like a decent person," it read, in part. "At some point in time darkness took his life over, his heart changed, and he began to associate with the more despicable groups in society."

Spencer's American Border Patrol was one of the first border groups to openly court white supremacists like Ready, according to the Southern Poverty Law Center, which described Spencer as "a vitriolic Mexican-basher and self-appointed guardian of the border who may have done more than anyone to spread the myth of a secret Mexican conspiracy to reconquer the Southwest." Once he migrated from California to southern Arizona, Spencer unleashed his conspiracy theories while ramping up his patrols (including airplane flyovers) of the border region. He didn't halt at Mexicans: in an on-line essay, "Speaking the Unspeakable: Is Jew-Controlled Hollywood Brain-washing Americans?" Spencer warned, "I think it is now time that Americans be forewarned that they are probably subject to clever pro-illegal alien prop-aganda every time they watch something produced in Hollywood."

President Obama's election in 2008 nearly pushed Spencer over the ledge. "Obama represents the greatest threat to the United States of America since the Civil War," he touted on his website. "Brainwashed Americans have just voted to commit national suicide."

Nonetheless, the epic battle to hold off the hordes of invading Mexicans remained Spencer's main focus. In 1999 he told supporters, "Every illegal alien in our nation must be deported immediately. . . . If we can bomb the TV station in Belgrade [in the former Yugoslavia], we can shut down [US Spanish-language TV networks] Telemundo and Univision." A year later, he ramped up the volume on his American Patrol website, warning readers, "Our country is being invaded by Mexico with hostile intentions. When it blows up, they can't say we didn't tell them, when the blood starts flowing on the border and in L.A. We're [talking] about *la reconquista*."

Such crackpot conspiracies would be laughable—if they did not inspire the bloodthirsty actions of deranged gun-toters like Forde and Ready. Or shape the narrative and policies of Arizona legislators like Pearce, Horne, and Brewer.

In the spring of 2012, State Senator Sylvia Allen and her wall-building col-league Steve Smith invited the unrepentant Spencer to address a special Sen-ate Committee as an expert on the topic of "border security." Embracing his role as an elder statesman and border expert, he lectured the legislature on the need to create a "sonic barrier" as part of a beefed-up technological effort on the border. Democratic members of the chamber walked out.

How much longer would Arizona allow this Tea Party to take the state to such an extremist fringe?

Randy Parraz. (Photo courtesy of Dennis Gilman.)

CHAPTER SIX

RECALL: THE FIRST SHOWDOWN

We have looked into the future, and the future is ours. . . . Once social change begins, it cannot be reversed. You cannot uneducate the person who has learned to read. You cannot humiliate the person who feels pride. You cannot oppress the people who are not afraid anymore.

CESAR CHAVEZ, ADDRESS TO THE COMMONWEALTH
CLUB OF SAN FRANCISCO, NOVEMBER 9, 1984

WHEN THE RAINS COME

Nathan Allen always referred to it as the "time of change." As streaks of lightning cascaded down the Estrella Mountains to the vast western stretches of the Akimel O'odham Nation, we would stroll the dusty trails toward the seemingly lifeless banks of the Gila River. Swirls of dust devils chased each other around the brush and cactus; saguaros somehow limped in the oppressive heat. We were waiting for the rains; the claps of thunder that rolled into the late afternoon and shook the monsoon storms onto the earth. Within minutes, the *akimel* river would be flowing, what Allen called the "ribbon of life."

The creosote exuded a pungent aroma, a rush of invisible steam. The frogs eventually emerged on cue, as signs of life revamped a dormant desert world.

"*Oigie thoth huibak*," he would say. "Come, let us rest. This is the time of change."

As those same summer monsoons gathered for their daily barrage in the Sonoran Desert in August 2010, Democrat Randy Parraz held a press conference for his insurgent US Senate campaign. He planned to officially hand-deliver a lawsuit against Sheriff Joe Arpaio at his office for his 2008 false arrest.

Not exactly a textbook event for a Senate candidate in the Democratic primary, but then again, this was Arizona in the summer of SB 1070. Parraz's campaign cast a most unflattering light on the state Democratic Party's head-in-the-sand approach to the most-talked-about issue in the state. This was the role he had always played as a community organizer and lightning rod. Hence the arrest by Arpaio's deputies.

Parraz wasn't alone. His arrest was the entry point for Chad Snow, the co-founder of Citizens for a Better Arizona, into a whirlwind campaign that would devour the next few years of his life.

In the spring of 2008, after a short period of organizing immigrant construction workers for the Laborers' International Union, Parraz decided to launch his first battle in the Phoenix area to expose civil rights abuses, including racial profiling. Parraz was not dealing with Russell Pearce's legislative policies but with the dragnet practices of Sheriff Arpaio, whose immigrant crime sweeps had been spiraling unchecked in targeted Latino neighborhoods. Establishing the Maricopa Citizens for Safety and Accountability, Parraz and his supporters appealed to the Maricopa County Board of Supervisors to address Arpaio's twenty-year reign of fear and clampdown. Over several months, Parraz's group filed petitions and complaints, and turned out in scores at board meetings, but never managed to nudge the equivocating board into action.

And perhaps for good reason. Arpaio had teamed up with disgraced Maricopa County Attorney Andrew Thomas to launch a bizarre witch hunt against county employees and supervisors who had questioned his reign of terror. It took years and a few destroyed careers before Thomas was finally called before an ethics hearing, tried for fraud and dishonest conduct in filing frivolous criminal and civil cases to harass his rivals, and disbarred from the courtroom.

When Parraz and others spoke out at a Board of Supervisors meeting on September 26, 2008, knowingly without the permission of the board chairman, they understood that the rules required a warning and then ejection from the meeting. After Parraz delivered a six-second appeal for the board to place the group's concerns on the agenda for public consideration, he left the chambers.

A moderate Republican attorney, Snow had attended the meeting out of curiosity. Arpaio's antics had perked up his ears; he felt the sheriff had evolved over the years into an increasingly corrupt self-promoter. Snow had never met Parraz; in fact, he could not have identified him in the room without someone's help. Once the board meeting was adjourned, Snow rose to leave, but he found himself sandwiched between two sheriff deputies.

"They grabbed me, grabbed my stuff," Snow told me, leaning back in his chair at his Phoenix office, where he deals with workmen's compensation suits. "They threw handcuffs on me, and I'm wondering, What the hell is going on?"

Five minutes of confusion ensued. Snow asked why he was being detained, and if the two deputies knew he was an attorney. It wasn't until a third deputy came down the hallway, looked at him, and announced, "Oh, that's not him," that Snow was released.

These are the perils of being a tall, physically fit attorney in your forties, with a fashionably clipped haircut. Although Snow may have some passing resemblance in profile to Parraz, they couldn't have been more different in background. A lifelong Republican and subscriber to the Rush Limbaugh newsletter, Snow grew up in Glendale, Arizona, in a traditional Mormon family.

"As I'm walking out the hallway," Snow recalled, "I see Randy walking down in handcuffs." Realizing he had been mistakenly cuffed in a ploy to silence Parraz, the outraged Snow and his partner immediately hopped in their car, went down to the police station, and offered their legal services to the community organizer.

Snow never looked back. As the conservative Republican to Parraz's liberal Democrat, the two joined forces in a campaign that arguably owed its birth to Sheriff Joe's excessive actions.

Even with his charges dropped, Parraz still had no plans to let Arpaio off the hook. He was not alone in this matter. From 2004 to 2007, over 2,700 lawsuits of wrongdoing were filed against Arpaio in county and federal courts—more than the combined total of several cities, including New York City, Los Angeles, Chicago, and Houston. Over the next few years, keeping tabs on the lawsuits against Arpaio and his office would be like playing the lottery; the stakes not only grew exponentially but also cost Maricopa County more than $45 million in damages. By the end of 2011, more than $176 million in damages and claims were being pursued in court.

Basing their actions in the historic El Campito barrio, Parraz and his Maricopa Citizens for Safety and Accountability launched a weeklong fast in the fall of 2008 at the Santa Rita Hall, the historic location of Cesar Chavez's United Farm Workers fast in 1972.

"Our top cop in Maricopa County should not be under investigation for civil rights violations," Parraz said, chronicling Arpaio's documented abuses. "He needs to step aside so we can have a real top law enforcement officer who really cares about people's concerns."

Three months later, in an extraordinary act of reproach, the Department of Homeland Security stripped Arpaio of his special powers under the 287(g) program, which had effectively granted the sheriff and his county troops unchecked authority (reserved for federal jurisdiction) to target suspected undocumented immigrants.

It didn't bother Arpaio in the least. He immediately took the stage on the *Glenn Beck* show and reminded the Obama administration that even though he had signed off on canceling the agreement with the Department of Homeland Security, "nothing has changed. I'm still going to do the same thing."

How can this happen, Beck wondered aloud, repeating his mantra that Phoenix was the city with "the highest kidnapping rate in the country."

"It's all politics," Arpaio said in a huff. "They probably don't know about it," he said, referring to the federal government, but he still planned to enforce federal laws. "It's gonna be great not to be under the federal umbrella," he went on, attempting to explain to a flummoxed Beck his interpretation of his self-ordained authority. If Arpaio's deputies came on some "people looking erratic," he explained, "if they have their speech, what they look like, look like they came from another country, we can take care of that situation."

Beck smirked in laughter, "that sounds like profiling." Beck's irony wasn't lost on the viewers. Within a year, SB 1070 would finally give Arpaio the justification that even Beck had mocked.

DEAR PATRIOTS

There were three stories about Arizona and his life that made their way into virtually every stump speech and interview with Russell Pearce, and all of them turned the leatherneck politician's voice into a puddle of pity, if not spurring a rare moment of humanity.

First, Pearce wanted everyone to know that he had been shot in the line of duty in 1977. On the slim chance you hadn't read about it, the Medal of Valor from the Maricopa County Sheriff's Office for his "brawl with three teenagers" in the neighboring town of Guadalupe—a Yaqui and largely Mexican American area between Phoenix and Tempe—hung on his office wall. Despite being shot through the chest and hand, Pearce had managed to apprehend the suspects.

Raised by his mother in a big Mormon family in what he described as a "Hispanic neighborhood" in Mesa, his alcoholic father largely missing from the picture, Pearce always fought back tears at the memory of his second story: a neighbor delivered a bag of food during a particularly rough period, and his mother commanded the children to not touch the groceries. As he recounted this story in 2003 to college instructors in Mesa, who had objected to Pearce's role in slashing state job-training adult education budgets, Pearce's hardscrabble example demonstrated that real Americans didn't accept handouts. "We've become a socialist state," he lectured the group of educators. "We ought to rely on family, church, and community first."

The third anecdote, according to many observers, accounted for his decade of deportation mania and informed the back story of SB 1070. Speaking at the Brookings Institution on the issue of illegal immigration in Arizona on a cold December day in 2004, Pearce was notified mid-speech that his wife had called and left an urgent message. Pearce stopped, stepped away from the podium, and phoned home. His son Sean, an eleven-year veteran of the Maricopa County Sheriff's Office and the SWAT team, had been shot in the gut after he broke through the door of a mobile home to serve a search warrant. The twenty-two-year-old shooter, who eventually received a fifty-one-year prison sentence, had been an undocumented resident from Mexico. "It verified what I'm trying to do down here," Pearce told a local journalist. He added hauntingly, "You couldn't have scripted it any better."

A year later, after speaking at a Minuteman Project rally at the Arizona state capitol and receiving a "rock-star cheer," Pearce weaved that script into a chronicle of a deportation policy foretold. "If I was the governor," he told the *Arizona Republic,* essentially mapping out a strategy that would eventually ensnare Governor Jan Brewer into the SB 1070 campaign, "the first thing I'd do is put the National Guard on the border, assign patrols and really beef it up." In an eerie foreshadowing of the Secure Communities program, Pearce called for local law enforcement agencies to be fully empowered with the ability to arrest immigrants without proper documentation. (Secure Communities, launched by the Bush administration in 2008 but dramatically ramped up under Obama, builds on the Bush-era 287(g) federal initiatives—which deputized county and city agencies to enforce immigration law—by giving local agencies access to federal criminal and immigration databases.)

And then came the kicker: "I'd declare an emergency under federal law," Pearce said, "because of the impact of a billion-dollar cost to the criminal justice system, to the health care system and the education system."

OPERATION WETBACK

Mr. Welty: Have you any wetbacks in Arizona?
Mr. Hayden: No, sir; that is a term with which I am not familiar.

ARIZONA DEMOCRAT CARL HAYDEN, ANSWERING A
QUESTION FROM OHIO DEMOCRAT BENJAMIN WELTY IN
TESTIMONY BEFORE THE HOUSE COMMITTEE ON
IMMIGRATION AND NATURALIZATION'S HEARING ON
THE "TEMPORARY ADMISSION OF ILLITERATE MEXICAN
LABORERS," FEBRUARY 2, 1920

"While SB 1070 has garnered unprecedented national attention," Pearce told *Politico* readers in the spring of 2011, "it was not the law that 'started it all.'" Five years earlier, on a warm fall morning, NPR listeners en route to work in Phoenix heard then State Representative Pearce discuss how he would reduce the flow of illegal immigration.

"We know what we need to do," Pearce said from Mesa. "In 1953, Dwight D. Eisenhower put together a task force called Operation Wetback. He removed, in less than a year, 1.3 million illegal aliens. They must be deported."

The media and Latino organizations jumped on Pearce for his use of the "wetback" moniker, but his brash call for a punitive deportation policy a half-century after Eisenhower's reckless campaign seemingly drew less criticism. In truth, Pearce was sowing the seeds for SB 1070's eventual harvest.

John Huppenthal, then a state senator from nearby Chandler, merely suggested that Pearce needed a "lesson in political correctness" to get his message across more effectively. Huppenthal had witnessed such a dragnet policy; in 1997, the police department in his district unleashed a five-day sweep and apprehended more than four hundred undocumented workers, ensnaring a passel of costly lawsuits over civil rights violations in the process.

But Pearce didn't really need a lesson in political correctness; his point, as he later explained, had more to do with a delusional '50s nostalgia. The term "wetback," which referred to the Mexican crossing over the Rio Grande River, was merely the disparaging tag du jour, not unlike the use of "illegal" today.

Only two years after Barry Goldwater went to Washington as an Arizona senator, troubling circumstances across the nation led to one of the most disastrous and shameful episodes in the history of US immigration policy. With the country reeling from the postwar recession, Eisenhower followed the easy route of scapegoating and ordered the forced deportation of an estimated 1.3 million immigrants (many with American-born children and spouses) to Mexico.

On the heels of the Immigration and Naturalization Act in 1952, which made it a crime to transport undocumented immigrants, among other measures, Eisenhower returned to his military roots for a drastic approach to dealing with Mexican laborers who had crossed the border through the Bracero Program during World War II. In 1942, while Eisenhower was serving as the supreme commander of Allied forces in Europe, the United States opened the border with Mexico in an attempt to fill a devastating labor shortage on some of the largest corporate farms in the South and Southwest. In truth, the influx of undocumented low-wage "braceros" overwhelmed the regulated numbers sanctioned by the two governments, and quietly provided the backbone for the nation's agricultural industries in the 1940s.

Once the war was over and General Eisenhower marched into the White House, the critical legacy of guest workers quickly vanished into the cloud of economic displacement, union criticism over nonunion laborers, and the renewed charge from the Hoover days that "our government has become a contributor to the growth of an illegal traffic, which it has the responsibility to prevent."

Eisenhower and his attorney general, Herbert Brownell, knew just the right man for the job: Army General Joseph Swing, who had cut his teeth in 1916 on the US invasion of Mexico and failed expedition to capture Mexican revolutionary Pancho Villa. Despite hundreds of missions by the First Aero Squadron (the first time Americans employed aircraft in battle), the first motorized combat vehicles, and five thousand troops from the American cavalry (including a young George S. Patton), Swing and famed General "Black Jack" Pershing exited from Mexico empty-handed. "We are now sneaking home under a cover like a whipped cur with his tail between his legs," Pershing wrote at the end of the eleven-month invasion.

Nearly fifty years later, Swing wasn't about to let the deviant Mexicans evade him again. In fact, his military blitz came on the heels of a decade-long shift in American border policy. As part of the conditions for the Bracero Program in the 1940s, the Border Patrol had already "committed itself to strengthen the Patrol force along the Mexican Border by the means of filling all existing vacancies and detailing approximately 150 Patrol Inspectors from other areas to the Mexican border," according to historian Kelly Lytle Hernandez. For the first time since the birth of the Border Patrol in 1924, more guards were protecting our southern border than the Canadian stretches (which, in fact, had presented a larger problem with bootleggers in the 1920s).

In a study on "Operation Wetback," Hernandez noted that the new focus on the southern frontier had historical ramifications: "First, the number of apprehensions of deportable aliens made by U.S. Border Patrol officers in the Mexican border region increased from 11,775 in 1943 to 28,173 in 1944. Although a rise in undocumented Mexican immigration certainly did occur during the 1940s, the quiet emergence of a U.S. Border Patrol priority to apprehend Mexican nationals combined with new strategies contributed to the dramatic boom in the number of apprehensions made in the Mexican border region."

It also set the precedent for a detention and deportation policy that would endure until today. Hernandez concluded:

> With cross-border collaboration, however, U.S. and Mexican officers were able to transform the line that marked the limits of their jurisdic-

tions into a bridge that linked rather than divided the two distinct systems of migration control. Upon that bridge the consequences for unsanctioned border crossing were merged. No longer were the detentions and dislocations that accompanied migration control isolated within one nation or territory. In the United States, those identified as illegal immigrants were subject to surveillance, detention, and deportation. In Mexico, they would face the disruptions and anxieties of forced dislocation to unfamiliar places. In each location, however, the consequences of having committed the symbiotic crimes of unsanctioned emigration and undocumented immigration were bound together through the collaborative practices of U.S.-Mexican migration control.

By the mid-1940s, the US had set up 4,500 feet of chain-link fencing near the border town of Calexico, California, as an experiment forcing illegal entrants to divert into more dangerous desert corridors. (President Bill Clinton's Operation Gatekeeper in 1994 took this approach to even further extremes.)

Utilizing all the military hardware available to him for the air, land, and sea, along with nearly 1,000 Border Patrol agents, Swing essentially ramped up what had been an increasing militarization of the border, and brought his dragnet of roadblocks and door-to-door sweeps primarily to Mexican American and immigrant communities in Arizona, Texas, and California. Bringing along the media, he intentionally turned his brutal sideshow into a media event that captured the nation's attention.

In the spring of 1954, before Operation Wetback, the *Stanford Law Review* published a controversial essay aptly titled "Wetbacks: Can the States Act to Curb Illegal Entry," which aired a sentiment about states' rights and immigration policy that hauntingly foreshadowed the SB 1070 debate. The *Review* asked: Could unilateral state policy on immigration ultimately impact federal decisions? "Obviously the problem is one which is within the power of the Federal Government to meet, and which the Federal Government is best able to meet," the legal journal noted. "Yet political pressures have been sufficient to forestall any forceful legislative attack on the situation. Congress even has evinced a willingness to weaken further its already over-extended border enforcement agencies to placate interest groups. Meanwhile the Wetback invasion in its current proportions constitutes a critical threat to the health, safety and general welfare of the people of the border states. Can the states act to

meet this threat? Or is the field one in which the doctrine of federal supremacy admits only the exercise of national power?"

The *Review* posited the case of the Chinese in California—"the original
wetbacks"—as a precedent for states' rights being used as an impetus for
greater federal action on immigration policy with Mexicans, the new wetbacks.

> In the latter part of the nineteenth century California faced a problem
> of Chinese immigration strikingly similar to that now posed by the
> Wetback. In 1891 a statute was passed making it unlawful for "any Chi-
> nese person," excepting only diplomatic envoys, to enter the state. All
> Chinese in California were required to secure certificates of residence
> which were to be exhibited, on demand, to any peace officer, and also,
> upon traveling, to any ticket agent or conductor. Failure to obtain and
> carry such a certificate was made an offense punishable by imprison-
> ment or deportation. The California Supreme Court, in a summary
> one-page opinion, struck down the statute, saying, "The power thus
> attempted to be exercised is one which belongs exclusively to the gen-
> eral government by virtue of its authority to regulate commerce with
> foreign nations."

A year later, of course, the Chinese Exclusion Acts passed through Congress, effectively outlawing migration from that country. A huge ocean
notwithstanding, the *Review* wondered, Why can't we carry out such a defin-
itive policy with Mexicans?

Swing would have agreed with such a sweeping approach. Placing Mexican
barrios "under a state of siege," he unleashed his campaign with the fervor of
ending migration from Mexico *forever*. However, his roundup or forced repa-
triation of more than 1 million Mexican immigrants was as effective as the il-
lusory attempt to capture Pancho Villa: a lot of military show that delayed
the inevitable. Villa became a hero; deported Mexicans would pack up their
belongings and return to the US.

Hernandez concluded, "Instead of being a major law enforcement campaign, the summer of 1954 can better be understood as a massive publicity
campaign for what had happened the year before and a public claiming of migration control by the U. S. government despite the critical contributions and
participation of the Mexican government."

"The so-called wetback problem no longer exists," Swing insisted in 1954. "The border has been secured."

More than fifty years later, the defiant Pearce floated this same banner in 2006, telling anyone who would listen that Operation Wetback was "a successful program for those who continue to tell you it's impossible to deport [illegal immigrants] in this country."

Arizonans would eventually listen to Pearce. Like the Californians' dalliance with their own private Chinese exclusion acts, SB 1070 challenged the nation with its attack on federal jurisdiction.

WE HAVE TO CREATE OUR OWN STORY

Randy Parraz sat in the meeting room of a local union headquarters in Phoenix, a picture of Martin Luther King Jr. above his head. Preoccupied, as if always in the middle of carrying out an action, he fidgeted in his seat, gazing intensely at the camera.

"It's not where you come from," he said, speaking at a machine-gun pace, "but what you dedicate your life to."

Parraz had dedicated his life to his two little girls, which brought him back to Arizona in 2007 after a divorce. He had first arrived in Arizona in 2002, signing on as the state director for the national AFL-CIO, but a career in the labor movement had left him dissatisfied with its effectiveness for change.

"Labor is so beat-up," he went on, shaking his head. "Lack of vision, lack of leadership, afraid to deal with immigration."

This frankness about Parraz, his brash take-no-prisoners approach to community organizing, had set him apart from the entrenched but paralytic Democratic establishment in Arizona. He remained the ultimate outsider who riled insiders with his indifference to protocol. Yet his passion and sense of purpose, and his brilliant organizing tactics, had attracted a growing following of young Latinos and liberal baby boomers that inspired a rebirth of activism in the state.

"We have to create our own story," Parraz offered.

Parraz's own story was impressive. Raised in Sacramento, California, he had earned a law degree from Boalt Law School at the University of California, Berkeley, then pursued a Masters in Public Administration at Harvard's Kennedy School. Inspired by Ernesto Cortés of the Industrial Areas Foundation

and the teachings of Harvard's Marshall Ganz, a legendary community organizer and colleague of United Farm Workers leader Cesar Chavez, Parraz
found himself easing into the stream of community organizing jobs in Texas,
Washington, DC, and then Arizona.

When he witnessed the faltering pushback on SB 1070, he shifted from
his behind-the-scenes community organizer role to that of a public figure.
"There are certain roles you have to take when no one else is ready to take it
on," he said.

Parraz was outraged by the Democratic Party's failure to "rise to the challenge" in Arizona and confront the misinformation over SB 1070. "They saw
it as a burden and walked away. I said, 'Hey, let's use this as an opportunity to
organize.' There were a lot of good people in the state who stayed quiet."

"The signing of SB 1070 was the turning point for Randy Parraz," the
Three Sonorans blog noted, introducing him to Tucson voters in the summer
of 2010. "As he said during his interview with *Arizona Illustrated*, his own personal threshold of injustice had been passed, and there was no strong voice
against the bill from the Democratic candidate against John McCain, a supporter of the bill, so Randy decided to enter the race."

Parraz failed to win the Democratic nomination for the Senate; but as he
predicted, the state Democratic Party lost every statewide race. In the meantime, Parraz had awakened the interests of a new generation of activists in the
state.

"One thing that becomes clear is that Randy Parraz is not your typical
politician," Three Sonorans continued.

> Parraz continues in the tradition of Cesar Chavez, with a proven record
> of fighting for civil and labor rights and fasting when needed. Not many
> politicians will go a day or two without food, but this type of dedica-
> tion speaks to the true motivations of Randy Parraz. His campaign is
> not about personal ambition, it's about fighting against injustice for
> the people. These are special times in Arizona, and whoever we elect
> this year will lead Arizona into its 100th birthday and second century
> of existence. Will we continue with the status quo, the likes of McCain,
> Brewer, Pearce, Arpaio, etc., or will Arizona bring in a new batch of
> leaders to take this state in a new direction?

"You drop a frog in boiling water," Parraz said, holding his hands together, "and it immediately jumps out. But if you put a frog in room-temperature water for eight hours and then gradually raise the heat, by the time the water is boiling his legs will be paralyzed and he wouldn't have noticed the change. That's what happened in Arizona."

"I'm trying to get people to behave differently," he went on. "To take risks. To protest. To tell the police to back off if they threaten your right to speech. I almost got arrested today for bringing people into the Arizona Capitol lobby. That's how insane it is here. We were just bringing people in to educate about the jobs bill. This place is on lockdown, and we have to change that."

For Parraz, that change came with the ascendancy of Russell Pearce to the State Senate presidency in the fall of 2010. Once the Tea Party president made it clear that he planned to pursue his radical agenda in the spring of 2011, Parraz and Chad Snow mobilized their supporters in the area to launch a recall.

Citing "insurmountable odds," the Democratic Party leadership and established media gave Parraz and his Citizens for a Better Arizona hardly any support or a sporting chance to take down the most powerful politician in Arizona. They didn't realize Parraz had done his homework. With the Republican Party increasingly in disarray, he saw that the Tea Party's grip on the conservative ranks was slipping; his early canvass teams reported back the surprising discovery that one out of every three or four voters in the district didn't even know Pearce.

"It takes a lot of work," Parraz admonished, especially to assemble a bipartisan effort. "What issue will drive them? How do you engage people in the act of politics? How do you create opportunities for people to act on their values?"

Parraz and Snow and their increasing ranks of volunteers mulled over these questions as they set up their tables in front of the Mesa Public Library to collect signatures, and then launched a door-to-door campaign. They set up a Facebook page that soon exploded with participants. Suddenly, they found themselves joined by a regular crew of retired educators and business people who were outraged by the toll that Pearce's ideological stance was taking on the economy and greater community, including disgruntled Republicans who found his Tea Party leadership out of step with traditional conservatism as well as Latino activists and younger voters anxious to take down the architect of SB 1070.

Little did they know that their efforts would snowball within weeks, thanks to social media networks that quickly spread the blogs, meeting updates, and recall petition achievements far beyond traditional political campaigns. "Randy had arrived in the precise moment," Snow said, "when we needed more profiles in courage."

SÍ SE PUEDE

A long-distance runner and Vietnam veteran, Alfredo Gutierrez once recalled outpacing security guards to deliver fliers and leaflets on behalf of Cesar Chavez's United Farm Workers in the 1960s. In fact, the Chicano activist hadn't stopped running since those days.

"I started registering voters in 1968," he told E. J. Montini at the *Arizona Republic*. "Always with the promise and the expectation that our time was coming. I never expected it to take this long." For the former Democratic State Senate leader, SB 1070 was just the latest in a long string of extremist anti-immigrant measures that had kept him in politics all these years.

"In the long run, this will blow up in Pearce's face," Gutierrez said. "With the national focus on our state and the damage to our reputation, some fair and some not, as the Mississippi of this century—that can't be good for business."

Gutierrez spoke from experience. In the 1970s he protested another Arizona law that had criminalized largely immigrant communities and inflicted punitive measures to keep them at large and afraid.

A pull quote from *BusinessWeek* in the summer of 1972 testified to the state's vanguard role in influencing the rest of the nation: "Arizona-type legislation is spreading to many other farm states, despite protests."

Chavez returned to his native Arizona on May 11, 1972, ostensibly to hammer out a compromise over labor rights with Governor John "Jack" Williams. Called "One-Eye Jack" by some, Williams had surmounted a hardscrabble past to become one of the most popular radio voices in Phoenix—eventually he became the city's mayor, and then governor. He had lost one eye as a child, and wore a dark lens over one side of his glasses. A conservative Republican, he famously signed off his radio programs with the line "It's another beautiful day in Arizona. Leave us all enjoy it." Of course, Williams wasn't promising a beautiful day for *all* Arizonans.

Spurning a meeting with Chavez, Williams hastily signed HB 2134, an anti-union bill that essentially banned secondary boycotts and strikes during harvest time, cracked down on collective bargaining rights and union membership procedures, and made it a crime to make "misleading" speeches about boycotted products. It also prevented the United Farm Workers from organizing a union in the country's second-largest lettuce-producing state.

Speaking in Tucson after signing the bill, Williams dismissed the growing crowd of farmworkers, union activists, and Mexican American and Yaqui representatives outside his building. He stated to the media, "For me, those people don't even exist."

Chavez immediately announced his plans to launch a boycott of Arizona's lettuce, and to conduct an open-ended fast in protest. He called it a "fast for love."

"The fast was started to create the spirit of social justice in Arizona and to try by our efforts through the fast and our sacrifices to erase the fears that the growers and the Republican legislators and the Republican governor have of the Union," he reported in *El Macriado*, the official news organ of the union. "The fast is to try to reach the hearts of those men, so that they will understand that we too have rights and we're not here to destroy, because we're not destroyers, we're builders."

For Chavez, whose grandfather had built the family's first home in Arizona three years before it became a state in 1912, Williams's act was subversive and "un-American." He declared the bill was "discriminatory" and aimed at "farmworkers who are Black, Brown and Indian." He added: "No other labor force is asked to live with these repressive measures."

Chavez, like every farmworker and many observers across the country, recognized the underlining focus of this bill—not unlike SB 1070, it was intended to keep the cheap labor of largely Mexican and Mexican American migrant workers in a state of fear.

"When 70 percent of the labor force lives in fear of being deported," declared *El Macriado*, "there are no cries to end child labor, no demands for drinking water, no petitions for toilets, no protests against the foul conditions of the labor camps."

By effectively outlawing the United Farm Workers' efforts to unionize, the newspaper went on, the state of Arizona "does not admit that 100,000 illegal aliens enter each year to slave in the fields, live in the squalor and be thrown out of the country penniless when the crops are harvested."

Arizona became the national "showdown" Chavez and the United Farm Workers had come to expect. But his campaign was not limited to simple collective bargaining demands. Nor did he see the farmworkers as in need of liberation—just the opposite. "Somehow," Chavez wrote, "these powerful men and women must be helped to realize that there is nothing to fear from treating their workers as fellow human beings."

Born in his family's home in Yuma in 1927, Chavez was no stranger to such a showdown. His grandfather had fled a fate in servitude to northern Mexico's most infamous land barons, the Terrazas family, who controlled an estimated 7 million acres of Chihuahua during the three decades of the Díaz dictatorship. (The Terrazas patriarch had once said, "I'm not from Chihuahua, Chihuahua is mine.") Chavez's father, though, was saddled with debt after a land deal went bad, and he eventually lost the family property and beloved fields in Yuma to a vindictive grower (or large farmer) in 1939. While his father struggled to collect enough loans to cover his back taxes, the grower bulldozed the trees on the property and filled in the irrigation ditches.

"When we were pushed off our land," Chavez said, "all we could take with us was what we could jam into the old Studebaker or pile on its roof and fenders."

Chavez's family crossed into California and into another state of existence. "When we left the farm," Chavez wrote, "our whole life was upset, turned upside down. We had been part of a very stable community, and we were about to become migratory workers. We had been uprooted."

Nonetheless, the young boy quickly learned that discrimination and civil rights had more to do with ethnicity than a home address. And he learned what citizenship meant in Arizona; the family had to dodge the Border Patrol and police, Chavez recalled, because "they don't distinguish between Mexicans and Mexican Americans. As far as they are concerned, we can't be a citizen even though we were born here. In their minds, 'if he's Mexican, don't trust him.'"

By the time he reached eighth grade, Chavez had dropped out of school to work full-time as a migrant worker in the fields of California. After a stint in the Navy, he returned to California, where he became an organizer with the Community Service Organization, dealing with labor rights and abuses. In 1962 he and Dolores Huerta cofounded the National Farm Workers Association, which became the United Farm Workers. Chavez drew national attention three years later, when the United Farm Workers led a successful national boycott of grapes in an effort to gain living wages and safer working conditions.

Like Martin Luther King Jr., Chavez was deeply influenced by the writings and life of Mahatma Gandhi. He used nonviolent strategies of boycotts, civil disobedience, and strikes to agitate for better working conditions for migrant workers. His most effective weapon, in the end, was his act of fasting, which he regarded as a spiritual endeavor as much as a political tool.

But first, he had to convince his own followers, especially in his native state.

In many respects, Chavez experienced the same level of apathy and the same vacuum of leadership that dogged Parraz's and other recall efforts. "In Arizona," he wrote, "the people were beaten. You could see the difference. Every time we talked about fighting the law, people would say, '*No se puede, no se puede*'—it's not possible. It can't be done."

Meeting with his union staff at a hotel in Wickenburg, west of Phoenix, Huerta flipped the lament on its head. "From now on," she said, "we're not going to say, '*No se puede*'; we're going to say, '*Sí se puede*.'" Chavez introduced this slogan at his next meeting in Phoenix—an inspiring and enduring sentiment that would be adapted by President Obama's "Yes we can" presidential campaign in 2008.

Basing his operations in Arizona at the Santa Rita Center, in a barrio on the south side of Phoenix, Chavez inspired the demoralized activists in the state with his determined campaign. The Santa Rita Center filled every evening with the air of a revival—not of some evangelical breakdown, but a reminder of the Chicano community's faith. Historian Christine Marin recalled attending the center's gatherings as a young student and the towering role of Chavez in that period:

> Large crowds packed into the Santa Rita hall, eager to catch a glimpse of the man who had dared to challenge Arizona's governor. Farm workers and their families from throughout the state came to the center, and to attend the nightly mass. There were rugged-looking men, many

with sunburned faces. They were working men. Their shirts, open at the collar, their sleeves rolled up. The women were dressed in simple, no frill dresses, many wearing blouses and skirts. Little girls held candles. Metal chairs were arranged in rows and rows, filling the hall, and every chair was filled. People stood along the walls, hugging every inch of space. When father Joe Melton blessed the wine for the sacrament, the priest told us that this was no ordinary wine, but wine harvested by men and women, working in dignity, under the protection of a union contract. And the hymns sung at the mass were union hymns, sung in English and in Spanish. . . . Then, a silence settled the room.

A group of people entered from another room, into the hall. You could hear a pin drop. And a short, small, weary-looking man appeared. He was assisted to his chair by others, their arms around his elbows and wrists. I wasn't sure what was happening. I didn't know who the men were. "Where is Cesar Chavez," I asked myself. "Is that him?" I wondered; no one said a word. No one announced his presence to the crowd. There was no podium from where he could speak. I expected to see Cesar Chavez address the crowd from a podium. He walked, ever so slowly, to the chair, steadying himself against the men so that he wouldn't fall. There was no voice from a microphone announcing his arrival, no applause from the crowd—just silence. It was like that almost every night: Cesar didn't speak. But the crowd was satisfied just to be in his presence, to hear mass with him.

Chavez, though, was not only protesting Williams's harsh legislation. Under his leadership, the United Farm Workers had launched an ambitious recall of the governor.

Another recall. Another Arizona campaign to send a message to the rest of the nation about right-wing extremism. The campaign transcended Williams. "Arizona continues as the political domain of the Goldwater machine," *El Macriado* charged, "a grower-based product of a Republican Party-John Birch Society merger."

"My major concern," Chavez wrote in an open letter published in the United Farm Workers newspaper on June 9, 1972, "is not this particular Arizona law and the fast is not out of anger against the growers. My concern is the spirit of fear that lies behind the hearts of growers and legislators across the country."

Barnstorming the state on flatbed trucks, setting up tables in the agricultural fields and barrio communities, volunteers with the farmworkers and their allies launched a major campaign to collect recall signatures and, more important, to register new voters in Chicano and Native American strongholds. The cry "*Sí se puede!*" rang out for the first time across the state—and the nation.

The evening meetings at the Santa Rita Center attracted national media, and social figures including Coretta Scott King, Joan Baez, and Democratic presidential candidate George McGovern. Huerta introduced Senator McGovern, declaring, "He does not stand with the Union only when the cactus is bearing fruit." For his part, McGovern called Arizona's bill a "regressive and unjust legislation that hampers the collective bargaining process and the rights of organized labor."

Debilitated by his water-only fast, Chavez eventually became confined to the Santa Rita Center. He struggled with speech, weakened by the strain. After twenty-four days, he ended his fast at a special memorial service in front of five thousand people.

Meanwhile, the recall effort exploded. Organizers employed the tactics Chavez had used in California, going door-to-door and canvassing people in the churches and shopping centers. Within a few months, more than a hundred thousand signatures had been collected, including many from new voters. Chavez and Huerta recognized that their efforts were changing the state's electoral demographics and reinvigorating the demoralized Democratic Party. For Chavez, the recall campaign had the effect of "waking up" the people. "It had never happened before in Arizona," he noted in his memoir, "or anywhere."

In the end, the organizers turned in more than 176,000 petition signatures, only 103,000 of which were needed to ensure the recall. In a bold manipulation of the process, though, county officials teamed up with the secretary of state to strike down 96,000 signatures as invalid. According to Attorney General Gary Nelson, "deputy registrars" were not legally permitted to collect petition signatures and register voters at the same time. Thanks to Williams's Republican cronies, the recall had been derailed.

Months later, an appeal to the federal court would reverse the attorney general's opinion. At that point, however, a recall election seemed futile in light of the upcoming elections. Nonetheless, "the effects on Arizona politics were tremendous," Chavez wrote later in his life.

Chavez may not have won the recall, but he had inspired a new generation of activists in Arizona. Although Williams's hard-line anti-union legislation would be fought in the courts for years, more than 150,000 new voters had signed up during Chavez's campaign, ushering in a new era in 1974. The political victories for the new movement would include Raúl Castro's election as the state's first Latino governor.

During his 2008 presidential campaign, President Obama recognized the legacy of the *Sí se puede* movement in his own life's work: "As farmworkers and laborers across America continue to struggle for fair treatment and fair wages, we find strength in what Cesar Chavez accomplished so many years ago. . . . And we should honor him for what he's taught us about making America a stronger, more just, and more prosperous nation. That's why I support the call to make Cesar Chavez's birthday a national holiday. It's time to recognize the contributions of this American icon to the ongoing efforts to perfect our union."

IT'S NOT THE MESA I WAS RAISED IN

They sat in the Citizens for a Better Arizona office like two bridge partners, giving each other a hard time for their individual tales. In many respects, the two women, Mary Lou Boettcher and Brenda Rascon, represented the diverse face of their hometown of Mesa. With large framed glasses, the white-haired Boettcher possessed the no-nonsense look of a librarian; in the 1960s, after arriving from Kansas, she had cofounded the first Republican Women's Club in the area. With a wide smile and a vivacious demeanor, the thirty-year-old doctoral student Rascon and her family had been among the first Mexican immigrants to integrate their neighborhood. Her family had moved from Los Angeles in the 1990s, like many California transplants, in search of a quieter and more affordable way of life.

"Russell Pearce made me an activist and taught me about state politics," Rascon said with a laugh. "The least I can do for my community is to make it better, especially in this period of negative rhetoric and . . . violence."

Taking part in the recall movement, her first political campaign, Rascon also discovered the wonder of the democratic experience. "At the beginning, people didn't know Pearce. Probably four out of ten had no idea who he was. Most people would say, 'I'm not political,' so I would go to the door, knock, tell what I'm doing, and then I would talk about education—and that would get their attention. People have the notion of politics as something dirty, and don't see it as civic engagement. Through our canvassing, we didn't just educate people about Pearce, but also the process of politics in their daily lives."

For Boettcher, a retired librarian and educator, the campaign was also an opportunity to restore a sense of balance to the community's school system, which had experienced draconian cuts under Pearce's leadership.

"He's too extreme," she said. "I'm not trying to make history. I'm trying to make sure we have someone willing to help people who need help through our state legislature—that our children receive a good education." Recalling Pearce, she added, was about the future of her grandchildren.

The wide streets of historic Mesa, lined with palo verde and palm trees, now gave way to the world they shared; once you pass the Tempe canal and head east on Main Street, the first *llanteria* (tire store) reminds you that the historic stronghold of the state's oldest Mormon temple is now composed of a diverse and growing community, with 40 percent from Latino families.

According to historical Mormon texts, Mesa was originally envisioned as a way station for polygamist colonies en route to Mexico. When their communities in Utah began burgeoning with immigration and overpopulation problems in the 1870s, Mormon leader Brigham Young called on veteran traveler Daniel Jones to seek out land opportunities in the Yaqui country of Mexico, with an eye on an area in the Salt River Valley that could be "a station on the road to those who would later go onto the far south."

In 1877, a year after Russell Pearce's family migrated from Utah to northern Arizona, a party of Mormons established themselves in the Mesa area, clearing creosote bushes, digging out prehistoric Hohokam irrigation ditches, and planting gardens, shade trees, and fields of Hollyhocks.

The key to Mesa, of course, was the ancient canal, which diverted water from the Salt River. The first task was to found the Mesa Canal Company, following the tradition of Phoenix founder Jack Swilling, a Confederate deserter who dug out the first prehistoric canal in 1867 and shoveled that city into existence. From the ashes of the ancient civilization, so rose Phoenix. Swilling, a troubled morphine addict who suffered from an enduring brain injury, died in prison in 1878 for an apparent bungled robbery. When Mesa officially incorporated in 1883, the church listed "389 souls of our people" in the township—along with twenty-four non-Mormons.

Persecution was undeniably brutal for the Mormons in the first decade of their Arizona residency. Perhaps as a forerunner of the state's trampling of federal jurisdiction, the territorial government of Arizona passed the Anti-Bigamy Act in 1885. The Edmunds Act in 1887 sent many polygamist Mormons across the border to Mexico; others were hauled off to prison. "Desperate diseases need desperate remedies," railed St. John's *Apache Chief* newspaper in 1884. "The Mormon disease is a desperate one and rope and shotgun is the only cure. The government refuses to do anything, and the 'people' of Apache County must do something or the Mormons will soon drive them out. Take the needed steps while it is yet time. Don't let them settle on any more of our lands; don't let them stop in Apache County; hang a few of their polygamous leaders, such as Jesse N. Smith, Udall, Romney, [John] Hunt and others of this nature and stop will be put to it."

According to pioneering Mormon Daniel Webster Jones, the Mormons had meted out their own version of frontier justice in Mesa and across Arizona. "There was scarcely a week passed but what there were miserable petty charges brought against the Indians, often on the slightest ground," he wrote. "Once the spirit ran so high against the Indian that it was determined to drive them away."

Although cooler heads eventually prevailed, Mesa residents struggled with the contradictions of ethnic discrimination and civil rights for the next century, just like the rest of the United States. Locals drove out Chinese merchants in the 1890s; the tragic death of a young Japanese student gave a local elementary school its motto to "Carry on"; German "slackers" were rounded up and imprisoned during the hysteria of World War I; the Ku Klux Klan thrived in the 1920s; and the swimming pool remained segregated in 1953, the same year the local newspaper named African American school principal Veora Johnson the "citizen of the year."

When Pete Guerrero was named Mesa's man of the year in 1942, the *Mesa Journal Tribune* noted that he was active in the Alianza Hispano Americana—the first national Latino organization, which had been founded in Tucson. "Pete is doing noble work as a missionary to keep constantly before the Spanish-Americans the virtues of Americanism."

At the time of Pearce's recall, Main Street still led to the monumental Mesa Mormon Temple, with roughly thirty thousand Mormons, including children, making up 17 percent of the district. The Mormon Church still held a powerful sway over the Mesa community and decision makers, though it no longer represented a monolithic front with a single voice. On the immigration issue, in particular, a broad range of opinions emanated from the various communities and states. "Pearce is in the vast minority and reactionary extremist wing" of the Mormon Church, said fellow Mormon Chad Snow of the recall campaign. Still, for Snow, this didn't mark a split in the church but rather a positive reflection of the wide spectrum of views.

In the summer of 2011, the Church of Jesus Christ of Latter-day Saints officials in Salt Lake City released an official "new statement" on immigration matters, stressing four areas of clear difference with Arizona and Pearce's punitive SB 1070:

Around the world, debate on the immigration question has become intense. That is especially so in the United States. Most Americans agree that the federal government of the United States should secure its borders and sharply reduce or eliminate the flow of undocumented immigrants. Unchecked and unregulated, such a flow may destabilize society and ultimately become unsustainable.

As a matter of policy, The Church of Jesus Christ of Latter-day Saints discourages its members from entering any country without legal documentation, and from deliberately overstaying legal travel visas.

What to do with the estimated 12 million undocumented immigrants now residing in various states within the United States is the biggest challenge in the immigration debate. The bedrock moral issue for The Church of Jesus Christ of Latter-day Saints is how we treat each other as children of God.

The history of mass expulsion or mistreatment of individuals or families is cause for concern especially where race, culture, or religion are involved. This should give pause to any policy that contemplates targeting any one group, particularly if that group comes mostly from one heritage.

As those on all sides of the immigration debate in the United States have noted, this issue is one that must ultimately be resolved by the federal government.

The Church of Jesus Christ of Latter-day Saints is concerned that any state legislation that only contains enforcement provisions is likely to fall short of the high moral standard of treating each other as children of God.

The Church supports an approach where undocumented immigrants are allowed to square themselves with the law and continue to work without this necessarily leading to citizenship.

In furtherance of needed immigration reform in the United States, The Church of Jesus Christ of Latter-day Saints supports a balanced and civil approach to a challenging problem, fully consistent with its tradition of compassion, its reverence for family, and its commitment to law.

In the spring of 2011, for example, the state legislature in Utah followed Arizona's state rebellion against federal jurisdiction over immigration policy but opted for a kinder, gentler approach to dealing with undocumented residents. Hailed as the Utah Compact, the law provided temporary residency permits for workers without proper papers, granted a limited form of amnesty for those who had entered illegally before a certain date, and narrowed obligatory residency status checks by law enforcement officials only in the case of felonies or serious misdemeanors. But like Arizona's SB 1070, the Utah Compact was immediately halted by the courts.

"It's not the Mesa I was raised in," Pearce lamented in 2005, referring to the impact of immigrants in his hometown. "They have turned it into a Third World country."

Not that everyone in Mesa agreed with his assessment. "It isn't the Mesa he grew up in because Mesa is a huge, diverse community," the town's vice mayor, Claudia Walters, told the *Tribune*. "Mesa used to be a small town. And we are now the fortieth-largest city in the country. We have everything from million-dollar homes to people who, unfortunately, are living in bad circumstances."

Indeed, it was Rascon's and Boettcher's Mesa, as well.

WHEN THINGS START TO COME UNDONE

Pearce's love of government, or rather *his* government, went too far in the spring of 2011. In the process, the first major crack in his invincibility made Arizonans sit up in their chairs for the first time in ages. For the Recall Pearce campaign, engaged in the tedious work of collecting petitions, it also signaled the beginning of the end of Pearce's grip on the business community.

President Pearce was stunned on March 17, when his own Tea Party supporters lost their nerve and failed to pass what he had trumpeted as the "omnibus bill" on immigration—the mother of all anti-immigration bills.

And what a package it had been: the bills required hospitals and public housing operators to verify legal residency status or evict undocumented immigrants; the Department of Public Safety would have been granted the right to check fingerprint backgrounds to verify citizenship or legal residency; the state constitution would have prohibited any language other than English to be used in official state business; undocumented children would have been prevented from attending school; citizenship would have been denied to children of parents without proper papers; and undocumented immigrants would have been banned from driving or purchasing vehicles, and if they were apprehended, their cars would have been put up for sale.

No child—or immigrant—was left behind. But the children in Arizona didn't let Pearce off the hook. On March 17, 2011, a parade of children dressed as firefighters, doctors, lawyers, police officers, pilots, and scientists, carrying signs including a thirty-foot banner of colorful hand prints, marched along the Arizona capitol grounds singing "This Little Light of Mine." On the eve of the Arizona state legislature's historic vote on this blockbuster bill, the kids held a symbolic sit-in on the capitol lawn with a reminder that no one would suffer more from the draconian bills than state's youngest.

It was a stunning defeat for the Tea Party president, and it bolstered the energy of the Recall Pearce campaign. Even some of Arizona's most conservative

CEOs and Chamber of Commerce stalwarts had written the legislature before the vote to inform Pearce that they "strongly believe it is unwise for the Legislature to pass any additional immigration legislation, including any measures leaving the determination of citizenship to the state."

Pearce took his stand. He was unmoved. "It took me a while on 1070, too," Pearce scolded his fellow senators, referring to the controversial immigration bill. "I introduced it in '05, '06, '07, '08, '09, and 2010 before we had a governor that would sign it. And we've become the envy of this nation, with twenty-five states writing legislation modeled after 1070."

In an interesting ideological barb aimed at the business community, Pearce chastised the "profits over patriots" interests of corporations that had been dependent on cheap undocumented labor for more than a century.

The children taught Pearce a lesson on that fine spring day, though. "Real education should consist of drawing the goodness and the best out of our own students," Cesar Chavez once reminded the nation. "What better books can there be than the book of humanity?"

On the heels of an unforgiving year of outrageous state rebellion, children in Arizona had to create their own book of humanity—if only to defend their state's diverse heritage and basic human rights. As part of the Repeal Coalition campaign in Arizona, a volunteer grassroots organization that was calling for the repeal of SB 1070 and other anti-immigrant laws, the children and youth opened a new chapter in the ongoing saga in Arizona. One banner simply asked, "Russell Pearce: Why Do You Hate Arizona's Youth?"

"While I was disappointed with last week's votes," Pearce would write later in *Politico*, "it was not the last word on illegal immigration in Arizona. I am not backing off from demanding our laws be enforced. . . . We have fought these battles before and prevailed. We will prevail again."

This time, however, Randy Parraz, Chad Snow, and their fervent recall movement presented the Tea Party president with an unprecedented challenge.

WHEN PEARCE COUNTRY WAS MECHAM COUNTRY

More than Parraz or anyone involved in the recall, Pearce must have been haunted by an earlier recall attempt: the campaign to oust one of his political heroes in Arizona in the 1980s. The two campaigns shared so many similarities that the first one served as a blueprint for handling the Tea Party takeover. It included a right-wing fringe politician who had captured the nation's attention for his racial calumnies; an energetic recall organizer who was denounced as a "dangerous" outsider; a division within the Mormon Church between hard-line fundamentalists and moderates; a national boycott of the state over controversial race-based policies; and the involvement of Jan Brewer, who defended the disgraced but loyal Republican ally from her adopted hometown of Glendale.

In 1987, Arizona became the laughingstock of the nation. As one Republican state senator from Tucson remarked, the state once again had "a lock on the bigot vote, the anti-intellectual vote and the homophobic vote."

The governor in question was Evan Mecham; his ghost still haunts the state.

It was his fifth attempt at the Arizona governorship—indefatigable car salesman that he was. While the endless delivery of the "Harold Stassen of the West" punch line provided some comic relief for the press (Stassen had been a perennial candidate for governor in Minnesota for decades), most cynical observers forgot one important detail: Stassen actually got elected as governor for one term in 1939.

So did Mecham, the Glendale auto dealer whose primary upset against Republican boss and Statehouse Majority Leader Burton Barr stunned the state in 1986.

With President Ronald Reagan's blessing and US Senator Barry Goldwater's endorsement, Mecham's long-shot candidacy turned into a Cinderella story for the nation's right-wing fringe. In a special appeal, Reagan told the voters of Arizona on October 14, 1986, "This year's election could mark a turning point in our country's history." He warned voters to choose the "right track" and turn away from policies of "weakness and ridicule abroad." Domestic ridicule would abound. "With me in the race," Mecham declared, "we're not just going to talk about water and air and nice things like that."

Taking advantage of a split vote between the Democrat and a liberal independent candidate, Mecham kept his word as he coasted to victory in the fall of 1986. In truth, the majority of Arizona voters (more than 60 percent) stayed home. Within days, the car salesman-cum-governor made good on his promise not to talk about "nice things like that" and managed to turn Arizona into a "Circus Maximus," in the words of venerable Arizona Congressman Morris K. Udall.

"Would You Buy a Used Car from This Governor?" The mocking headline by the *San Francisco Examiner,* nearly a year after Mecham's shocking victory, underscored a level of national scorn and derision that calls to mind the state's more recent debacle over immigration policies. Jon Stewart and *The Daily Show* would have had a bottomless well of material.

In Mecham's case, however, the nuttiness of his character somehow tempered the anger—or at least made it secondary to his nonstop tendency, as his press secretary once noted, "to put his foot in his mouth." Mecham was already known for his B-movie Pontiac car TV commercials; at first his folksy character and gaffes almost charmed cynics and pundits alike, providing a lifetime of jokes and one-liners. His descent into national buffoonery seemed inevitable—even welcomed.

Within days of his inauguration, though, the invective in the jokes mirrored the increasing division and extremist overtones in Mecham's train wreck of an administration. *What a shame to waste a $400 toupee on a two-bit head! Did you hear that Mecham ordered the U. of A. School of Agriculture to develop chickens with only right wings and all-white meat? Why did Mecham cancel Easter? He heard the eggs were going to be colored.*

Born in rural Utah in 1924, Mecham had a childhood that was fairly typical of the Mormon West. He served in World War II and earned a Purple Heart after being shot down in Europe. He returned to the States, got married, became a lay bishop in his Mormon church, moved to Arizona to raise his large family, and soon launched a car dealership in the remote mining town of Ajo, near the US-Mexico border.

After losing a race for the Arizona House of Representatives, Mecham moved to the Phoenix suburb of Glendale and opened a new Pontiac dealership. Cars may have been his business, but politics was his first love. He finally managed to get elected to the Arizona State Senate in 1960, only to launch an ambitious campaign for the US Senate against the state's (and arguably one of the Senate's) most legendary Democrats, Carl Hayden, in 1962. (Elected as the first Representative from Arizona in 1912, Hayden became the longest-serving member of Congress, lasting a full fifty-seven years, until

1969.) Mecham ran on an anti-communist campaign to get the United States out of the United Nations; he was trounced, but the loss opened the chute for a twenty-five-year escapade of nonstop losing campaigns.

Until 1986. Running largely to get payback for the "ambush" of an earlier run for governor, Mecham targeted the seemingly invincible Republican leader Barr. He blasted Barr for "perfidy" and proclaimed he would bring an end to an era of "hidden and secret government control." To the amazement of the Republican machine, Mecham won.

Not that it surprised Mecham, who reportedly told one of his assistants of his heavenly connections on the eve of the election: "I have assurance that I am going to win."

Mecham's appointees could have done with a bit more secrecy in ushering in a new era on January 6, 1987. Even *People* magazine couldn't resist running a list of Mecham's eyebrow-raising cabinet assignments: "Appointed to the state Board of Education a woman who reportedly described the ERA campaign as a lesbian plot. . . . Nominated as director of revenue a man whose company was $25,000 in arrears on unemployment compensation payments." Some appointments were almost uncanny in their contradictions: Mecham's main adviser on education lectured a legislative committee on the failings of schools and declared, "If a student wants to say the world is flat, the teacher doesn't have the right to prove otherwise." A convicted felon was asked to head up prison construction. The head of Mecham's fan club turned out to be a child molester. *Time* magazine called Mecham's nominee for a state investigator "a former Marine who had been court-martialed twice. The Governor's special assistant went on leave after being charged with extortion. Such blunders have prompted publication of a hot-selling Evan Mecham joke book. One entry: 'What do Mecham's political appointees have in common? Parole officers.'"

These were pardonable offices compared with Mecham's bullheaded implementation of the religious right wing's extremist ideas. Mecham's insurgent campaign, a precursor to the Tea Party, had railed against the Republican establishment in Phoenix and laid the foundations for a popular revolt "committed to the Constitution, traditional American values, and cleaning up our widespread drug problem and organized crimes," according to the right-wing president of the Arizona Eagle Forum.

This popular revolt was launched at his inauguration. With Church of Jesus Christ of Latter-day Saints President Ezra Taft Benson standing at the podium, a prodigious moment that recognized Mecham's "divine calling" to the seat of power, Mecham declared that his first major act in office would be to rescind former Governor Bruce Babbitt's last-minute decree to enact an official Martin Luther King Jr. Day in Arizona.

Mecham didn't simply rescind the holiday; he took one step further and declared, "I guess King did a lot for colored people, but I don't think he deserves a national holiday." Before too long, Mecham was also defending the use of the word "pickaninnies" for African American children in Cleon Skousen's book *The Making of America*.

Whether or not Arizona was fed up with Mecham, national organizations and a host of celebrities led by Stevie Wonder quickly orchestrated a boycott of the state over the governor's unabashed racism and holiday decision, and would even manage to get the National Football League to move the 1993 Super Bowl from Sun Devil Stadium in Tempe to Pasadena, California. Public Enemy sized up Arizona's reputation with their single "By the Time I Get to Arizona" mentioning the "fact" that "the whole state's racist."

Whether or not they took umbrage at Mecham's reckless appointments or discriminatory policies, it took little for the business community—still smarting from the defeat of their Republican stalwart Barr—to jump on the finger-pointing bandwagon.

One of the governor's earliest critics was real estate developer J. Fife Symington III, who claimed that Mecham's holiday debacle had resulted in at least forty-five convention cancellations and the loss of more than $25 million in revenue. He told *Time* magazine: "I think he's had a really adverse effect on the business climate," adding as an aside, "You'd have to live here to appreciate this comedy of errors." (Symington went on to become governor himself in 1991, only to resign in disgrace for bank fraud.)

"He's got the whole country laughing at us," lamented Udall, "and you just can't have that and attract the kind of new business you need."

No one would argue with Udall's liberal record, especially on civil rights, but his concern that Mecham had "damaged our image" spoke as much to the majority in the state that stayed at home during the elections and now rued Arizona's scarred reputation—a hauntingly similar situation, in many respects, to post–SB 1070 Arizona, where empathy for the casualties of the right-wing agenda placed a distant second to the pocketbook and the media's social register.

The coastal media in the Mecham era, as well, thrived on his gaffes and on the sociocultural implications of portraying Arizona as a backwater state. *Doonesbury* immortalized Mecham as a buffoon. Writing in the pop culture magazine *Spin,* Bart Bull updated the colorful portraits of New York City–based travel writers from a century ago:

> Arizona is where the Old West crawled off to die. Or if not actually to die, then at least to establish a cranky early retirement. Arizona is God's country, wide open spaces of desert so dry and hard and craggy that only the bravest, boldest and most devotedly crooked of developers dares plant a For Sale sign. Arizona is a man's man's No Man's Land, where bikers gripe when they have to check their hogleg pistols before bellying up to the go-go bar to hoot at the tattooed topless cuties. Arizona is where the cactus meets the palm tree at poolside just the way God intended, where the Official State Tie is shaped like a noose, where the Mormons and the Mexicans and the Mercury dealers can all get together to agree on just exactly what kind of people we need less of around here.

THE RECALL HAS DONE WHAT IT HAS DONE WITH GRASSROOTS PEOPLE POWER

Writing in the *New York Times,* Arizona-based author Alan Weisman transcended such caricatures and focused more on the transient "confusion of a state largely populated by recent arrivals whose self-interests replace roots and loyalties." He wrote, "In the restless way of the Sun Belt, for every four who arrive in Arizona in search of quick success, three others leave. Although many recall supporters believe all will be solved if they get rid of the Governor, the casual, rootless regard many Arizonans have for their state creates opportunities for someone like him to thrive. Amid the passions of the recall, an unpleasant fact has been mostly overlooked: this year, Arizona's legislature again failed to authorize a King holiday. And few frankly believe that it would pass a statewide referendum, which Mecham has proposed to settle the issue."

Enter Ed Buck, a thirty-three-year-old millionaire entrepreneur in Phoenix, who told the *New York Times*, "Never before has one man alienated so many people in such a short period of time." Buck was hardly alone. Beyond the Martin Luther King Jr. incident, the African American community didn't know what to think of a governor who said he would willingly employ black people "because they are the best people who applied for the cotton-picking job."

The Mexican American community took offense at Mecham's rationale for selecting a TV weather anchor as his liaison to the Hispanic community: "I was so dazzled by her beauty," he gushed, "I hired her on the spot." Indeed, Mecham's quip that his Pontiacs were "Mexican Cadillacs" always had people shaking their heads.

His views of those south of the border were not as sweet. Threatening to use the National Guard on the border, Mecham railed against Latin American revolutions and the "idea of communists parked in his nation's back yard." And when Japanese businessmen toured Phoenix with the governor, he remarked that they got "round eyes" when he showed off the city's golf courses.

Among numerous other matters, Buck was personally offended by Mecham's public disparagement of gays. The governor told one radio show, "If you are a member of the same church I am, you have evidently changed your lifestyle, because the church I belong to does not allow homosexuals to participate under any circumstances."

Within seconds of the official 180–day waiting period, Buck decided that derision and shame did little to solve the state's number-one nuisance: the Republican businessman, who happened to be gay, launched a recall campaign that sidestepped political affiliations and challenged Arizona's costly apathy. Buck took no prisoners. He called Mecham a "Neanderthal who breeds paranoia and is a tragedy for this state."

Everyone agreed. The Chamber of Commerce nodded in approval. Democrats turned their heads in glee. Nonetheless, Buck found himself alone on the next step: the Herculean task of collecting 220,000 verified signatures.

"Thirty days ago, when we started the Mecham recall movement, no newspaper, no political pro, no pundit, no columnist—no one except the participants gave us a chance," Buck lectured in an op-ed in the *Arizona Republic* on August 16, 1987. "We were written off as crackpots."

Within the first thirty days, he and a growing crew of volunteers had already gathered more than 103,000 signatures.

Buck didn't pull any punches. A Republican maverick and an outspoken gay activist at the beginning of the AIDS epidemic, he chastised state leaders for their "lack of courage." The business community was too timid, and couldn't get beyond "discussing" the recall to actually join it. The Democrats, paradoxically leery of losing Mecham as their target, were ineffective and "rent by infighting." The rest of the Republican leadership had succumbed to "political prostitution."

Buck issued a warning, which would resonate today in any state arena and certainly foretold a generation of lame Democratic politics in Arizona: "Those leaders who won't lead are in danger of finding that no one pays attention anymore. The recall has done what it has done with grassroots people power—thousands of volunteers, hundreds of thousands of man-hours of work, untold amounts of shoe leather and elbow grease and very little money."

And they always had Mecham for inspiration: "Whenever we think this recall movement may be losing steam," Buck joked, "Ev pulls us through."

The governor didn't just roll over and surrender. He countered every accusation; he defended his fiscal policies and balanced budget; he trumpeted his war on drugs and commitment to funding education. He was typically giddy when discussing the state's new trade office in Taiwan. He took the cartoon depictions and punch lines in stride; he placed himself in good company, in line with the rest of the nation's criticized leaders. "Who am I to be concerned about such attacks?" he told the *New York Times*. "Washington, a president elected by acclamation, was pilloried by journalists. And Lincoln: Terrible how they treated him. Jefferson's friends begged him to crack down on the press. Nothing that's worth doing ever comes easy. This doesn't surprise me."

Like Pearce, who attacked the "union thug" and "anarchist" Parraz, Mecham singled out Buck for his wrath—and his battle strategy. "The homosexuals sought me out," he told the John Birch magazine. "The first element that we know that joined the recall effort was the National Gay Rights Liberation Movement. And the Democrats. And the pornographers. And the drug people, too—it's a big business in Arizona, too big."

Mechamites, as they were eventually called, got vicious. They distributed bumper stickers with the words "Queer Ed Buck's Recall." They warned Arizonans to watch out for petition gatherers, especially the gay liberation forces: "Be warned, you may get AIDS if the person that offers you the pen and petition to sign is a homosexual with the AIDS virus."

Then they turned desperate. Once again like Pearce and his obsession with Parraz's band of anarchists and socialists, Mecham railed against a left-wing conspiracy and leaned on his hard-line supporters to donate funds to counter the "militant liberals and homosexual lobby" that was leading the recall. He also wanted his followers to consider a radical move, literally: he sent a mailer to 25,000 right-wing patriots asking them to "pick up and move to Arizona." Mecham wasn't kidding: "That's right. I want you to sell your house, pack up your belongings, quit your job, and come to the most beautiful state in the Union."

In the end, Buck pulled off a miracle, but all in vain. His volunteer operation turned in more than 350,000 signatures—6,000 more than the votes Mecham had won in the election. He had taught the state an enduring lesson. "It is clear that those to whom Arizonans have traditionally looked for leadership lack the courage of their convictions," he said. "It is clear that those who have captured Arizona—they of the rabid right—have used that apathy and lack of opposing leadership to ride their misguided, mean-spirited passions into the governor's office. What should now be dawning on both groups is that something is happening out here. Something stirs deep within the body politic they have so long taken for granted."

Before the scheduled recall election took place in the spring of 1988, the state legislature seized on allegations of improper loans and misappropriated campaign donations, and subsequent perjury charges, and slammed through a special impeachment trial in the spring. It provided an even greater media circus. Mecham was convicted for a handful of relatively minor charges, including the misuse of government funds and obstruction of justice. He was kicked out of office, and the recall was canceled. Secretary of State Rose Mofford, best known for her beehive hairdo, became the governor.

It took Arizona four more years before it finally passed Proposition 300, which made Martin Luther King Jr. Day a paid holiday. Mecham ran again for governor and the US Senate. He lost both elections. Buck eventually moved to West Hollywood, California.

"Truth be told," concluded Pulitzer Prize–winning political cartoonist Steve Benson (the grandson of Mormon leader Ezra Benson), "Mecham was forcibly extracted from the governor's chair after having been in office only 15 months and was later confined to the dementia unit of the Arizona State Veteran Home (suffering from a form of the affliction similar to Alzheimer's disease), before dying in February 2008, a beaten, humiliated and broken man."

Gonzo journalist Hunter S. Thompson predicted that Mecham would never really go away: "The only problem now is how to make him disappear without heaping more scum and ridicule on Arizona's image. . . . But Mecham will not go away. He is like one of those big pack rats. . . . Welcome to Phoenix: This is Mecham country."

Or perhaps one could say: Mecham country became Pearce country. More important, a right-wing philosopher provided both men with the bedrock of their extremist ideas—and his legacy, thanks to Glenn Beck and Pearce, was once again shaping politics in Arizona and across the nation.

SKOUSEN, ARIZONA

In the winter of 1987, while the snowbirds were ensconced in their rounds of golf, the precocious twenty-three-year-old Glenn Beck cruised into a new job in Phoenix in a DeLorean after successful stints as a shock jock in Corpus Christi and Louisville. Applying his zoo-show antics to the KOY airwaves, Beck sought to bring the FM station into first place among its competitors.

An admitted drug user and boozer, Beck was hardly the Christian warrior in those days. His brief radio hitch in Phoenix was a classic mix of rock 'n' roll antics and gags, fueled by the excess of Arizona's suburban sprawl.

It would take him another twenty years before he realized he had missed a titan of right-wing extremist philosophy in his very neighborhood. But Beck would more than make up for it. By 2007, the radio host had set out to make sure the rest of the nation discovered iconic fringe hero Cleon Skousen and his best-selling book, *The 5,000 Year Leap*.

Arizonans were a few leaps ahead of Beck. Although a few eyebrows were raised when Mormon President Ezra Benson appeared at Mecham's divine-right inauguration, only a handful of people would have recognized another elder Mormon figure in the background of the Capitol celebrations. By the end of Mecham's first year, though, Skousen had become almost a household name. Mecham's gaffes made sure of that.

A Canadian by birth, Skousen has been described variably as a crackpot historian, an anti-communist conspiracy theorist, a constitutional scholar, and a latter-day conservative Mormon visionary. In the 1950s, after a fifteen-year stint as a clerk at J. Edgar Hoover's FBI headquarters in Washington, Skousen launched a lifelong career as a special agent in the battle against the invasion of godless communism in everyday life. He called out President Eisenhower as a communist sympathizer; he railed against the plot for a worldwide collectivist society. In 1961 *Time* magazine hailed him as the "guiding light" among "rightwing ultras" and as "one of the busiest speakers in the rightist movement." *Time* also mentioned that in 1960 Skousen had been fired as chief of the Salt Lake City police department, which he had operated "like a Gestapo," according to the former mayor.

The darling of the John Birch Society, Skousen also cranked out a series of books that undeniably shaped two generations of extremist followers. In *The Naked Communist,* he called for a "war of ideologies" against a communist menace hell-bent on "the total annihilation of all opposition, the downfall of all existing governments, all economies and all societies." In his speeches, he warned, "We should not sit back and wait for our boys and girls to be indoctrinated with materialistic dogma and thereby make themselves vulnerable to a Communist conversion when they are approached by the agents of force and fear who come from across the sea."

By 1979, however, Skousen's extremist views had alarmed the Mormon leadership enough that the church president's office issued a special letter prohibiting any announcements of Skousen's lectures under the auspices of the church or the use of church facilities for his followers' meetings, though it did note that "this instruction is not intended to express any disapproval of the right of [Skousen's] Freemen Institute and its lecturers to conduct such meetings or of the contents of the lectures."

Just after rescinding Martin Luther King Jr. Day in Arizona, Mecham dropped another verbal bomb that kept him as a national punch line for days. When the Arizona governor casually defended the use of the word "pickaninnies" for African American children, he set off an investigation into the intellectual makeup of his increasingly wacky statements. The Mormon governor, in fact, was defending the work of his mentor Skousen, a regular visitor to Mesa and the Phoenix area, and someone Mecham considered a hero.

Only months before his election victory, Mecham had raved to the *Arizona Republic*, "I would enjoy being known as a protégé of Cleon Skousen. I have all of his books, suitably autographed. I'm a great fan of his, and we're very dear friends."

The "pickaninnies" gaffe had come from Skousen's controversial book *The Making of America*, which invoked the term from a 1934 essay. As Alexander Zaitchik revealed years later in his extraordinary exposé on Skousen and Beck for *Salon*, "Quoting the historian Fred Albert Shannon, *The Making of America* explained that '[slave] gangs in transit were usually a cheerful lot, though the presence of a number of the more vicious type sometimes made it necessary for them all to go in chains.'"

In line with Mecham's derogatory statements about King, Skousen believed that the civil rights leader was "a man who courted violence and night riding and broke the law to achieve his purposes; who found it expedient openly to collaborate with totalitarian Communism; and whose personal life was so revolting that it cannot be discussed."

Nearly a quarter of a century after the Mecham debacle, Russell Pearce and his brother Lester joined ranks with Beck to make Arizona a hotbed of Skousenian disciples, revamping the old man's soiled reputation and reintroducing his philosophies to a new generation of Tea Party activists in search of a handbook.

"Even before Obama's inauguration," Zaitchik wrote, "Beck had a game plan for a movement with Skousen at the center." Introducing his "September 12th" movement, Beck informed his radio listeners that the first imperative was to "get *The 5,000 Year Leap*. Over my book or anything else, get *The 5,000 Year Leap*. You can probably find it in the book section of GlennBeck.com, but read that. It is the principle. Please, number-one thing: inform yourself about who we are and what the other systems are all about. *The 5,000 Year Leap* is the first part of that."

Thanks to Beck, Skousen's books and seminars flourished among Tea Party offshoots across the country, including the Arizona Mainstream Project, which also focused on the communist conspiracy theories of Tucson's Ethnic Studies Program.

A profile in the *LA Times* in 2011 noted that Pearce had "attended lectures by W. Cleon Skousen, a right-wing author and former FBI agent," and shared Mecham's sense of a "divine calling," according to State Representative Bill Konopnicki, a fellow Republican who had challenged Pearce on immigration policy. (In retaliation for his opposition, Konopnicki claimed, Pearce instigated a series of threats against his family, an allegation Pearce denied.)

"I believe government is a creation of God," Pearce had told an interviewer in Mesa. "It just must be limited."

In the spring of 2011, in an article in *The Nation,* author Garrett Epps wrote about his experience at one of Lester Pearce's Skousen trainings, where he learned that the "constitution is based on the Law of Moses; that Mosaic law was brought to the West by the ancient Anglo-Saxons, who were probably the Ten Lost Tribes of Israel; and that the Constitution restores the fifth-century kingdom of the Anglo-Saxons." Lester Pearce also noted: "Virtually all of modern American life and government is unconstitutional. Social Security, the Federal Reserve, the Environmental Protection Agency, the Civil Rights Act of 1964, hate crime laws—all flatly violate God's law. State governments are not required to observe the Bill of Rights, and the First Amendment establishes 'the religion of America,' which is 'nondenominational' Christianity."

Arizona Congressman Trent Franks, who listed his education at the Skousen-founded National Center for Constitutional Studies in Idaho as his main academic background, made national headlines in the fall of 2009 when he referred to President Obama as "an enemy of humanity." Echoing Skousen's depiction of slavery, Franks defiantly told a conference on abortion that "far more of the African American community is being devastated by the policies of today," referring to reproductive choice, "than were being devastated by the policies of slavery."

Looking back at his short time in office in a 1988 interview in the John Birch Society's *New American* magazine, Mecham concurred: "I'm a Constitutionalist. . . . The Constitution was inspired by God through people He raised up to give us the right amount of government. God gives us our freedom—if we're smart enough to listen to Him, He'll see that we have a type of government that will maintain that freedom for us. But, if we aren't, He doesn't send a legion of angels down to fight for us."

For Pearce, those angels didn't really include Mexicans or Mexican Americans or progressives. At the Skousen seminar, he reminded attendees, "I wrote a bill when I was in the legislature to give [the Gadsden Purchase] back to Mexico, because we had people in Tucson who were socialists."

But the angels were fighting beside a lot of Skousen disciples—not just Glenn Beck and Russell Pearce. On the presidential campaign trail in Iowa in 2007, former Massachusetts Governor Mitt Romney, a Mormon, praised Skousen as an influence during a radio interview. Like Romney's ancestors, Skousen's grandparents had fled to the Mormon colonies in Mexico. In fact, Pearce and Romney had both buried a secret about their ancestors' arrival in the territory of Arizona.

THE BLOOD OF SOME ARIZONA PROPHETS

As a fifth-generation Arizonan, Russell Pearce would never be confused with a carpetbagger, and he often invoked that history as a badge. But although Mexican American Studies advocates had to justify their history and counter interminable charges that Mexican American students were somehow outsiders or newcomers to the American experience, hardly anyone turned the mirror on a self-avowed nativist like Pearce.

A closer examination of Pearce's family history revealed a dark tradition of violence and paranoia reminiscent of today's approach to "outsiders." The same could be said for the Romney family; few political observers knew of his ancestors' dubious past in Arizona. Not that Romney had been forthcoming in his memoirs.

Statehood, secession, or theocratic empire—those appeared to be the three options facing Brigham Young and the Mormons in Utah in 1856, living on the harrowing edge of economic and agricultural ruin. When two Mormon apostles journeyed to Washington, DC, with their statehood petition, they hardly received a glance. Young went into overdrive and borrowed a page from Martin Luther, leading the Mormons into a spirit of Reformation. Bloody reformation.

As Will Bagley notes in his award-winning history, *Blood of the Prophets: Brigham Young and the Massacre at Mountain Meadows*, "Perhaps the most troubling aspect of the Reformation was the Mormon leadership's obsession with blood. Their rhetoric dripped with sanguine imagery, and their Old Testament theology incorporated this dark fascination in a perplexing doctrine known as blood atonement. . . . Of all the beliefs that laid the foundation of Utah's culture of violence, none would have more devastating consequences."

John D. Lee carried out this doctrine better than any follower. Abusive, ruthless, hated by his own community, the commander of the Mormons' Fourth Battalion in southern Utah had an "autocratic style" matched only by the captain of his first company: Harrison Pearce.

A Georgia native, Pearce had converted to Mormonism in his twenties, and then migrated west with the exodus. A dedicated polygamist whose three wives would be listed on his tombstone, he settled in the fledgling cotton corridors of southern Utah. A carpenter by trade, he also served as a sheriff in Washington, Utah.

As the resentment against "gentiles" festered and talk spread that the US military was sharpening its bayonets for a possible invasion, stalwarts like Lee and Pearce readied themselves for a holy war. The presidential campaign of 1856 had set the stage: the time had come to end "the twin relics of Barbarism—Polygamy and Slavery." The Mormons had staked their claims on the state sovereignty hopes of Senator Stephen Douglas. When President James Buchanan rode to victory, rumors of a Utah War—a Mormon War—spread like messengers across the plains.

To their great misfortune, a wagon party of Arkansas travelers knew nothing of the brewing storm over Zion. They just wanted to make it across the great desert and mountain range to the futureland of California. They set off in the spring of 1857 with their horses and cows, their children and wives, toting their rifles and the gullibility of those who believed in the great American migrant dream.

For Mormons like Lee and Pearce, the travelers represented an official invasion—or, simply, easy targets. Bagley posits, "If Brigham Young did not intentionally provoke a war with the United States, by early 1857 he was busily preparing for it." Young braced his Mormon followers for an assault by President Buchanan's federal troops just as his kingdom was unraveling on all sides.

As the Arkansas travelers unwittingly passed through Cedar City on their way to the Mountain Meadows, the Mormon leaders concocted tales of the travelers' abuses and offenses, and fomented the suspicion that they planned to poison the local livestock and water sources. Lee assembled his troops; he recruited local bands of Paiute Indians. Regardless of the travelers' intent or the lack of any acts of disparagement to the locals, the Mormons had drawn a delusional line in the sand and were determined to protect it.

Pearce declared his wish to "see all the Gentyles strippt naked and lashed on their backs and have the Sun scorch them to death by inches." Paiutes and Mormons dressed as Indians launched the first attacks on the wagon train. Pearce and his son James, along with other Mormon militia reinforcements, soon arrived at the battleground. Over the next five days, the dwindling Arkansas parties held off the repeated attacks, even as their ranks diminished to a handful of men and mainly women and children. Lee eventually orchestrated a white-flag truce, claiming he would lead the party out of danger from the Indians if they disarmed. He ushered out the children and their mothers on a march for the last horrific minutes of their existence. The final call was made. The Mormons and their Indian allies swept down and carried out the massacre.

Years later, one of Brigham Young's wives recounted her version of a story—never proved but often told—that Harrison Pearce had shot his own son when he attempted to save a young girl from a bloody death on that day. She cited a scar on his face as proof. One of Lee's sons claimed that the elder Pearce had shot down the last standing child—a ten-year-old girl—when the son refused to carry out the dishonorable deed. In the end, 120 children, women, and men were massacred at Mountain Meadows. Their bodies were left to the ravages of birds and wolves and other wild animals.

Reports of the dark massacre eventually made their way to outer edges of newspapers in California; the Mormons manufactured denials, placed the blame on "savages," or fabricated stories of attack and poisonous treachery by the travelers.

More than a year and a half after the disaster, an appointed judge and federal investigators waded among the blanched bones in Mountain Meadows, collected affidavits, and issued arrest warrants for the key militia leaders, including Pearce and his son. The judge declared that crimes had been committed by the "order of the council." It would take another two decades before a single person—John D. Lee, who had fled to Arizona—was brought to justice.

Meanwhile, Brigham Young championed the prophetic outbreak of war back east. "There is no Union to leave; it is all disunion," he declared. "Our Government is shivered to pieces, but the Kingdom of God will increase."

With the masterful lies of an ancient mariner, and acting at Young's behest, Lee took his wives (eight, according to some accounts) and extended family and moved to Arizona, where he established a crucial ferry on the Colorado River. Pearce did the same. In 1876, the same year Lee was sentenced to die for his solitary conviction of murder at the Mountain Meadows massacre, Pearce set up the historic "Pearce Ferry" on the northern edges of Arizona. Settlers began to pour into Mesa.

A bitter old man who finally admitted his mistakes, Lee was taken out to the desolated remains of the abandoned Mountain Meadows and executed by a makeshift firing squad on a brisk spring morning in 1877. Five years later, the elder Pearce petitioned his church to return to southern Utah. His son James, among others, had already launched a new era in Arizona history.

ARIZONA OUTLAWS AND SANCTUARY SEEKERS

Mitt Romney's family struggled to adjust to a new era in that same period. Their practice of polygamy was hardly news, of course. In the summer of 2011, as the Republican presidential primaries were heating up, the *Washington Post* ran a feature on Romney's sizable family community in northern Mexico and the role of his great-grandfather Miles Park Romney, "who came to the Chihuahua desert in 1885 seeking refuge from U.S. anti-polygamy laws."

But that was not quite the full story. Nor did a critical chapter on his family's lawlessness in Arizona appear in Romney's official version.

Only hours before one of the contentious Republican debates in the fall of 2011, Arizona Governor Jan Brewer formally petitioned the US Supreme Court to consider an appeal to a lower court's decision on SB 1070. Brewer invoked state jurisdiction over immigration and police enforcement issues, just in time to thrust Arizona's extremist immigration laws back into the national political arena.

Romney, in fact, had been the first Republican contender to speak in support of SB 1070, declaring that "Arizona's new immigration enforcement law is the direct result of Washington's failure to secure the border and to protect the lives and liberties of our citizens." He did add, though: "It is my hope that the law will be implemented with care and caution not to single out individuals based upon their ethnicity."

More than a century ago, Romney's family wouldn't have shared his concerns about border security. Consider his great-grandfather's dalliance with Arizona laws. In his 2004 memoir, *Turnaround: Crisis, Leadership, and the Olympic Games*, Romney recounts his version of his great-grandfather's removal to Mexico:

> Miles Junior was asked to move again, this time to build a settlement in St. Johns, Arizona. To every request, Romneys were obedient. And leaving behind all that they had worked to establish, they yet again pitched themselves against the arid terrain, the cactus, the alkali, quicksand, and rattlesnakes. They built schools and libraries. Miles Junior was the founder of a theatrical society on the frontier. He dug irrigation ditches and plowed up the desert soil.
>
> Eventually Miles was called upon to settle in northern Mexico, where his son, my grandfather Gaskell, would wed and my father George would be born.

Romney concludes the story of his great-grandfather, who died in Mexico in 1904: "Despite emigrating, my great-grandfather never lost his love of country." He may never have lost his love of the United States, but he didn't leave Arizona on good terms—or legal ones.

In the 1880s, Mormons in Arizona didn't just face persecution for their polygamy practices; they also faced resentment over their aggressive land deals and encroaching settlements. Five Mormons, including William Flake— the great-great-grandfather of Arizona Republican Representative Jeff Flake, who ran for a Senate seat in 2012—were convicted of unlawful "cohabitation" in 1884 (instead of violating the Edmunds Act, which outlawed polygamy) and sent to prison. In a related land claims dispute involving Miles P. Romney, Mormon leader David Udall—the great-grandfather of US Senators Tom Udall, a Democrat from New Mexico, and Colorado Democrat Mark

Udall—was sent to prison in Detroit on perjury charges. (Udall, who had apparently considered fleeing the country, was later pardoned by President Grover Cleveland.)

Romney's ancestor took a different option. Faced with the same perjury charges over his land claim in St. Johns, Arizona—rivals had accused of Romney of failing to reside continuously on a 160-acre ranch—Romney went on the lam in the spring of 1885 and forfeited more than $2,000 in bond when Udall warned him that federal marshals were en route to his home (according to Udall's diary). A local newspaper wrote that Romney's flight left his community "in the lurch."

Writing in the *Journal of the Southwest* in 1977, in their article "Prosecution of the Mormons in Arizona Territory in the 1880s," Mormon historians JoAnn Blair and Richard Jensen spelled out Romney's break from Mormons who willingly faced the legal system in Arizona: "Romney had fared well in the earlier legal proceedings for the same alleged offense, partly because, he claimed, he had paid 'several hundred dollars to grease the wheels.' But this time he was less confident of success. . . . Fearing he would be prosecuted for polygamy, as well as for the earlier charge of perjury regarding his land claim, Romney skipped bond and fled to Mexico."

Years later, Mitt Romney attempted to use the same issue to bolster his immigration hard-liner bona fides. Calling out New York City, San Francisco, and other cities for passing sanctuary policies in the past, he declared, "Sanctuary cities become magnets that encourage illegal immigration and undermine secure borders." In his memoir, he casually overlooks the reality of Mexican sanctuary cities and his family's history, and picks up the story from the border as seen through the eyes of one of Miles P. Romney's wives: "Theirs was a life of toil and sacrifice, of course, of complete devotion to a cause. They were persecuted for their religious beliefs but they went forward undaunted. Despite emigrating, my great-grandfather never lost his love of country. He had an abiding loyalty to America and a deep interest in politics." Romney concludes: "These were the same values and commitments that animated my grandfather and my father and my mother. They were the same values that were passed along to me."

Values, as in seeking out sanctuary cities? Or supporting Arizona's SB 1070 and strict enforcement of the border?

Romney's ancestors had a slightly different take on border security and sanctuary. Having sided with Mexican dictator Porfirio Díaz, Romney's Mormon clans fled their homes and ranches in 1912 when the Mexican Revolution came to town. Fleeing back across the US border, the thousands of Mormons appreciated the porous border and sanctuary cities—and more than $20,000 allocated by the US government for aid and relocation efforts.

In the heat of the Republican primary Romney declared, "It is my hope that the law will be implemented with care and caution not to single out individuals based upon their ethnicity. . . . It is increasingly clear that the time has come for Washington to fulfill its responsibility for border security." When he emerged as the Republican presidential candidate, he went one step further: taking on SB 1070 author Kris Kobach as his immigration policy adviser, he embraced an "attrition through enforcement" policy that held up Arizona as a role model. Romney and the Republican Party would strongly base their immigration policies on SB 1070.

To be sure, in the spring of 2012, Russell Pearce announced to Tea Party activists in Gilbert, Arizona, that Republican presidential candidate Mitt Romney's "immigration policy is identical to mine."

TURNING THE TIDE

The opening salvo in the 2012 elections arguably came on May 30, 2011. That day, scores of people representing Citizens for a Better Arizona poured into the cramped foyer of the secretary of state's office with the rush of a rave. The room swelled as media cameras flashed from the corner posts; state employees peered from the receptionist's open counter to witness the intrusion. Even the security guards smiled.

A stand of children suddenly emerged, a grinning mob in pink ribbons and dresses and tennis shoes, as frosty-haired elders and a dizzying array of parents and activists in their formal best lined themselves in rows. Milk crates passed through the crowd with the unbroken rhythm of veteran delivery workers. Crates of petitions. Papers, please, for sure: 18,300 hard-won signatures in bins that dotted the floor with black-on-yellow placards:

RECALL PEARCE—CITIZENS FOR A BETTER ARIZONA

Demanding the recall of the State Senate president, the bold architect of SB 1070, the Citizens for a Better Arizona effort marked the culmination of a campaign that had defied expectations, and signaled a watershed moment for the beleaguered state—and the nation.

Once the state and Maricopa County recorders verified the legal requirement of at least 7,756 signatures from the traditionally conservative and Mormon-founded Mesa district, Pearce would become the first State Senate president in American history to be recalled. A new election would be scheduled for the fall of 2011. The Tea Party's grip on the Republican Party and its most impor-tant staging ground in the nation would either be solidified—or broken.

The rows parted on cue, as Citizens for a Better Arizona cofounder Randy Parraz swept to the front in his hurried manner. Dark-rimmed glasses and a dark stylish suit framed his ramrod posture and intense gestures; as always, he was flanked by his equally svelte Citizens cofounder, Chad Snow. Parraz looked around the packed room as more people squeezed inside and every-one attempted to widen the walls. Retired librarian Mary Lou Boettcher pursed her lips in a serious view of the scene as she stood near Brenda Rascon, the doctoral biology student and daughter of Mexican immigrants, who could barely contain her enthusiasm. Progressive Democrats of America activist Dan O'Neal, a gray-haired retired history teacher, tugged at his tie.

Coming only days after a Supreme Court decision had upheld the first in a series of controversial immigration laws originating in Arizona—in this case, the imposition of penalties on employers who knowingly hired undocu-mented workers—the recall campaign had national implications. As the na-tional Tea Party hero, the de facto governor of Arizona, and the motivating force behind the state's notorious blitz of extremist policies on border security, education, health, guns, the environment, and immigration, Pearce had in-fluenced legislators and government officials in other states and had done more than any other Tea Party politician in the nation to peddle a nativist and antifederal political brand shaped by the powerful American Legislative Exchange Council, among other corporate lobby interests.

The tide was turning in Arizona. Working door-to-door in the desert heat over the past four months, against the backdrop of the state's floundering image and economy, Parraz and Snow and their volunteer shock troops intended to make Pearce's policies a national referendum on immigration and civil rights.

"We want to send a message to Senator Pearce, to every legislator down here at the Arizona legislature," Snow told the media, "that this kind of extreme, ideologically driven policies will no longer be tolerated in our state."

"Extremist politics only result in short-term gain," added Parraz, who called Pearce an "outright embarrassment to the state." The recall effort stood as a warning for right-wing extremists across the country that there would be "consequences" for their policies and rhetoric. Throughout the campaign, Arizona activists stressed that the recall effort transcended the hot-button immigration issue, reminding residents that *all* of Pearce's draconian measures were out of touch with the values and interests of Arizonans. In an official statement, Citizens for a Better Arizona focused on Pearce's "reckless disregard" for public education; his support for drastic cuts in health care for the poor, including the state's widely denounced termination of the organ transplant program; and his role in diminishing the state's reputation and economy.

Calling Pearce a "real demagogue," retired educator John McDonald, who lived in the state senator's district and had joined the door-to-door campaign over the past 120 days, said Pearce's "meanness goes too far." He criticized Pearce for what he called punishing measures against immigrants, the poor and indigent, as well as schools and children. An active Mormon, Snow charged that Pearce was even out of step with the majority of Peace's fellow Mormons in the district and around the nation.

Trying to stave off a meltdown, the Tea Party president's defenders had brought him even more embarrassment in the days leading up to the recall. Former US Representative J. D. Hayworth had just sent out a nearly incomprehensible email to Pearce supporters, calling the Citizens for a Better Arizona campaigners a group of "socialist thugs who carry swastikas."

"Arizona has been in the headlines for all of the wrong reasons," Parraz told the crowd in the lobby. "We need a victory now. If we come together, we can hold Pearce accountable and win." The children went first, a fistful of signed petitions in their hands. They tiptoed their way to the counter and dropped the petitions into a pile, and then a seemingly endless line of participants followed with the same expressions of astonishment. Everyone watched, the cameras flashed, and Parraz looked on with his intense expression as the stack of petitions grew high enough to block the view of the state employees.

Now the real campaign would begin. The secretary of state and Maricopa County Recorder's Office had to verify the petition signatures over the next ninety days, at which point Governor Brewer would issue an announcement for a recall election in the fall of 2011.

"If you can recall Pearce," Parraz shouted to the crowd, and to the viewers on national television, "you can recall anybody."

A feeling of victory already hovered over the Capitol in Phoenix that day, as the crowd scattered into the lobby and flooded the grounds. Within minutes, photos and updates and schedules for the next recall events exploded on Facebook and across the blogosphere. Having lit a fire under a new movement in Arizona—one that was likely to grow and become more powerful—Parraz and the Citizens for a Better Arizona knew they stood to be the most organized and inspiring political force in the state.

GAME ON, PRESIDENT PEARCE

Within five weeks, the Citizens movement received a swift affirmation of its new power. Secretary of State Ken Bennett notified Governor Brewer on July 8 that Pearce had officially been recalled. Bennett confirmed that the petitions "exceeded the minimum signatures required by the Arizona Constitution."

According to Bennett's statement, Pearce had two options: resign from office within five business days, or become a candidate in the recall election. Either way, Pearce became the first State Senate president in recent memory to be recalled.

"No one expected this or picked up on this political earthquake," said an excited Parraz, fully aware of how his grassroots-led campaign had electrified a bipartisan effort in Pearce's district. Parraz credited Pearce's extremist leadership with prompting a "dramatic shift" over the past six months.

"We had people pouring into the office," Parraz said, citing the role of Republicans, Democrats, and Independents in the canvassing initiative, "and they told us: Russell Pearce is too extreme for our district and state."

The recall campaign had racked up a record number of signatures from discontented Arizonans. The secretary of state's office confirmed that an additional one-third of the necessary signatures had been properly collected and verified.

Within fifteen days, Governor Brewer had to set the date for the recall election. When the Arizona Supreme Court gave the final green light for the November 8 election date, one thing became clear: Citizens for a Better Arizona had galvanized a new era in Arizona politics.

Soon the historic recall of Pearce exploded into a spectacular display of high-road and low-road politics. Moderate Republican accountant, educator, and Mormon leader Jerry Lewis from Mesa emerged to claim the frontrunner's position, and the Tea Party president started to look desperate. While a bipartisan community effort for Lewis spread quickly across Mesa, emphasizing a positive campaign for jobs, education, and a "balanced approach to immigration," Pearce and his Tea Party supporters openly flaunted a series of dirty tricks, all of which backfired.

Thanks to the legwork of *Phoenix New Times* reporter Stephen Lemons, legendary Phoenix videographer Dennis Gilman, and a legion of Pearce watchers, virtually every attempt by Tea Party activists and Pearce supporters to intimidate, mislead, litigate, and even plant a bogus Mexican American candidate to confuse voters and derail competing votes was exposed.

The dirty tricks had started even before Lewis entered the race. A day before his announcement, while he was out jogging in his Mesa neighborhood, the fifty-four-year-old former Boy Scout leader was struck in the groin with a padlock thrown from a passing pickup truck. (The Pearce campaign denied any knowledge of the attack.) Within days, Lewis saw other signs of trouble on his jogs. Mysterious campaign signs invoking Cesar Chavez's "*Sí se puede!*" slogan started appearing around the district in support of Olivia Cortes, a phantom Latino candidate who had never appeared in public.

As Pearce replaced three members on the state's Ethics Committee over an investigation of a colleague's domestic abuse charges, his campaign spiraled deeper into allegations of fraud and ethics violations. Compounding this, a series of blatantly fraudulent efforts by his supporters to set up Cortes's sham candidacy to undermine his main opponent's support among Latino voters unraveled into a damaging comedy of errors.

Along with the Cesar Chavez signs, a new campaign website for Cortes emerged that invoked Superman's pursuit of "Truth, Justice and the American

Way." But in a strange act of either plagiarism or mockery, an accompanying statement emailed by Cortes and widely circulated by Pearce supporters and websites borrowed text from Randy Parraz and the Recall Pearce campaign Facebook site.

Unraveling the Pearce campaign's bungles, Lemons and Gilman methodically connected Pearce operators to most of Cortes's campaign endeavors. In apparent violation of the Arizona Code of Judicial Conduct, Pearce's brother Lester Pearce, a justice of the peace, had assisted in his brother's campaign hijinks. So had his daughters, who had collected petitions for Cortes. Franklin Bruce Ross, the plaintiff on behalf of Pearce in the failed lawsuit to challenge the recall petitions, also solicited petitions for Cortes. And East Valley Tea Party chair Greg Western turned them in to the secretary of state's office.

Once Citizens recall campaign organizer Mary Lou Boettcher and her attorney Tom Ryan filed suit in the Superior Court of Maricopa County for a "verified statement of election contest," the party for the fake candidate was over. Cortes was, in fact, a real person. A retired and bewildered, if not amused, Mexican immigrant in Mesa who had joined the Tea Party cause, she emerged at the hearing and quickly withdrew from the race. The Pearce team had been shamed.

With less than six weeks to go until the November 8 election, it was hard to imagine how much lower Pearce's campaign could sink.

In a sign of things to come, right-wing Arizona Representative Trent Franks sent out a fundraising letter, which breathlessly (and erroneously) declared that "liberal groups from all over the country," along with "left-wing open-border activists," are "expected to spend more than one million dollars" to smear "the hard work and good reputation of our friend Russell Pearce." Calling on all patriots to prevent Pearce from becoming "the first State Senate President in American history to be recalled," Franks threw down the gauntlet: "They will do anything to defeat the author of SB 1070."

LAST DANCE ON THE TEA PARTY LOVE BOAT

Only days before the recall election, Minnesota representative and presidential contender Michele Bachmann brought her floundering campaign to Arizona, giving a special shout-out to the embattled Pearce for his role as the architect of SB 1070. But Bachmann's dismal ranking behind Republican front-runners Mitt Romney, Herman Cain, and Rick Perry only served to remind Arizonans that Pearce's ship was set to sink on November 8.

In one of the biggest campaign flops in recent memory, an estimated four hundred true believers barely covered the first rows in the thirteen-thousand-seat Hohokam baseball stadium for a Pearce rally in Mesa on October 14, 2011, a Friday night. The self-proclaimed "Tea Party president" had heavily advertised and touted the event as the mother of all political rallies in Arizona, featuring a who's-who lineup of extremist right-wing lawmakers—including perennial candidate and former American Constitution Party leader Tom Tancredo, who declared "the American way of life" was at stake. Maricopa County Sheriff Joe Arpaio swaggered to the stage and addressed the largely empty stadium with his usual aplomb. State Superintendent of Public Instruction John Huppenthal, now leading the charge on the crackdown of Mexican American Studies in Tucson, praised Pearce for his commitment to education.

Although Pearce had defiantly declared at a recent debate with Jerry Lewis that his extremist policies had placed Arizona "at the front of the parade," that parade had gone elsewhere, apparently. Pearce had outspent Lewis three to one, but his grassroots support appeared to be unraveling.

"I felt as though I was surrounded by political has-beens, by people who had been damaged by their own destructive brand of politics," said Citizens volunteer Brenda Rascon. "There was a feeling of sadness in the air accompanied by halfhearted speeches that bordered on pathetic and didn't seem to give State Senate President Pearce the encouragement and peace he may have been seeking."

RUSSELL PEARCE HAS BEEN RECALLED

Almost a year to the day after he took power and thrust Arizona's hard-line immigration and antifederal laws into the national arena, State Senate President Russell Pearce watched in bewilderment on November 8, 2011, as an extraordinary citizens campaign dethroned him.

"Today marks the beginning of a new era in Arizona politics," declared Parraz. "The reign of Senate President Russell Pearce has finally come to an end."

As the darling of the right-wing American Legislative Exchange Council and an influential ideologue in the nativist-tinged anti-immigrant movement, however, Pearce was not the only loser in the election upset. With more than 90 percent of his campaign funds coming from corporate lobbyists and out-of-district contributions, allowing him to vastly outspend his opponent, Pearce lost by a nearly 10 percent margin—53.4 percent to 45.3 percent—to Jerry Lewis, a moderate Mormon leader and Republican newcomer who largely ran his grassroots campaign as a referendum on Pearce's extremist views.

Pearce's downfall stood as a looming cautionary tale for the 2012 presidential election and placed the hotly charged issue of immigration policy back onto the front burner. While the state's controversial SB 1070 immigration law had been embraced by all Republican presidential candidates, and replicated in battleground states like Georgia, the question remained whether Democrats would join Parraz and his new bipartisan campaign approach or stay in the shadows on immigration reform like Arizona's reticent and failed Democrats in 2010.

Endorsing Romney for the Republican nomination for president, a defeated but defiant Pearce told the *Washington Post* five months after his recall loss: "Attrition by enforcement. It's identical to mine—enforce the laws. We have good laws, just enforce them."

"[Democrats] thought they were going to take over the Senate and the House two years ago," Pearce added. "We got the largest majority ever in the history of the state of Arizona in the Senate and the House. And you know what brought it there? SB 1070. Everybody ran on SB 1070. We won districts that Republicans have never won before. So, it's nice to have hope and dreams, you know, but it ain't gonna happen."

"This is a huge shift for the Republicans as much as the Democrats," Parraz said, standing in front of the Citizens office in Mesa. "But it will only have a sustainable impact if we continue to get out and do the work, and not sit back and wait for the change."

With an estimated five hundred campaign volunteers taking part in door-to-door canvassing efforts, and a full-scale get-out-the-vote operation, the Citizens group signed up 1,150 new voters—a number that appeared at first to be insignificant but ultimately proved pivotal, considering that Pearce represented one of the most conservative districts in the nation—and amassed a dedicated online following that could mobilize within a minute's call.

"Immigration issues are not Republican or Democratic," said Parraz, who went to great lengths to stress that the recall transcended a single issue, showcasing Pearce's leadership role in a states' rights agenda that cut education and health care, and oversaw the state's economic decline. "We have to work together to make effective change."

"Russell Pearce is too extreme, but he is not alone," said Parraz, who often chastised state and national leaders for allowing the Tea Party figurehead and other hard-liners like Arpaio to go unchallenged. "This election shows that such extremist behavior will not be rewarded, and will be held accountable."

Galvanizing a huge turnout of bipartisan voters, including the growing numbers of retiring baby boomers, Latino youth, and immigrant communities, Parraz and his Citizens group had taught Arizona a compelling lesson on how to stand up for truth and justice.

"This election sends a message to other Democratic efforts," announced Dan O'Neal, a key volunteer on the recall campaign and activist with the Arizona chapter of the Progressive Democrats of America, "to not be afraid to take on issues and races in red states."

The clarion call had been made for the 2012 election—and far into Arizona's future.

TUSD superintendent John Pedicone addresses media as UNIDOS
activists take over the school board on April 26, 2011, in Tucson.
(Photo courtesy of Chris Summitt, Summitt Photography.)

CHAPTER SEVEN

OUTLAWING HISTORY: THE SECOND SHOWDOWN

I am of the Chicano Generation. We grew up in the 1950s and early 1960s, when American society viewed Americans of Mexican descent as foreigners and there was a concerted campaign by society, particularly the schools, to make us feel inferior and treat us as interlopers in our own land. . . . But history is cyclical, and the Mexican haters have resurfaced. We again find ourselves having to prove our legitimacy in our own country.

SALOMON BALDENEGRO SR., "MY TUCSON:
CHICANO MOVEMENT IMPROVED TUCSON,"
THE TUCSON CITIZEN, JULY 28, 2006

STOPPING LA RAZA

While the national fallout over SB 1070 still dominated the news headlines, Governor Brewer sat down at her desk on May 11, 2010, and signed a lesser-known bill that opened another front in Arizona's assault on Latinos and

Native Americans. Known as HB 2281 (officially signed as ARS 15-112), the new law prohibited schools from including courses that "promoted the over-throw of the government" or advocated ethnic solidarity or resentment against another race or class of people. It also outlawed any curriculum "de-signed primarily for pupils of a particular ethnic group." As a thinly veiled ex-tortion tactic, the law allowed the state to withhold 10 percent of the district's state budget if it refused to comply. (Two weeks earlier, the Arizona Depart-ment of Education had issued a mandate for schools to remove any teachers with heavily accented English from classrooms still learning the language.)

In launching one of the most strident anti-Latino campaigns in Arizona history, Brewer's spokesperson announced that the governor believed stu-dents "should not be taught to resent or hate other races." (Within days of this statement, Brewer defiantly declared on TV that "most illegal trespassers" entering her state from Mexico were "drug mules.") As the architect of the bill, then Superintendent of Public Instruction Tom Horne—who would use the law's passage as a victory against "La Raza" in shaping his successful elec-tion campaign as attorney general that fall—took Brewer's rationale to its sur-real limit, comparing Mexican American Studies to segregation in the 1950s: "It's just like the Old South, and it's long past time we prohibited it."

As the nation watched the unfolding of the bizarre witch-hunt fervor of Arizona's new law, the first misnomer in the media came with the framing of HB 2281 as an attack on "ethnic studies." In truth, Horne and his eventual successor, John Huppenthal—a state senator who would also campaign that fall on the need to "Stop La Raza"—exclusively targeted a single "ethnic" pro-gram in the entire state: the Mexican American Studies program in the Tuc-son Unified School District (TUSD). They didn't consider other classes in African American Studies, Native American or Asian Studies, or any of the various curriculums in the state public schools that examined issues of race and oppression or political controversy.

Nor did it matter that Tucson's twelve-year-old Mexican American Studies program had undeniably succeeded in its mandate to narrow the achievement gap for underserved youth in a school district where more than 60 percent of the students came from Mexican American households. According to the district's records, students in the program had higher test scores and graduated at nearly 90 percent rates. In fact, two days after Brewer's announcement, the Pew Hispanic Center released a nationwide study showing that 52 percent of foreign-born Latinos and 25 percent of US-born Latinos were high school dropouts. But the issue of achievement was not at the heart of this crackdown.

"A small group of radical teachers, anti-capitalists, anti-Western civilization, anti-free enterprise" had infiltrated the Mexican American Studies program, Horne charged on CNN one evening, creating a crisis that required his intervention.

The nearly pathological obsession of Horne, who had never once visited a Mexican American Studies class in his four-year offensive, could be dated back to 2006, when seventy-five-year-old United Farm Workers leader Dolores Huerta made an off-the-cuff remark as a visiting lecturer at an assembly at Tucson High School. Huerta had joked that Republicans "hate Latinos." Horne was offended.

As a follow-up to Huerta's visit, Horne sent one of his Latino underlings to speak in an attempt to show the students that Huerta's comment had been off-base. In an offense to the Latino community and other longtime civil rights advocates, Horne referred to the esteemed Huerta as the "girlfriend" of union cofounder Cesar Chavez. Unlike Huerta's visit, though, the one from Horne's associate came with a stipulation: the students were informed that no one would be allowed to ask a question or make a comment. Abiding by the rules, a group of Mexican American Studies supporters simply taped their mouths shut, raised their fists in protest, and eventually walked out.

That was the last straw for Horne. Free speech and dissent—or even a silent protest—had gotten out of control.

"These kids are being taught not to deal with civil disagreements in a civil way, but to deal with everybody by getting into people's faces and being rude, and that means they are going to be unsuccessful adults," Horne fumed. "So it's a dysfunctional education, and I fought hard to get the legislature to put a—to pass a law so that I can put a stop to it."

Embracing the conspiracies spread by Russell Pearce and border militias, of a Mexican plot to take over Arizona, Horne added to the *New York Times*, "They are teaching a radical ideology in Raza, including that Arizona and other states were stolen from Mexico and should be given back."

THE TEMPEST

The tragic shooting of Arizona Representative Gabrielle Giffords and eighteen other Tucson residents later in 2011 greatly exacerbated the crisis. Only days after the January 8 shooting, CNN descended on the Mexican American Studies literature class of Curtis Acosta, who had been singled out as one of the radical instigators in Horne's witch hunt. But the cameras had come to Acosta's classroom to note his unique role in helping students handle the fallout from the bewildering massacre at the Safeway supermarket.

The class began, as always, with a Mayan poem interpreted by Chicano theater legend Luis Valdez: "You are my other me," the students said in unison. "If I do harm to you, I do harm to myself. If I love and respect you, I love and respect myself."

The CNN cameras remained on the students as they picked up their copies of Shakespeare's *The Tempest* and launched into a discussion about the characters' clashing views. "In a divided town struggling to heal," the CNN reporter concluded, "the double meaning was hard to miss."

Almost exactly one year later, a different scene of clashing views took place. This time, however, Acosta and his students stood in utter confusion and silence. As part of the state-mandated termination of the Mexican American Studies program, the Tucson school district released an initial list of books to be banned from Acosta's and ten other classrooms. According to district spokesperson Cara Rene, the books were to be "cleared from all classrooms, boxed up and sent to the Textbook Depository for storage."

Facing a multimillion-dollar penalty in state funds, the governing board of Tucson's largest school district had officially pulled the plug on the acclaimed program in an attempt to come into compliance with the state ban on teaching "ethnic studies."

The list of removed books included the twenty-year-old textbook *Rethinking Columbus: The Next 500 Years,* which features an essay by famed Tucson author Leslie Silko, who had been an outspoken supporter of the program. "By ordering teachers to remove *Rethinking Columbus,* the Tucson school district has shown tremendous disrespect for teachers and students," said the book's editor, Bill Bigelow. "This is a book that has sold over 300,000 copies and is used in school districts from Anchorage to Atlanta, and from Portland,

Oregon, to Portland, Maine. It offers teaching strategies and readings that teachers can use to help students think about the perspectives that are too often silenced in the traditional curriculum."

Along with the entire Mexican American Studies curriculum, which included scores of texts, films, and documents, other books to be banished from the classroom included *Pedagogy of the Oppressed,* by famed Brazilian educator Paulo Freire, and *Occupied America: A History of Chicanos,* by Rodolfo Acuña. The Chicano historian's forty-year-old textbook, now in its seventh printing, had been singled out by Horne and his successor, John Huppenthal, who assumed the position of superintendent of public instruction in 2011 after Horne was elected to the attorney general post, despite an independent audit that praised it as "an unbiased, factual textbook designed to accommodate the growing number of Mexican-American or Chicano History Courses." The Tucson administrators also removed every textbook dealing with Mexican American history, including *Chicano!: The History of the Mexican American Civil Rights Movement,* by F. Arturo Rosales, which features a biography of longtime Tucson educator and Chicano icon Salomon Baldenegro Sr.; *500 Years of Chicano History in Pictures,* by Elizabeth Martinez; and the textbook *Critical Race Theory,* by scholars Richard Delgado and Jean Stefancic.

At a community gathering soon after the book confiscations, TUSD school board member Adelita Grijalva expressed her "awe" at the actions of her colleagues. "We are banning books in this district, not even anything controversial. We're banning pictures."

"The only other time a book of mine was banned was in 1986, when the apartheid government in South Africa banned *Strangers in Their Own Country,* a curriculum I'd written that included a speech by then-imprisoned Nelson Mandela," said Bigelow, who serves as curriculum editor of *Rethinking Schools* magazine, and who co-directed the online Zinn Education Project. "We know what the South African regime was afraid of. What is the Tucson school district afraid of?"

"In regards to this double-speak about these books being banned," said Cholla High School teacher Lorenzo Lopez, "it is irrelevant if these books are banned from the entire district or just from our classes. If our kids can't have access to that knowledge, and it was urgent that these books be removed immediately from our classes, they are, in effect, banned."

According to one teacher, the mandated roundup of texts included teachers' personal libraries in the classroom. "We were told by our principal that we need to comply with the law, and that meant that with the suspension of Mexican American Studies classes we had to remove the listed books from our classrooms immediately," said Pueblo High School teacher Sally Rusk. "Our own personal copies were not to be on our bookshelves either. It seems obvious to us that being made to take certain books out of the classroom—even when used as reference books and not class sets—is censorship. How can not allowing teachers to use these books, even as reference material in a traditional US history course, not be interpreted as banning those books?"

Unbelievably, copies of the very book in Acosta's classroom that had been championed for its healing in Tucson a year ago—*The Tempest*—had to be packed away as well. In an earlier meeting with administrators that had been tape recorded, Acosta had been warned to stay away from any units in which "race, ethnicity, and oppression" were central themes, including the teaching of Shakespeare's classic.

"What was very clear was that *The Tempest* was problematic for our administrators due to the content of the play and the pedagogical choices I have made," Acosta said in an interview. "In other words, Shakespeare wrote a play that is clearly about colonization of the new world, and there are strong themes of race, colonization, oppression, class, and power that permeate the play, along with themes of love and redemption.

"At the end of the meeting it became clear to all of us that I need to avoid such literature, and it was directly stated. Due to the madness of this situation and our fragile positions as instructors who will be frequently observed for compliance, and be asked to produce examples of student work as proof of our compliance, I couldn't disagree with their advice. Now we are in the position of having to rule out *The Adventures of Huckleberry Finn, The Great Gatsby,* etc., for the exact same reasons."

Fellow Mexican American Studies teacher Lorenzo Lopez said that when his daughter, Korina, heard that the texts had been taken to a storage facility, she asked him, "Isn't that the book graveyard where they send all the old books, never to be seen again?" Lopez said he replied, "Yes, it is."

The "madness" of the great Tucson book banishment, as it would come to be known, had come at the end of a year of protest, upheaval, and massive confusion over the celebrated and suddenly controversial Mexican American Studies program.

While Kansas school board members had made national headlines in 1999 for their brief ban on teaching Darwin's theory of evolution, Tucson school board member and Tea Party activist Michael Hicks propelled the city to national disgrace when he stumbled through his reading of the motion to kill what some educational experts and renowned scholars, like Christine Sleeter and Henry Giroux, had defended as "the nation's most innovative and successful academic and instructional program in Ethnic Studies at the secondary school level."

IS THE CONSTITUTION A HOLLOW DOCUMENT?

"In any state but Arizona, the enhanced 'academic success of Latino students' would be seen, not only as a crucial educational goal, but as a federal mandate," Acosta's attorney Richard Martinez wrote in a federal district court motion challenging the constitutionality of Arizona's new law. "Yet, Superintendent Huppenthal pounces on the language to justify withholding more than $1 million per month in order to bully TUSD into eliminating Mexican American Studies (MAS). Accordingly, these aspirations for Latino students cannot be tolerated and HB 2281 stands to prevent TUSD from promoting the achievement of Latino students through the vehicle of learning about Mexican Americans."

Martinez charged that the vagueness and breadth of HB 2281, and its enforcement by Huppenthal and Horne, violated the plaintiffs' constitutional rights of equal protection, free speech, and substantive due process:

> Among the many flaws contained in HB 2281 is the unmistakable message to our youth that the promise of the Constitution to protect them all equally is a myth; that the history, literature and culture of at least one group is not worthy of being taught in school. If the State of Arizona can take away the right of students to learn about the historical, literary and artistic contributions of Mexican Americans to the American experience, then the Constitution is a hollow document. The fact that the teachers "are educating the young for citizenship is a reason

for scrupulous protection of Constitutional freedoms of the individual, if we are not to strangle the free mind at its source and teach youth to discount important principles of our government as mere platitudes." Whatever legitimate role the State may have in setting curriculum standards in Arizona, it must be "within the limits of the Bill of Rights."

In appealing for a preliminary injunction, which was turned down, the student plaintiffs in Martinez's case won standing for a historic federal showdown in what would ultimately decide the fate of the Mexican American Studies program—and the legalities of the state's witch hunt.

"Arizona's current political climate is hostile to Mexican Americans," Martinez pleaded. "The Supreme Court has warned that 'times can blind us to certain truths and later generations can see that laws once thought necessary and proper in fact serve only to oppress.' Should the State be successful in its efforts to eliminate MAS, the stigma to Latino students, as well as to Mexican Americans in general, would be inevitable, as was the stigma that attached to the Texas law criminalizing homosexual conduct in *Lawrence v. Texas*. There is no legitimate state interest that can justify this type of intrusion into students' lives and educational choices."

Horne and Huppenthal, of course, had other views.

OUR CITIZENS MUST UNDERSTAND THEIR HISTORY (EXCEPT MEXICAN AMERICAN HISTORY)

On a lovely fall afternoon in 2011, when most public officials were working on public matters, Horne downloaded a sixteen-month-old video about a Tucson street theater performance, which he tagged as "AG Tom Horne killed in effigy," and then posted it on Twitter. He had posted a link to the same video several months earlier, in a special press release referring to Mexican American Studies protesters as a "thuggish mob." Reminding readers that the protesters were peaceful and within their First Amendment rights, the *Arizona Republic* ran an editorial that called out Horne for a "pattern of recklessness" for the unfair reference.

"The Raza Studies program teaches irrational mob behavior as a matter of habit," Horne wrote. "For example, they did a street play called 'the killing of

Tom Horne' which was filmed by channels 4 and 9 in Tucson, and broadcast." Problem was: despite the fact that the brief excerpts from the video had been withdrawn by the television station because of concerns over inaccuracies, Horne refused to correct his misrepresentation of the play—a classic bit of Chicano street theater that depicted Horne as the predator, not the prey. Several participants and witnesses responded to the station's video posting, including a detailed exchange on the "Save Ethnic Studies" Facebook page. "There was a street theater performance," one witness noted:

> One guy had on a "Tom Horne" mask. The other performers had skulls painted on their faces with face paint—to symbolize cultural genocide. Those students were also wearing t-shirts that said, "You can't kill my spirit." "Tom Horne" was going around, hassling the students in face paint, and taking their books away. He kept telling them that Chicano history isn't real history. The students in face paint continued to run from him and kept opening their books to read. At one point, a student went up to Tom Horne to try to get her books back from him. They had a little theatric tussle. Then "Tom Horne" fell to the ground, unconscious. It was obvious that he was unconscious as a symbol of the fact that he is UNCONSCIOUS of so many things: 1) the effect his actions are having on our community as a whole; 2) the fact that Ethnic Studies is a treasured and necessary part of the curriculum; and 3) that Ethnic Studies wouldn't even be needed if standard social studies classes included the history, culture, and values of the many non-white communities who live within the Untied [sic] States.

It didn't matter to Horne. The threat was real for the former state superintendent of public instruction and current attorney general, who had obsessed over Tucson's Mexican American Studies program with intransigence reminiscent of former FBI chief J. Edgar Hoover's hounding of Martin Luther King Jr. and other civil rights leaders.

Horne didn't have time for the federal government, either. Speaking to the conservative Heritage Foundation in 2007, he had compared the Bush administration's No Child Left Behind policy to the Soviet bureaucracy, "as dysfunctional in attempting to micromanage a complex continent-wide education

system, as was true of the Soviet bureaucracy trying to micromanage the Soviet economy."

Horne's main beef was with the standards required for English learners—
the burden of all those Mexican immigrants. Given that "there has been a tidal
wave of illegal immigration into Arizona," he posited, it was unfair for his state
to be judged by national standards.

Falling in line with the anti federal policies of future governor Jan Brewer
and Tea Party State Senate President Russell Pearce, Horne made the case
for state systems, which he considered "far more rational than the federal
system."

A rational state system, however, was not necessarily based on its unique
history and ethnic diversity, apparently, for Horne. On the other hand, as the
Canadian-born son of Eastern European Jews who had fled wartime Poland,
Horne paradoxically championed the importance of his own ethnic and cultural legacy in teaching education and history in Arizona:

> I am the only Jewish person ever elected to statewide office in the his-
> tory of Arizona. What does being Jewish have to do with being the
> elected state superintendent of schools? It is pretty well known that I
> have brought a renewed emphasis on academics and rigor to education
> in Arizona. There is a long cultural tradition in Judaism of valuing
> scholarship. Max Dimont, in his book *Jews, God and History*, tells a
> wonderful narrative of this long tradition. As long ago as the first cen-
> tury C. E., Jewish pregnant women would stand in the front yard of a
> scholar, hoping the fetus would absorb some scholarship through the
> air. I have put a lot of emphasis on having students learn more history.

As long as American history lessons followed his Judeo-Greco-Roman
basis for Western civilization, Horne seemingly had no problem encouraging
young people to study history and heritage. The question was: whose history
and heritage, and did Native American and Mexican American cultures fit
within his framework? As Horne told the Heritage Foundation in 2007, students need to understand their history, starting with Christopher Columbus
and George Washington: "A country that does not know its history is like an
individual who has lost his memory. He does not know where he has been;

he does not know where he is going; and he does not know how to deal with problems. If we are going to be able to preserve our free institutions, our citizens must understand their history. If they are going to have pride in our institutions and want to preserve them, they must know our history in depth."

In his Nobel Prize address in 1990, Mexican author Octavio Paz examined the literary interpretations of historical identity: "In Mexico, the Spaniards encountered history as well as geography. That history is still alive: it is a present rather than a past. The temples and gods of pre-Columbian Mexico are a pile of ruins, but the spirit that breathed life into that world has not disappeared; it speaks to us in the hermetic language of myth, legend, forms of social coexistence, popular art, customs."

Yet this was where Horne drew the line: the indigenous, Mexican, and Mexican American histories that helped give birth to Arizona should not be a presence within the modern-day borders, nor did they fit in his Western canon (or had presumably been taught at his Mamaroneck High School in Westchester County, New York, where he had immigrated from Canada and headed up the school's Anti-Smoking Committee in the early 1960s). In fact, Horne went one step further in his revisionist views in a televised interview and dismissed the cultural-relevancy curriculum of the Mexican American Studies Program as being based on a "primitive part that is tribal."

"My point of view is that these kids' parents and grandparents came, mostly legally," he told the *New York Times*, "because this is the land of opportunity, and we should teach them that if they work hard, they can accomplish anything."

A line in Horne's stump speech merits repeating: *These kids' parents and grandparents came, mostly legally*. All Mexican American students (including those of mixed ancestry), in essence, were immigrants—or, more precisely, foreigners—in their native land of Arizona. Unlike the Canadian Horne, apparently. Herein lay a blatant disregard of history and geography, and the underpinning denial of reality in Arizona: Tucson's Mexican American and Native American communities, including more than 60 percent of the students in the Tucson Unified School District, traced their heritage back centuries, to a time when their ancestors founded the presidio, missions, and ranches in southern Arizona under the Republic of Mexico. It reached even further back to the Spanish Empire, not to mention the centuries-old province and cultural realm of the O'odham and other tribes, and the heavily documented prehistoric Hohokam Empire, which stretched across modern-day Arizona and northern Mexico for more than two thousand years. In a chilling parallel to the admittedly racist sentiments behind the abduction of Irish orphans from so-called "un-American" Mexican American households in Clifton-Morenci, Arizona in 1904, despite pleas by one Mexican American citizen that "the 'low-down' Mexicans whom you refer to . . . are nearly all native-born American citizens and voters" who "were born and raised in Arizona under the American flag," the transplanted Horne simply didn't accept—or know—the roots of Mexican American and Native American histories inside his adopted Arizona borders. And besides, he didn't even have his own Jewish history in Arizona in order.

Jews, in fact, were at the forefront of Arizona's immigration politics before the ink had dried on the Gadsden Purchase. Herman Ehrenberg, a Jewish engineer from Germany, had accompanied Charles Poston on his groundbreaking mining expedition in southern Arizona in 1854. Three of Arizona's most prominent copper barons in the nineteenth century came from Jewish families; the Freudenthals and Lesinskys laid the first irons for the territory's railroad. Isador Solomon was the first of many Jewish financiers and bankers in the state; Jewish immigrant Abraham Frank from Germany played a key role in the territorial legislature. Territorial representative Selim Franklin ensured the legacy of education in Tucson by securing the funds for the University of Arizona in 1885. Barry Goldwater's granduncle helped to found the Democratic Party in Arizona, served as a mayor for more than a quarter of a century, and took a leading role in the budding state's 1910 constitutional convention as vice president—a statewide position for the soon-to-be-state.

More than a century before Horne left behind the East Coast to reinvent himself in Arizona, the state was Goldwater country—or at least it had been since the senator's Jewish ancestors revolted against the czar in Russian-occupied Poland and fled to the United States. By the 1860s, Goldwasser had become Goldwater, and Barry's grandfather and granduncle had crossed the Colorado River as pioneering merchants.

Although Goldwater's Jewish past never really emerged in his political campaigns, his ancestors' role as power brokers in early Arizona politics served as a reminder of Horne's frequent self-aggrandizing boast of his own breakthrough role as a pioneering Jewish politician in the Wild West of 2012. (Much to Horne's chagrin, Representative Gabby Giffords, of course, was Arizona's most notable Jewish politician.)

In the footsteps of his Jewish ancestors, Goldwater (who was raised as an Episcopalian by his mother) entered Phoenix politics in the 1940s and was elected to the US Senate as a Republican in 1952.

Born in pre-statehood Arizona, Goldwater loved history and never missed a chance to spin tales about his Jewish ancestors' struggles in the territory. Elected to the school board for a township named after Ehrenberg and nearby La Paz, Goldwater's granduncle "spoke with an accent and spelled English phonetically and sometimes misplaced his verbs and adjectives," Goldwater told a meeting of the Arizona Pioneers Historical Society in 1962. But "like many immigrants . . . nobody accused him of [an] inability to make himself completely understood."

The same was true for Charles Meyer, the namesake for the main avenue through Tucson's historic Barrio Viejo and one of Tucson's first territorial magistrates. A Jewish pharmacist from Germany, Meyer spoke in heavily accented English—he referred to jail as "yug." But that didn't prevent him from holding office for nearly a decade in the 1870s.

Such an accent would not have been permissible in contemporary Arizona. It took a class-action suit with the federal Education Department and a Justice Department investigation in the fall of 2011 to get Huppenthal to back off a state policy of replacing any English teacher who spoke with an accent. Huppenthal, like Horne, had deep reservations about the life-changing impact on students of teachers who said "da" instead of "the" or "anuder" instead of "another." Huppenthal, who had no educational background, once told a group of university scholars that he based his pedagogical approach on the success and failure of Fortune 500 companies.

The accent game, of course, was simply another scare tactic to counter the pivotal role of Mexican American and immigrant teachers in the classroom. The same week that the feds reprimanded Arizona for its discriminatory accent policy, which Huppenthal declared he would challenge, the superintendent spelled out his true feelings about the Mexican American Studies program in Tucson with chillingly racial undertones. During his guest speech at a Pima County Republican luncheon, he compared the program to the

Nazi-era Jugend, a paramilitary organization that had trained German youth in weapons and assault tactics and propagated white supremacist beliefs.

In an astounding affront to Mexican American veterans and military families, the disturbing comments were issued a week after the sixty-first anniversary of the awarding of the Medal of Honor to Arizona war hero Silvestre Herrera, whose famous capture of Nazi troops was hailed as one of numerous acts of bravery by Mexican American soldiers during World War II—many of whom had taken part in the liberation of Europe.

Most likely unbeknownst to Huppenthal, an Indiana native whose German American family came to Arizona in the 1950s, Nazi POWs famously tried to escape from a prison at the Papago Park Camp near Phoenix on Christmas Eve in 1944.

Had they lived in Arizona, in fact, Huppenthal's grandparents wouldn't have been welcome in Russell Pearce's Mesa district. The *Mesa Tribune* reported several arrests of travelers for "looking like a German," and subsequent sweeps of German "slackers" by "home-front patriots," whose "over-zealous actions" were "only milder manifestations of the Boston Tea Parties."

Huppenthal was no stranger to inflammatory speech-making, but this latest episode made Mexican American Studies advocates in Tucson openly question whether the extremist Arizona politicians and their Tea Party supporters had gone too far in their attacks on the Mexican American Studies program. At what point, many wondered, would the Civil Rights Division of the Justice Department be summoned for an investigation? At the very least, didn't Huppenthal owe Mexican American veterans and supporters an apology? (In the fall of 2011, Huppenthal apologized to Equality Arizona, a nonprofit advocacy group, for including gays in a speech on "inappropriate behaviors" that included neo-Nazis.)

The comment was particularly disturbing in light of the fact that the Arizona Anti-Defamation League, a worldwide organization dedicated to fighting anti-Semitism, had come out against the state's controversial ethnic studies ban and declared that the Mexican American Studies program "obviously resuscitated the desire to learn in so many students." Incensed at the rebuke of his campaign, Horne had quit the ADL board in Arizona after the decision.

Longtime Chicano leader Salomon Baldenegro Sr. confronted Huppenthal at a theater in Tucson a few weeks after the bizarre Hitler charge. "Huppenthal owes not only the Mexican American Studies students, their parents, their teachers, and all of us who support MAS an apology for his abject 'Hitler Youth' libel," said the Tucson educator, "he needs to get himself a dictionary and go to the letter 'H' and look up 'hypocrite'; Huppenthal is in bed with State Senate President Russell Pearce, and as is well known, there is video footage of Pearce embracing J. T. Ready, a known neo-Nazi (who marches under the Nazi swastika flag), and white supremacists on the grounds of the State Capitol!"

CARTHAGE MUST BE DESTROYED

It would be hard to imagine how Barry Goldwater could have fit in among such Tea Party extremists, especially on issues of Mexican American history and immigration.

In 1978, Goldwater made it clear that he sided with the federal government over states' rights and believed the feds "should bear the main responsibility of determining who is here legally and who is not." Far from any punitive measures, Goldwater had introduced legislation that would have established a temporary labor permit program, allowing Mexicans to enter Arizona and the United States legally. Despite attempts to close off the border, Goldwater wrote, "with the incentive for a better life people will brave laws and obstacles to come here."

To be sure, Goldwater had distinguished Arizona as a hotbed of extremists in his own time. His famous pronouncement had given birth—or rebirth— to the more radical conservative Republican movement in the 1960s: "I would remind you that extremism in the defense of liberty is no vice. And let me remind you also that moderation in the pursuit of justice is no virtue."

Those words lit up the libertarian Republicans at their party's convention in 1964, sparking an insurgent movement that could easily be seen as the antecedent for today's Tea Party. Shaking down the "establishment" Republicans—including moderate stalwarts like New York Governor Nelson Rockefeller—Goldwater both embraced and dismissed the movement's radical ways as a natural step toward reclaiming the nation. "What's happened here," one Republican delegate told *Time* magazine, "is a real revolution. We aren't a bunch of extremists. All we are is a fast-growing group of people interested in law and order."

Republican moderates were so concerned about this fast-growing insurgency that they even introduced an "anti-extremism" plank in the platform. Goldwater delegates shouted it down. When Rockefeller addressed the convention and admonished the party to "repudiate here and now any doctrinaire militant minority, whether Communist, Ku Klux Klan, or Bircher," the crowd booed in return and drowned out his speech with chants of "We want Barry!"

Many critics viewed Goldwater and his insurgency with the same contempt reserved for contemporary Tea Party leaders like Pearce and even Huppenthal. In an essay on "Goldwaterism," columnist Emmet John Hughes called the movement "almost neurotically fearful of critical scrutiny." He traced its roots beyond any American conservative origins to the "stale jargon of ultra-rightist movements in Europe over the last quarter century. And so it is no coincidence that it has there evoked some approving response in only two regions: conservative Bavaria and totalitarian Spain."

Goldwater lost in a landslide to Lyndon Johnson in the 1964 presidential election, of course. But his movement "in search of a program, a mood in want of a doctrine . . . a credo without content," Hughes noted, took root—and revolutionized the Republican Party for the next generation.

Whether Horne, Huppenthal, Pearce, Governor Brewer or others among the new generation of hard-line Republicans could claim to be the heirs of Goldwater's legacy, the senator's progeny had parted ways with the anti-immigrant rhetoric that ruled the state's airwaves. In an op-ed in the *Arizona Republic* in 2007, Barry Goldwater Jr. expressed his dismay at what had emerged:

> Speeches soaked with hateful, angry racist tones and dialogue. Eyes closed, listening to the roar of inflammatory rhetoric and sermonizing, I could have easily mistaken myself to be at one of David Duke's Ku Klux Klan rallies in Baton Rouge, La. "Deportation, deportation, deportation" was the chant of the incensed crowd. Illegal immigration has, like so much of our political system, become so polarized—left and right. Politicians on both sides of the aisle have painted themselves into

a narrow corridor in the political spectrum, unwilling to breach the middle ground and seek the reasonable and compromising actions the people of this great nation and state so desperately crave and deserve.

Having long since abandoned the middle ground, Horne always delivered his stump speech on the TV network circuit with a soft voice. He admired the literary work of Ayn Rand, and as an accomplished concert pianist who often entertained at Republican Party benefits, he frequently played Rachmaninoff's Piano Concerto No. 2, a Tea Party and right-wing cult favorite that had been mentioned in Rand's novel *The Fountainhead.*

Speaking to a sparse crowd at the Phoenix Marriott Hotel on September 10, 2011, the attorney general drew on his admiration for Greco-Roman teaching and invoked the infamous words of Roman statesman Cato when he called for the destruction of Tucson's Ethnic Studies and Mexican American Studies programs.

Horne made this alarming admonition while participating in a special public panel on the Mexican American Studies program hosted by the so-called Arizona Mainstream Project, a Tea Party offshoot that hailed "America's exceptionalism" and peddled books by Glenn Beck and notorious right-wing extremist Cleon Skousen on its website. The panel was also broadcast live online via streaming video.

"The only thing they can do to come into compliance is to terminate the program," Horne told a questioner from the audience, who had asked how the program could meet the demands of Arizona's controversial Ethnic Studies ban. Horne said the program must be "destroyed," invoking Cato's obsessive call for warfare as a punch line: "Carthage must be destroyed."

All irony aside, Cato's war with the Phoenicians in Carthage is considered one of the bloodiest episodes in ancient Roman history. As the *Wall Street Journal* noted in a view of Richard Miles's new book, *Carthage Must Be Destroyed,* Cato's declaration of war eventually came to fruition: "The city was demolished and the site formally cursed by Roman priests. The oft-repeated story of the ground being sown with salt is a much later invention, but the destruction of Carthage as a political state was total."

Coming a day before September 11 anniversary events, Horne's use of such violent imagery to describe the ban was unsettling, to say the least. In many respects, the panel seemed like an eerie flashback to the witch-hunt actions of the House Un-American Activities hearings in the 1950s. Hardly representative of "mainstream" Arizona, several members of the audience referred to the Mexican American Studies program as a tool of Marxist-Leninists; one woman declared it was part of a larger "Islamic" Catholic plot from Mexico to reconquer Arizona. "Don't laugh!" she warned the audience. State Senator Lori Klein addressed the panel from the floor, commending the participants for fighting against "communism," and declared, "The cold war is not over."

PREPARING YOUTH FOR A NEW CIVIL RIGHTS MOVEMENT

Glenn Beck understood the cold war dimensions of the debate over Tucson's Mexican American Studies program. On his televised program one day, he froze the frame of a video from Fox News showing a young Chicano student pumping his fist at an extraordinary Tucson school board protest and sit-in on April 26, 2011, that gained national media attention. Beck wagged his finger at the kid. "See that, that kid is frightening," he exclaimed.

With his usual assuredness, Beck repeated Horne's false charge that the school district "separated people, so you would be—if you were Mexican, you'd go into that class. If you weren't, you would stay in the other." He completely misrepresented a historic takeover of the Tucson school board by a cadre of Mexican American Studies students who had been pushed to the brink that spring. "This racist, communist class," Beck railed, "the kids took over the city council . . . Treasonous. They're teaching our kids to overthrow the United States government, and that is not an understatement."

Watching his own footage, Beck seemingly overlooked the fact that among the nine protesters at the sit-in, there were Anglos, African Americans, Native Americans, and a Pakistani American student. "These students are angry, and they are pounding on the—they've taken over the council chambers," Beck said. "And they're sitting where the council sits. And they are protesting that the class is being reconsidered. It's Mexican studies or whatever, and they want to restore it."

The frightening kid's name was Danny Montoya, a shy senior at Tucson's Rincon High School. Struggling to find his place in school, he had credited the Mexican American history courses with enlivening his study habits and preparing him to work his way through college, where he planned to study economics.

A step ahead of everyone, Morales at the Three Sonorans blog had informed his readers that a so-called "compromise resolution" offered by Tucson School Board President Mark Stegemen would effectively dismantle the Mexican American Studies program by demoting it to an elective instead of a course that fulfilled core curriculum requirements.

Three Sonorans posted a video of the April 26 sit-in that went viral, bringing mixed responses in the process. For many in the nation, the student takeover inspired the feeling of a new civil rights movement or, at the very least, the awakening of a new era of protest on a par with the more recent uprising in Wisconsin over collective bargaining rights. The event attracted national praise—how often do you see high school kids protesting to keep their courses available? But for Fox News viewers and the followers of Glenn Beck and other trash-talk radio and TV hosts, the video proved the danger of exposing schoolkids to a radicalized curriculum.

Three Sonorans seemed overwhelmed by the historic event captured by the video: "How to describe tonight's actions with so much emotion? I'll let the video above convey emotion, and I will stick to the facts here. The TUSD board meeting was to start at 6pm. About 5:40 the doors were opened. Around 5:50 is when the students took over the board seats. The rest of the crowd immediately filled the boardroom. The students chained themselves to the chairs and to each other immediately."

Danny had been one of the organizers of the new student group UNIDOS, which operated on its own and outside the purview of teachers or parents. "Nobody was listening to us, especially the board," said high school student and UNIDOS activist Lisette Cota. "We were fed up. It may have been drastic, but the only way was to chain ourselves to the boards' chairs."

"I'm very moved by their passion and commitment to maintain these courses and curriculum," said Sally Rusk, one of their surprised teachers. "They're brilliant. This is not a one-time event. It looks like they're not going to stop until they have an impact on this decision."

And that was what actually frightened Tea Party and Tucson School District officials. For the first time, attention shifted from Horne and Huppenthal to the administrators who had to make the final call to defy or surrender to the extremist state officials.

TUSD Superintendent John Pedicone canceled the board meeting that evening, but students vowed to keep returning to the district office for as long as it took to make the district defend the Mexican American Studies program—whatever the cost. "We'll keep coming back, with twice as many people next time, each time," added Cota. "We're not going to let this happen. We're going to make it impossible for them to vote."

Through the evening, the students and their community supporters chanted: "Our education is under attack! What do we do? Fight back!"

"Just like the people of Wisconsin took a stand and said, 'Enough is enough,' the youth of Tucson are standing up and letting it be known that they are fed up with these attacks on their education and on their future. They have been under relentless assault by Tom Horne, John Huppenthal, and by the Arizona state legislature, and they have had enough," said Sal Baldenegro Jr., a Mexican American Studies alum. "As Arizonans, we absolutely must stand behind our youth and say, 'Enough is enough' with these attacks on their education. There has never been a more critical time to stand behind our children as they fight for their rights and for their futures."

Stumbling further into the quagmire of a national public relations disaster, the Tucson school officials issued drastic new measures that essentially turned the "manufactured crisis" into a troubling moral crisis for the city—and the country.

As the controversy escalated in the spring of 2011, school officials appeared to unravel, while the UNIDOS youth activists emerged as the calm standard bearers of civil discourse for the community. "As Ethnic Studies students we envision a society based on the values of respect, equality, justice, diversity and equitable education for all," MAS alum Leilani Clark noted in releasing the group's "Ten Point Resolution." She added, "We want an educational system, not just in Arizona, but beyond, where many cultures fit in." In an op-ed following the sit-in, two students made a simple request: if the TUSD officials were truly interested in dialogue, they should table the controversial resolution that had divided the community and sit down with the students, teachers, and community to hammer out a true compromise.

Instead, in an alarming crackdown on the nonviolent UNIDOS student campaign, the backpedaling TUSD superintendent Pedicone shocked the community by hiring costly armed guards to attend the next board meetings. As extreme new security measures were introduced with each school board meeting, a photo of a tiny Latino child being patted down and wanded by armed security officers at one meeting aired on CNN and soon went viral, becoming the image of Pedicone's excessive police actions.

Only months before, Pedicone—who had recently been hired and was clearly unable to make the administrative leap from heading a tiny local school district to leading TUSD's nearly 53,000 students—had referred to the draconian state crackdown on Mexican American Studies as unconstitutional, declaring that TUSD would challenge the law as "the first hurdle" and battle it "to the end." In a candidate's forum the previous fall, he had noted, "If you look at the data, it is hard to argue with the success this program has with a historically underserved population."

Within days of the board takeover, Pedicone, a Chicago transplant who lived out of the district in the affluent suburb of Oro Valley and once served as vice president of Tucson's shadowy corporate lobby front, the Southern Arizona Leadership Council, seemed to have changed his mind about the program. He published an incendiary op-ed in the local newspaper that offensively labeled the students "pawns," blamed adults for "abhorrent" behavior, and falsely categorized the widely denounced resolution vote as only a "discussion."

Meanwhile, attorney Richard Martinez, representing the Mexican American Studies students and teachers in their lawsuit against the state, hailed the entire state of affairs in Arizona—from SB 1070 to the shameless Mexican American Studies witch hunt by extremist state officials—as a "manufactured crisis" in a television debate with the school board president. Martinez charged that the TUSD administrators had triggered a "moral crisis" by blatantly disregarding the reality of the district's majority of Mexican American students and the city's fervent and deeply rooted Mexican American and Chicano heritage.

His timing was perfect. The crisis erupted on the anniversary of the 1963 "Children's Crusade," when students stood at the forefront of Martin Luther

King Jr.'s Birmingham campaign; in Tucson, brave kids like Danny and the other Mexican American Studies students from UNIDOS were not only ramping up their efforts to keep the district's acclaimed program alive but teaching the faltering administrators a lesson in civility and democracy.

As Danny reminded the naysayers in Tucson, King wrote his famous "Letter from Birmingham Jail," on "why we find it difficult to wait," as he faced similar criticism that his protests were "unruly." King wrote, "For years now, I have heard the word 'Wait!... This 'Wait' has almost always meant 'Never.'" Nearly a half-century ago, Alabama students recognized King's call "to create a situation so crisis-packed that it will inevitably open the door to negotiation."

After the uprising at the April 26 meeting brought national notoriety, Pedicone planned a different route for the May 3 meeting. Flanked by nearly one hundred police in riot gear, a helicopter swirling above, paddy wagons and armed reinforcements lurking behind the school administration building, Pedicone embraced Horne's and Huppenthal's "Stop La Raza" campaign by setting up an armed blockade and ordering the arrest of veteran Chicano leaders who had sought to speak after the time limits imposed on the public comment period, including one elderly woman who had wanted to read King's Birmingham letter.

In a chilling whisper that only the Three Sonorans blog picked up from the microphone, Pedicone turned to board chair Mark Stegemen and quipped, "We'll just arrest them all until it's just us left."

In another blog video that went viral, Three Sonorans placed the excessive show of police brutality in the context of the "us vs. them" ethnic conflict at play: "At a TUSD board meeting to dismantle Mexican-American History, Pedicone showed his complete disregard for the Latino community by having a 69-year old Mexican-American History professor, Lupe Castillo, who walks around with two crutches due to a disability, arrested by a swarm of about a dozen police in full riot gear and helmets, guns."

The display of condescension by Pedicone, who literally sat elevated on the board dais with the steely expression of a veteran showman, outraged the audience. An amateur nightclub crooner, Pedicone swiveled in his seat as if he had stumbled upon a difficult crowd at a busy Friday night show.

For many longtime community members, the student uprising in Tucson recalled the Chicano student walkouts in the community in 1969 and marked the beginning of a new civil rights movement. Salomon Baldenegro Sr., who had been one of the leaders of the walkouts in the late 1960s, spoke about that historic event a week later, when he rose to his feet to defend the beloved Chicana historian Lupe Castillo as the riot police hauled her off, one hobble after another with her walker. The elder Chicano leader found himself snared in the roundup, as well.

A few days later, Baldenegro sat on the front porch of his home, within view of his old haunts at Tucson High School, and reflected on the recent events. Growing up in the copper smelter town of Douglas, he had been forced to enroll in "IC" courses, just like all children of Mexican heritage, despite the fact that he was native born and a native English speaker, and placed in the school's top ranks (he had been an honor student). The IC program essentially sought to take the "Mexican" out of Mexican American and inculcate "American values" and English-only teaching. In the process, a large part of the Mexican American students were detained, often leading to higher dropout rates and social problems.

More important to Baldenegro, the IC program "viewed Americans of Mexican descent as foreigners, and there was a concerted campaign to make us feel inferior and treated as interlopers in our own land." The IC program endured into the 1960s, and its troubling connotations returned cyclically thereafter, as the actions of Horne, Huppenthal, and Pedicone showed so well.

"We had two choices," Baldenegro recalled. "We could acquiesce and shuffle through life, hat in hand, picking up society's crumbs. Or we could resist and assert our humanity. We resisted."

The attack on the Mexican American community on May 3 struck Baldenegro in a hard way, as had the past waves of discriminatory action by state officials, including the state ban on bilingual education. "We keep finding ourselves in the same place," he said, "having to prove our legitimacy in our own country."

Looking back at Pedicone that night, the police locked onto his arms as he was hauled out of the school board meeting, Baldenegro had declared, in sheer bewilderment at the excessive use of force, "I've been coming before this board since 1969. Never have I seen our community treated in the manner you have treated us tonight." He paused, and then added, "We founded public education in this town. And we will be here when you're gone."

Baldenegro's reference addressed not only the Mexican American community's enduring struggle for decent public education in Tucson but also its legacy of honor in defense of the city. He was speaking about the role of Estevan Ochoa, the Mexican immigrant who stood up to the Confederate occupation of Tucson. Ochoa's other great contribution to Tucson came in 1872, eight years after Lincoln recognized Arizona as an official territory, when he served as Tucson's mayor—the first and only Mexican American—and president of the school board. In a haunting parallel with contemporary events, with his pioneering school district in total disarray and unable to educate the majority Mexican American study body, Ochoa upstaged a recalcitrant territorial legislature and domineering Catholic bishop when he single-handedly raised the funds and donated the land to build the town's first public school.

The legislature didn't see any reason to dispense funds to educate the overwhelming majority of kids who came from a Mexican heritage, but Ochoa marched on with his campaign. In essence: it took a Mexican immigrant to overrule the interests of carpetbaggers and make the first solid attempt at public education in Tucson.

In the spring of 1876, the *Arizona Citizen* declared, "Ochoa is constantly doing good for the public," concluding, "Ochoa is the true and useful friend of the worthy poor, of the oppressed, and of good government." When a new school was completed in 1877, with Ochoa placing on the last "shingles to build a ramada on the front side" of the schoolhouse, the same newspaper raved, "The zeal and energy Mr. Ochoa has given to public education, should give him a high place on the roll of honor and endear him more closely than ever to his countrymen. He has done much to assist in preparing the youth for the battle of life."

For Baldenegro and supporters of the Mexican American Studies program, Ochoa's legacy—and that of all Mexican Americans in Tucson—was under assault. In fact, like Ochoa's historic Congress School, which had been demolished as part of urban renewal, it was in the process of being erased from the historical record altogether.

TO BE IN COMPLIANCE

A few days after college-bound Mexican American Studies graduates collected their diplomas in the summer of 2011, the increasingly isolated state superintendent of education, John Huppenthal, announced his plans to release the results of a greatly anticipated independent audit over compliance with Arizona's controversial law.

With the city barely recovering from the school district's notorious bungling of two school board meetings, Mexican American Studies teachers, students, and supporters brought together diverse communities to heal the community and open a channel of civil discourse.

At a heartfelt forum at the Most Holy Trinity Catholic Church in Tucson, four members of the TUSD board—including critics of the program—and intergenerational citizens from across the district heard from a panel of distinguished education experts on the program's longtime mandate and documented success in alleviating the achievement gap among area students.

Soundly debunking the state's charges that the program taught children to "overthrow the government" and promote ethnic chauvinism, university scholars and administrators explained the widely accepted approach of teaching culturally relevant curriculums. Asiya Mir, a Mexican American Studies high school student, UNIDOS activist, and Tucson native of Pakistani American origin, spoke on how the courses transcended ethnic barriers, improved her and fellow students' academic performance, and assisted their intellectual and emotional growth.

Even the Arizona State Board of Education distanced itself from Huppenthal's extremist crusade that week, when members were deemed "nominal or passive parties" in the Mexican American Studies teachers' filing for a motion for summary judgment in federal court, in a case that sued Huppenthal on the basis of the state ban's unconstitutionality.

Huppenthal's absence at the forum was no less noticeable than that of TUSD Superintendent John Pedicone, whose use of unwarranted police force and conflicting communication with various community interests had been widely denounced as a disgrace and a public relations nightmare for the city and school district. In his recent "State of the District," Pedicone had dismissed the Mexican American Studies crisis as a "distraction." And in a breathtaking revision of events, he claimed that "threats made against our students and the audience at the next board meeting resulted in the Tucson Police Department having to make several arrests."

The Mexican American Studies teachers weren't pulling punches, though. As a follow-up to Huppenthal's announcement that he would "stress accountability" by issuing letter grades for school performances, the teachers delivered their own report card on Pedicone's 2010–2011 school year. At a press conference, the teachers noted that he had failed to respond to nine letters—including a hand-delivered letter—seeking dialogue and clarification. The longtime Tucson educators gave Pedicone, who had been in office for only six months, an F for honesty, genuineness, connection to community, leadership, and overall performance. In calling for his resignation, they concluded, "Supt. Pedicone has proven to lack the courage, skills or abilities to lead TUSD in a critical time, one when the challenges are at an unprecedented number. He divides our community when we need unity, lies when we need honesty, and uses deception to hide his true intentions."

Like Pedicone, Huppenthal wasn't taking the bait of civility either. He appeared ready to revamp the state's radical descent into extremism and escalate the manufactured crisis.

And then something quite odd happened. At one of the most bizarre press conferences ever staged, Huppenthal kept his campaign promise to "Stop La Raza" at the Arizona Department of Education in Phoenix, and declared the Mexican American Studies program to be out of compliance with the state's controversial ban. Speaking in a nervous voice, having already announced that he had another pressing engagement and had little time for questions from the media, Huppenthal introduced the long-awaited and costly audit as proof that the Tucson program promoted resentment, was designed primarily for a particular race, and advocated ethnic solidarity. Within a few minutes, Huppenthal and his associate superintendent had hastily exited the press conference for other engagements.

There was just one glitch: the audit contradicted Huppenthal's claims and ultimately found the Mexican American Studies program *to be in compliance.*

"This decision is not about politics, it is about education," Huppenthal had read nervously from a printed statement. He proclaimed his "responsibility to uphold the law and a professional imperative to ensure every student has access to an excellent education." But the audit questioned Huppenthal's judgment and integrity. And it found that students in the program "graduate in the very least at a rate of 5 percent more than their counterparts in 2005, and at the most, a rate of 11 percent more in 2010." The audit added, "MASD programs are designed to improve student achievement based on the audit team's finding of valuable course descriptions aligned with state standards, commendable curricular unit and lesson plan design, engaging instruction practices, and collective inquiry strategies through Approved State Standards."

In terms of Huppenthal's points of violation, a brief review of the audit results flat-out rejected the superintendent's justification for terminating the Ethnic Studies Program:

DESIGNED FOR PARTICULAR ETHNIC GROUP

A majority of evidence demonstrates that the Mexican American Studies Department's instruction is NOT designed primarily for pupils of a particular ethnic group. As previously indicated, every current course syllabus states: "At the core of this course is the idea that ALL people should not be required to give up their ethnic and cultural traditions in order to become part of mainstream society."

ETHNIC SOLIDARITY

No evidence as seen by the auditors exists to indicate that instruction within Mexican American Studies Department program classes advocates ethnic solidarity; rather it has been proven to treat students as individuals . . .

ETHNIC RESENTMENT

No observable evidence exists that instruction within Mexican American Studies Department promotes resentment toward a race or class of people. The auditors observed the opposite, as students are taught to be accepting of multiple ethnicities of people.

So what was the violation? Huppenthal had dropped the state's earlier claims that the courses promoted the overthrow of the government. His team had patronizingly dismissed the program's curriculum development and excerpted a handful of short, allegedly troubling quotations from various books, but this paled in comparison to the audit's hugely complimentary assessment. The auditors mainly questioned whether some of the curriculum material—such as renowned historian Howard Zinn's *A People's*

History of the United States—should be taught at the high school academic level.

According to the audit's summary: "During the curriculum audit period, no observable evidence was present to suggest that any classroom within Tucson Unified School District is in direct violation of the law A.R.S. 15-112."

The auditors additionally noted that MAS, far from being a controversial program, had the required backing of a majority of the board members: "three board members interviewed by the audit team are clearly supporters of this program." The auditors concluded, "No evidence exists in any format that Arizona Revised Statue 15-112 (A) is being violated in any of the six American History from Mexican American Perspective courses visited." The audit echoed the same judgment for the five Latino Literature courses, the four American Government/Social Justice courses, and the Chicano art courses.

Despite Huppenthal's charges to the contrary, the 120-page audit concluded "no observable evidence" fell in direct violation of the state ban. In the end, what did Huppenthal's auditors recommend? "Maintain Mexican American Studies courses as part of core curriculum for high school course: US History, American Government and Literature."

THE MATERIALS THE AUDITORS REVIEWED

For Mexican American Studies students in Arizona, the scandal just kept getting stranger.

The TUSD board voted immediately to appeal Huppenthal's decision on the state level, and attorney Richard Martinez also announced his intention to file a preliminary injunction in district court to halt Huppenthal's sixty-day deadline for the school district to bring the program into compliance or lose 10 percent of its state funding. In a red flag of the school district's backpedaling of support for its own program, though, the TUSD school board and administrators refused to join the federal lawsuit of Martinez on behalf of the Mexican American Studies students and teachers.

Although the occasional spasms of extremist rhetoric and legislative initiative were often dismissed as nutty episodes in Arizona Gone Wild politics, advocates began to wonder if Huppenthal had crossed the line of lawlessness in his latest bombshell announcement. If Huppenthal had knowingly misrepresented the results of the independent audit in order to justify his ruling that the program was out of compliance with the state's controversial Ethnic Studies ban, did he break the law?

Specifically, did Huppenthal violate Arizona Article 38–423? The law stipulates: "A public officer authorized by law to make or give any certificate or other writing, who makes and delivers as true such a certificate or writing containing a statement which he knows is false, is guilty of a class 6 felony."

At his press conference and in a written statement, Huppenthal noted, "The materials gathered by, and submitted to, the Arizona Department of Education, *as well as the materials the auditors* reviewed, contained context promoting resentment towards a race or class of people." However, the audit results contradicted every one of Huppenthal's charges, including his misrepresentation above. According to the audit, "No observable evidence exists that instruction within Mexican American Studies Department promotes resentment toward a race or class of people. The auditors observed the opposite, as students are taught to be accepting of multiple ethnicities of people."

To be fair, Huppenthal did note that "two-thirds of the final audit report was beyond the scope of the legal determination I am making today." But what was beyond the scope? Answer: academic achievement. The audit verified that Mexican American Studies students did better than their counterparts, and concluded the Ethnic Studies programs "are designed to improve student achievement based on the audit team's finding of valuable course descriptions aligned with state standards, commendable curricular unit and lesson plan design, engaging instruction practices, and collective inquiry strategies through Approved State Standards."

Huppenthal's teachers were held accountable by the Arizona Board of Education for "unprofessional and immoral conduct." Specifically, the state board was obliged to investigate any actions that "deliberately suppress or distort information or facts relevant to a pupil's academic progress" or that "misrepresent or falsify pupil, classroom, school or district-level data from the administration of a test or assessment."

Although Huppenthal's elected position did not fall within the jurisdiction of these guidelines, some wondered if he should be investigated by the Board of Education or the state legislature for similar violations of "unprofessional and immoral conduct." These were reasonable questions that deserved an-swers—or more specifically, a state or federal investigation.

It took six months to mobilize its members, but the Congressional His-panic Caucus finally called Huppenthal's bluff and formally appealed his de-cision on TUSD's compliance to the civil rights divisions of the Education Department and the Justice Department, asking for an investigation into the state of Arizona's attack on the Mexican American Studies program and to "ensure state compliance with federal law."

"This is not about one group of people wanting special treatment," said US Representative Raúl Grijalva, who sent a letter on behalf of the caucus. "This is about a successful educational program with a high graduation rate being shut down for purely ideological reasons. Public education isn't sup-posed to be politicized in this country, but that's exactly what's happened in southern Arizona, and the students are losing out because of it. The Depart-ment of Education would do a great public service by conducting a full and fair investigation into whether this power grab is authorized under federal law."

On April 18, 2012, the Office of Civil Rights in the Education Department finally opened multiple investigations into possible violations of Title VI of the Civil Rights Act of 1964, in response to a complaint by longtime Phoenix education activist Silverio Garcia. (The TUSD communications director and superintendent, however, did not divulge the information to the public until Three Sonorans outed the news in a follow-up blog on May 3.) Probing is-sues of racial and language discrimination and access to school board meet-ings, unfair restrictions on Latino events at public schools, and potentially extraordinary civil rights violations over the dismantling of the Mexican American Studies program, the federal action was hailed as a breakthrough in both holding Huppenthal's state office and the Tucson Unified School District accountable.

"The hateful, anti-immigrant political climate in the streets of Arizona has created a climate of irresponsibility and complete disregard for civil rights on federally funded TUSD1 administrative offices, school facilities and/or cam-puses and this is the basis of the federal complaint," said Garcia, director of the Civil Rights Center in Phoenix, which had taken the lead in other suc-cessful petitions before the Education Department. "The manner that a quorum of the TUSD1 School Board has publicly displayed itself along with its unchecked militaristic law enforcement tactics takes us back to the '50s and '60s when we speak of blatant civil rights violations against our communities, parents and youth. It is far past time that the federal government came into TUSD1 and balanced the tables of equal access and justice for all."

"Pedicone is the Sheriff Arpaio of TUSD education," said Tanya Alvarez, a TUSD parent. "He has no respect for our community's strengths, needs, and culture. He lacks cultural sensitivity, uses excessive police monitoring. While extremist Arizona State Superintendent John Huppenthal squandered school funding on audits, Pedicone ignores the results and fails to understand his neglect and abuse of power."

While Huppenthal's latest episode brought head-shaking comments of disgrace from nationwide educators, it drew raves from right-wing commentators like Glenn Beck, who applauded the education chief for standing up to this "ethnic studies program—you remember, the one we told you about that called for the overthrow of the United States government and had these students chanting for it because they were all revved up by former hippie revolutionaries."

THIS JOB IS NOT FUN

On a hot August night in 2011, no one in his or her right mind would have been attending the Tucson Unified School Board meeting. No controversial issues were on the posted agenda. The relatively small chambers, in fact, had plenty of seats available. A handful of students from the embattled Mexican American Studies program chose to remain outside with their placards. If anything, after a raucous spring of controversy and demonstrations and excessive use of riot police, the community needed a breather from the charged atmosphere inside the chambers.

Eight months after Giffords's tragic shooting and only days after her dramatic return to the floor of Congress to vote in the debt ceiling debate, the indefatigable Three Sonorans blogger David Morales stood with his camera framed on the speaker at the podium.

It was the part of the meeting when community members were allowed to address the board for three minutes on any topic. The speaker was no stranger to the school board, especially the board chair, Mark Stegeman. Introducing himself with the fictitious name Juan Blanco, the gray-haired speaker was part of a cadre of anti-immigrant extremists who haunted the meetings with the wild-eyed urgency of true believers. They approached the "call to audience" period with the verve of *American Idol* contestants. They didn't simply worry about the radical curriculum of the Mexican American Studies program; they saw themselves as the righteous remnant defending the modern-day Alamo of Arizona against the "invasion" and "*reconquista*" plot of Mexicans and their allies, and as the shock troops in Russell Pearce's defense of the great American Dream.

Security officers had already apprehended the speaker for attempting to enter the board meeting with a six-inch buck knife that evening. Such a knife is not an uncommon accessory in a state that allows unregulated concealed weapons to be taken into bars, but given the tension around the Tucson school board meetings that year, it should have set off an alarm. After he left the knife in a friend's vehicle, the man—a Vietnam vet—returned and then passed through the metal detector and stand of guards without any other concern. When Juan Blanco's name was announced, he stood and delivered.

"There'll be no time-out when the civil war comes," he declared to the board members. He continued with a rant about the impending Mexican invasion and "bloodshed," and then he flipped off board member Adelita Grijalva, referring to her father, Representative Raúl Grijalva, as a "traitor."

As people catcalled from the audience, Stegeman overruled board member objections, disregarded board policy, and allowed the self-proclaimed Tea Party activist to continue an inflammatory tirade on the coming civil war between Mexicans and American patriots. The speaker was unequivocal: "We don't care about law enforcement."

A month earlier, Juan Blanco had circulated a conspiracy video on Facebook claiming that Giffords's attempted murder was a scam set up by the Department of Homeland Security. On a Tea Party website, he had written, "Demorats [*sic*] are a cancer and you do not cure cancer you cut it out and KILL IT DAMMIT. They are NOT ONE OF US. I was trained to kill Communist. ALL of them. I say CIVIL WAR if you have the guts."

The audience, which included students and young children, teetered between a state of outrage and bewilderment, especially with Stegeman's defiant bending of district policy to accommodate the diatribe on "slaughter" only days after Giffords had courageously stepped back into the public eye.

The board president's act appeared especially duplicitous in the eyes of many who had witnessed Stegeman's and Pedicone's excessive police crackdown and arrest of elderly nonviolent Mexican American activists earlier that spring. One student piped up: "What was Stegeman waiting for—another tragedy?"

Stegeman, whose contentious behavior on Facebook and public forums was increasingly concerning observers, had dropped a bombshell at a recent state administrative hearing when he referred to the Mexican American Studies program as "cult-like." He objected to the fact that the students clapped their hands in the tradition of a United Farm Workers meeting.

"These teachers excel at the very principles the district has promoted: rigor, relevance, and relationship," local educator Kristel Foster said at the board meeting that night. "The school board president now says that rigorous books are inappropriate, that social justice is irrelevant, and that the relationship, this strong community of learners, is a cult. Every move he makes shows his lack of experience and understanding of what quality, effective education is."

The board meeting adjourned. The shell-shocked audience didn't know what to think, let alone do. Everyone went home and logged on to his or her computer. With no local news media on hand, Morales immediately posted his footage with commentary and links to the speaker's nefarious associations and statements. The next Three Sonorans headlines were typically provocative: "Stegeman and Pedicone Treat the White Man Differently." "Should Weapons Be Allowed in School Parking Lots?" "Profiles of the Tucson Right-Wing: Fearful Christian Men With Guns Who Are Ready to Kill." The information and background research, though, provided more than enough evidence for action.

Forwarding Morales's blogs, a small group of parents and advocates for the Mexican American Studies program launched a Facebook page to call for the removal of Stegeman, an economist at the University of Arizona, as board chair. A groundswell of students, parents, and community members answered this call and pressed for the resignation at the next board meeting.

"As school board president, Stegeman has redefined failure," said Becky Harvey, whose African American daughter had graduated from the program and now attended the University of Arizona. "His disgraceful actions and words have escalated tensions and created a volatile atmosphere."

"Dr. Stegeman's characterization of our classes as 'cult-like' is a very serious accusation; moreover, grounds for libel," said Jose Gonzales, one of the two teachers who had been branded as "cult-like." "Our MAS teachers are experienced, dedicated professionals who have had stellar careers with TUSD, and are renowned nationally in the educational profession. To characterize our MAS teachers' years of dedicated experience to Tucson Unified School District as a 'cult' is negligent at best and bigoted at worst."

Curtis Acosta, the teacher noted on CNN for bridging ethnic divisions and turmoil during the Giffords shooting, ripped into the board chair and his accusations: "Dr. Stegeman's comments about his visit to my classroom were not only inaccurate and irresponsible but spiteful. His testimony disregarded eighty minutes of my instruction, the entire content of the class, and all my interaction with the students. He even inaccurately represented the poem we recite, which is based upon loving and seeing all human beings as equal."

Within days, the impact of the Facebook and blogging campaign was undeniable. A City Council representative returned a campaign donation to Stegeman, who was an active member of the Democratic Party. The student group UNIDOS announced plans to protest.

Harvey continued to ramp up the Facebook entries. She posted an email exchange with Stegeman in which he wrote, "Anyone who organizes a recall is probably doing me a favor. This job is not fun." Harvey agreed, and she wasn't alone. "His reckless leadership and now this horrible attempt to discredit successful students and teachers are unacceptable," she posted.

At the next school board meeting, Morales stood on the right side of the room, camera in hand. Community members packed the chambers this time. Within the opening minutes of the meeting, the board voted to demote Stegeman as chair. The crowd cheered. A motion by Michael Hicks, a Tea Party member of the school board, to make Stegeman the board clerk, failed. The crowd cheered ever louder.

In the face of the extremist anti-immigrant tide that had swept across the state, it was a small victory for Three Sonorans and the supporters of the Mexican American Studies program. But it was a victory nonetheless, and a reminder of their ability to organize a rapid-response network through social media, blogging, and new forms of activism. As battle-worn as they felt, though, they knew the main trial had yet to come.

BARRIO VIEJO

A profound sense of Arizona history had emboldened Sean Arce, the esteemed director and cofounder of the district's Mexican American Studies program, to withstand the daily attacks on his work. In some of the most trying times, he had gone to the well of his family's Mexican American history in Tucson, which predated the creation of the territory in the mid-nineteenth century. He did this while struggling to rescue the floundering school district's reputation from an embarrassing desegregation court order dating back to his youth in the 1970s, which had been placed back on by a federal judge in the late summer of 2011. MALDEF (Mexican American Legal Defense and Educational Fund) president Thomas Saenz called the court's decision "much-needed protections for Latino and other minority students in a state that has too often demonstrated hostility toward these students."

All politics aside, Arce and a host of other scholars had methodically developed a nationally acclaimed curriculum that reversed troubling dropout rates among Latino students, especially in the lower income areas, and he had overseen one of the most successful academic programs in the state.

Despite the extraordinary stress and uncertainty over Arizona's controversial law, which Arce and his fellow Mexican American Studies teachers and students were challenging in a landmark case in federal court as a violation of constitutional rights, the famously calm program director remained an inspiring figure for educators across the country.

"Mr. Arce has an exceptionally gifted intellect and is a highly competent administrator," noted Dr. Devon G. Peña, former chair of the National Association for Chicana and Chicano Studies. "Under his leadership, MAS-TUSD has become the nation's most innovative and successful academic and instructional program in Ethnic Studies at the secondary school level."

His dedication also went beyond the classroom lessons for Tucson's students, according to Jesus "Tito" Romero, a 2007 alumnus of the Mexican American Studies program: "Arce has been in the business of saving lives for many years, whether he realizes it or not. It wasn't until I had him as a history teacher that I discovered what it meant to be a student, and I soon realized that Mr. Arce had not only saved my life, but had changed and touched so many others."

Although Arce was raised in Oakland, his parents and their extended families had shaped the history of Tucson's Barrio Viejo and the surrounding neighborhoods. His mother had served as a translator and mentor; his father helped to support a community endeavor that sent local music legend Lalo Guerrero, "the father of Chicano music," off to fame in California. Returning to visit the bulldozed ruins of the Arce family's beloved neighborhood in 1990, which had been destroyed under a real estate development scheme largely promoted by Pedicone's colleague and Southern Arizona Leadership Council cofounder S. L. "Si" Schorr, Guerrero composed the ballad "Barrio Viejo" as an anthem for Tucson's Chicano community:

> Viejo barrio, old neighborhood,
> There's only leveled spaces
> where once there were houses,
> where once people lived.
> There are only ruins
> of the happy homes
> of the joyous families,
> of these folks that I loved.

Returning to Tucson to study at the University of Arizona, Arce soon replanted himself in the local school system as a popular mentor and curriculum specialist. After a brief stint at the United Farm Workers, he cofounded Tucson's Mexican American Studies program in 1998.

In the spring of 2011, Arce's life history played out on the big screen in front of him with a compelling reminder of his cutting-edge role. The documentary *Precious Knowledge* reveals the ideological and political fervor afoot in Arizona and underscoring the anti–ethnic studies ban and anti-immigrant measures, and places the founding of the ethnic studies program in the larger historical context of the long struggles by Tucson's Mexican American community for better education and an end to discriminatory policies. A sign from the famed 1969 walkouts, led by Chicano activists, resonates today: "We dare to care about education."

Arce watched in the theater that night as his city finally transcended the radio show banter and saw the role of culturally relevant material and critical pedagogy in challenging the student to read the word, and the world. "The freedom to ask questions," says Mexican American literature teacher Acosta, "that are the most pertinent in the way they view the world."

The attendants at the theater shook their heads as Horne first denies at a Senate hearing that he had ever been invited to a Mexican American Studies classroom, and then backsteps when challenged by a legislator and admits that he had indeed been invited but refused. Horne's accusation that the Mexican American Studies program is "dividing students by ethnicity" and preaching ethnic resentment is rebuked by the sheer number of non-Latino students who take the classes, testify at various hearings, protest, and eloquently describe their experience to visiting lawmakers and TV reporters.

Far from any protests or debates, the documentary showed that night what the rest of the state had been missing: Huppenthal and Horne possessed a hyper-aversion to anyone addressing past social injustices in the United States, especially among the founding fathers. Instead of viewing historic campaigns for civil rights, women's suffrage, or child labor laws, for example, as inspiring lessons of change and transformation in the American democratic process, Huppenthal and Horne effectively demanded that a censored presentation of American history be taught to Arizona children, one that casts modern society as colorblind and flawless—and our founders as infallible.

After visiting Acosta's class at Tucson High School in the film, Huppenthal reports back to a Senate hearing that a Mexican American Studies administrator has "trashed Benjamin Franklin." Yet as viewers witness for themselves, the adviser had only repeated Franklin's very famous "Observation" in 1753 in which he expressed his concern that there were too many "tawny" people. (One little footnote: Those "tawny" people included Huppenthal's German ancestors, whom Franklin also disparaged as "the most ignorant stupid sort," unable to learn English; but the adviser assumingly skipped that part to avoid hurting Huppenthal's feelings.)

Such duplicity never seems to bother Horne or Huppenthal, who soon ramp up the powder-keg rhetoric of their obsessive campaign with the help of the infamous Russell Pearce. After hearing African American student Mariah Harvey's passionate and compelling description of a program that "doesn't teach us to be anti-American" but to "embrace America, all of it, flaws and all," Pearce shrugs his shoulders and grumbles that the program preaches "hate speech, sedition, anti-Americanism."

In the end, Acosta tells community members at a rally, "we have taught you to love."

Sean Arce wept with the rest of the theatergoers that night in Tucson. As he watched the documentary on the role of transformative education alongside his son and father—who had been forced, like all Mexican Americans, African Americans, and Native Americans, to view film screenings at the same theater from the segregated balcony seats as a student—the historic role of Arce's work had come full circle.

YOU CAN'T PADLOCK AN IDEA

The final decision came down on January 10, 2012.

With the Tucson Unified School District already under an embarrassing federal desegregation order, the Governing Board acquiesced to the demands of Huppenthal and his Tea Party state officials, and voted four to one to terminate the Mexican American Studies program.

Less than two months before the 140th anniversary of the opening of the first public school in Tucson by Estevan Ochoa, Sean Arce and his teachers were instructed to halt their Mexican American history and literature courses. They were given seventy-eight hours, in some instances, to adopt unofficially approved "American" literature and history courses, including European History.

"The good news is, we have a vehicle to challenge immediately the constitutionality of HB 2281," said attorney Richard Martinez the day after the school board decision came down.

Although he denied a motion for a preliminary injunction, US Ninth Circuit Court Judge A. Wallace Tashima, who had spent part of his childhood at a Japanese internment camp in Arizona during World War II, granted plaintiff and Mexican American Studies student Korina Lopez standing in her claims that the state ban violated constitutional rights. Tashima had been assigned the case after John Roll, the federal court justice who had been assigned to it originally, was killed in the Giffords shooting.

By granting Lopez standing, he ensured that the Mexican American Studies program would have its day in federal court. "The students here have made a plausible showing of a First Amendment violation based on allegations in the Complaints that viewpoint-discriminatory criteria are being used to remove certain texts and materials from the MAS curriculum, which represent 'willing speakers' to which the students would have otherwise been exposed," he wrote.

The significance of an inevitable rendezvous with the Ninth Circuit Court was not lost on Martinez, a Tucson native who had cut his teeth in the Chicano movement of the 1960s and emerged as one of the most eloquent spokespeople in the Latino community. In 1947, the same court had upheld a lower federal court ruling in a segregation suit filed by the Mendez family in California, whose children had been denied enrollment. Onetime migrant cotton pickers in Arizona, the Mendez family had moved to California and eventually took over management of a farm owned by a Japanese family, who had leased to it them during their internment in World War II.

"From a legal perspective, *Mendez v. Westminster* was the first case to hold that school segregation *itself* is unconstitutional and violates the 14th Amendment," noted legal scholar Maria Blanco. "Prior to the *Mendez* decision, some courts, in cases mainly filed by the NAACP, held that segregated schools attended by African American children violated the 14th Amendment's Equal Protection Clause because they were inferior in resources and quality, *not* because they were segregated. From a strategic perspective, Thurgood Marshall's participation in *Mendez* paid critical dividends for years to come. Marshall, who later would successfully argue the *Brown v. Board of Education* case before the U.S. Supreme Court and eventually become the first African American Justice on the Supreme Court, participated in the *Mendez* appeal."

"We are no closer to knowing what HB 2281 prohibits or allows," Martinez added. "This is a fundamental flaw in the statute that should result in finding it invalid due to the impermissible vagueness of the law. After tonight's decision by the TUSD Governing Board, to eliminate MAS in TUSD, there will likely be a new effort made to reverse that action. We are far from a final decision, and the legal challenges will continue."

The challenges to the demoralized Tucson school board would go beyond the courts, as well. Three of the four members who voted to dismantle the program were up for election in the fall of 2012, and campaigns for their ouster were launched immediately after the announcement.

"In the '90s we asked why our students were last to be considered for an ethnic studies program," wrote community leader Miguel Ortega, who had run for the school board in the past and planned to mount a new campaign. "Now we ask why we are the first to lose it. After successfully creating the Mexican American Studies program at TUSD in 1998, we knew we would need smart, ethical and courageous leaders to protect it. That fact hasn't changed."

In announcing her candidacy for the school board, longtime educator Kristel Foster said, "Do they realize what tight bonds they're creating? No one was broken. No one has given up. We're informed, we know the process. We're more united than ever, and will work together to elect new members of our community to represent us."

Pima College freshman Mayra Feliciano, who had been one of the leaders of the controversial UNIDOS takeover of the school board, didn't even have time to dwell on the latest episode in the Mexican American Studies witch hunt that week. "I took the Mexican American Studies course and my life turned around for the better," Feliciano wrote in an email, juggling full-time college and work. "I was struggling to graduate, and I didn't care because I knew people were expecting me to fail. But, this class taught me that we all live in a society where we all struggle and that knowledge and facts are what help get you through. On the correct side of history."

On track to fulfilling her dream of becoming a civil rights attorney, Feliciano—like thousands of young Tucsonans who had graduated in the beleaguered state's upper tier and gone on to college, thanks in large part to the Mexican American Studies program—considered herself "on the correct side of history" in Arizona.

Examining the thirteen-year track record of the program, which had served 5,726 Mexican American and 712 non-Latino students, esteemed emeritus professor of education Christine Sleeter wrote in *Education Week*, "On Arizona's achievement tests in reading, writing, and math, its students also outscore students of all racial and ethnic groups in the same schools but not in that program—a remarkable record. As schools nationwide struggle to close racial achievement gaps, Tucson's Mexican-American studies program should be one from which we are learning."

"Then why was the Mexican-American studies program in Tucson terminated? And why did Arizona ban ethnic studies?" Sleeter concluded:

> I believe the core issue is fear of the knowledge Mexican-American students find precious and empowering. Ethnic studies names racism and helps students examine how racism works in their everyday lives, how it was constructed historically, and how it can be challenged. For students of color, ethnic studies draws on knowledge from within racially oppressed communities, and affirms what students know from everyday life, taking the concerns of students seriously and treating them as intellectuals. In so doing, well-designed programs (like Tucson's), taught by well-prepared teachers who believe in their students, connect students' ethnic identity with academic learning and a sense of purpose that takes racism into account.

In an extraordinary move, educators, writers, and advocates from across the country rallied to make sure Tucson's calamity would not go unnoticed or unchallenged. A caravan of *librotraficantes*, or book smugglers, set out from Texas to deliver banished and censored books to Tucson students and create underground libraries. In an editorial, the *New York Times* commended the book smugglers: "School officials say the books are not technically banned, just redistributed to the library. But what good is having works from the reading list—like *Los Tucsonenses: The Mexican Community in Tucson, 1854–1941* and *The House on Mango Street*, by Sandra Cisneros—on the shelves if they can't be taught? Indeed, the point of dismantling the curriculum was to end classroom discussions about these books."

From the new immigration hot spots like Georgia and Alabama, to the high plains of Wyoming and Colorado, spanning to the urban centers of Los Angeles, Atlanta, Chicago, and New York City, hundreds of schools launched a historic teach-in movement in the spring of 2012 to incorporate lesson plans from the banished Mexican American Studies program in their own classrooms.

Organized by Teacher Activist Groups and joined by Rethinking Schools and other educational networks, the "No History Is Illegal" initiative came on the heels of unusually strong statements by more than two dozen of the nation's largest librarian, publishing, literary, and education organizations. Together they called on the Tucson Unified School District and Arizona state education officials to recognize First Amendment rights, "return all books to classrooms and remove all restrictions on ideas that can be addressed in class."

Despite the fact that there were less than three copies of several of the removed Mexican American Studies textbooks in the district libraries, which served more than 52,000 students, thousands of books remained behind lock and key in the district's warehouse.

"Our history is not over," Tucson scholar Guadalupe Castillo, who had been arrested at a school board meeting, told a gathering in the historic Barrio Viejo. "It is very much with us. We live it every day. It is a history that is profound, deeply rooted. And it is very difficult right now, because there are those who want to take it away from us. The people who are saying the end of this must occur are profoundly wrong, and they are racists and they have to be called what they are. To say that we do not have that history, and a right to that history and a right to have it spoken loudly in all of the schools like all other histories—it is, as Rodolfo Acuña says, not just simply about a discipline. It's about our right, and our way of life."

Nearly half a century ago, in a similar move, segregationists in Tennessee attempted to shut down the Highlander Folk School for its pioneering curriculum and for its efforts to desegregate local schools. Despite shuttering and padlocking the doors to the school, and auctioning off its books and property, the state learned an enduring lesson. "A school is an idea," Highlander cofounder and educator Myles Horton declared. "And you can't padlock an idea."

Invoking Horton's towering legacy, on April 2, 2012, the Zinn Education Project bestowed its national Myles Horton Education Award on embattled Mexican American Studies director Sean Arce for his leadership role in "one of the most significant and successful public school initiatives on the teaching of history in the U.S."

"Tucson's Mexican American Studies program gets it absolutely right: Ground the curriculum in students' lives, teach about what matters in the world, respect students as intellectuals, and help students imagine themselves as promoters of justice," Zinn Education Project codirector Bill Bigelow said in the press release. "Mr. Arce has begun work that we hope will be emulated by school districts throughout the United States."

The day after receiving the national honor, Arce was formally notified by Superintendent Pedicone that his contract would not be renewed with the district. The retribution under Pedicone's leadership had just begun. After sixteen years of teaching—including twelve years of shepherding the Mexican American Studies program—Arce was essentially fired. Rene Martinez, a middle school Mexican American Studies teacher and son of the plaintiffs' attorney Richard Martinez, was the next to be let go as part of a "reduction in force." In a *Los Angeles Times* profile, Martinez attempted to address the concerns of his bewildered students. "Why are they getting rid of this class? Can you explain?" Martinez told the reporter. "We do our best to explain the history of the law, but it's hard to comprehend how we've come to this point."

Highlander eventually reopened and continues to flourish today. Few doubted that Arce and Tucson's Mexican American Studies program would fail to rise again, as well. The question was, of course: how long it would take, and through what legal avenue?

"The immediate future of Mexican American Studies will be decided by a federal judge, a circumstance that has existed many times before," Martinez concluded. "The fight to achieve constitutional equality is never easy, predictable or direct, but like every other group one we must travel and ultimately be successful in."

SB 1070 protest in Phoenix.
(Photo courtesy of Dennis Gilman.)

WHAT HAPPENS IN ARIZONA DOESN'T STAY IN ARIZONA

Life in Arizona for undocumented immigrants since SB 1070 passed is a combination of basic survival under a climate of hate and inspiring organizing that will one day turn hate to love.

CARLOS GARCIA, PUENTE ARIZONA

A BROKEN IMMIGRATION SYSTEM

Governor Jan Brewer kicked off her book tour in the fall of 2011 in Alabama, as if to give her signature of Arizona's role in influencing the states' rights rebellion on immigration policy across the nation. Driven by SB 1070 author Kris Kobach's approach of "attrition through enforcement," Alabama's HB 56 actually went a few steps further than Arizona. It required schools to check and report the immigration status of their students; kept undocumented students from attending public colleges and universities; required police checks of citizenship or valid immigration status from suspects stopped for any infraction, including routine traffic stops; and made it a felony for an unauthorized immigrant to enter into a contract with a government entity.

Declaring that states' rights had been "disrespected" by the Obama administration, Brewer praised Alabama's move and trumpeted her state's singular role in "paving the way" for the rest of the nation.

"President Obama's administration had done nothing—*nothing*—to work with us to secure the border," Brewer's memoir declared. In Alabama, she remained resilient and even more convinced that a post–SB 1070 Arizona "won't be intimidated, and we won't back down."

In that same period, the *Arizona Capitol Times* headlined former Arizona governor and Department of Homeland Security (DHS) Chief Janet Napolitano's announcement of a deportation milestone. For the third straight year, the federal agency Immigration and Customs Enforcement (ICE) had posted a new record, deporting 396,906 illegal immigrants in the fiscal year that ended September 30—since his inauguration, President Obama had removed more than 1.1 million people from the United States.

Writing in the *Huffington Post*, immigrant rights advocate Joshua Hoyt attempted to place these statistics into a human realm beyond Arizona's borders: "What does this very large number of 396,906 mean for families and U.S. citizen children? Let us assume that at least two-thirds of the deportees are married, with an average of 2.5 children. Thus, from the perspective of ICIRR [Illinois Coalition for Immigrant and Refugee Rights], the impact of this year's accomplishments by ICE is that 654,895 children—most of them U.S. citizens—have lost a parent during just the past year due to deportation."

In the spring of 2012, ICE released its first-ever report to Congress on the impact of deportation policies on US-born children. In the first six months of the previous year, the federal government had deported 46,000 parents of children who were American citizens; another 21,860 parents had been given orders to leave. The fate of these American children was unknown.

"We have made the enforcement of our immigration laws smarter and more effective," Napolitano said, testifying to the Senate Judiciary Committee. The administration had focused "our finite resources on removing those individuals who fit our highest priorities," and pursued undocumented residents with criminal backgrounds. They weren't simply deportees; they were criminals.

While Brewer railed about the "backdoor amnesty" policies of the Obama administration, the administration had placed a priority on pursuing undocumented residents all, with or without criminal records. In fact, no other recent administration—except for Eisenhower, who launched Operation Wetback—had gone to such levels to deport residents. (In the 1930s, Hoover "repatriated" nearly 500,000 Mexican laborers.) For Ali Noorani, executive director of the National Immigration Forum, the record figures highlighted "a failure of our government to come to grips with our broken immigration system."

The broken immigration system went far beyond Arizona's front lines. In the summer of 2011, ICE announced new rules that effectively required all municipalities and states to cooperate in Secure Communities (S-Comm), a high-tech program that allows FBI and law enforcement agencies to share fingerprinting records with ICE to check against immigration databases. Several states, such as Illinois, New York, and Massachusetts, had attempted to withdraw from the program, claiming that it had led to unfair sweeps of nonviolent offenders or working immigrants—such as those parents with US-born children and spouses—without a criminal past. According to Illinois Governor Pat Quinn, less than 20 percent of the undocumented residents apprehended as part of the Secure Communities agreement in his state had been convicted of a serious crime.

"The heart of the concern is that the program, conceived of as a method of targeting those people who pose the greatest threat to our communities, is in fact having the opposite effect and compromising public safety by deterring witnesses to crime and others from working with law enforcement," wrote New York Governor Andrew Cuomo.

As the linchpin in the Obama administration's aggressive approach to deportation, Napolitano, whose Department of Homeland Security oversaw ICE, didn't relent. ICE's announcement rebuked the states that had announced plans to opt out of Secure Communities with a friendly reminder that they didn't have a choice.

"Today's announcement confirms ICE's status as a rogue agency," said Chris Newman of the National Day Laborer Organizing Network, an immigrant rights group. "The level of deception involved in S-Comm so far has been alarming, but this moves things to another level. A contract is a contract—but apparently not when it comes to ICE.

"A federal judge already found that DHS and ICE went out of their way to mislead the public about Secure Communities. Today's announcement shows that ICE also systematically misled the states, engaging in protracted negotiations—at substantial cost to the American public—for what it now claims are sham contracts. But all the deception in the world can't hide the fact that S-Comm is horrible policy."

In many respects, S-Comm reminded us that we all lived in Arizona's post–SB 1070 world now.

At a special congressional hearing on border security on May 8, 2012, Michael Fisher, head of the US Border Patrol, announced the agency's "New Strategic Plan and the Path Forward" and an accelerated approach to work more closely with local law enforcement agencies. With deportations at record highs and apprehensions of undocumented entries by migrants at their lowest since 1970, the new four-year plan signaled an increasing push in the Obama administration's immigration efforts and called for "expanding the use of consequences to punish people who enter the country illegally instead of the revolving-door policy of the past," according to the *Arizona Republic*. In an interview with Terry Sterling at the *Daily Beast*, immigration attorney Ezequiel Hernandez concluded, "That would mean detaining migrants who were formerly caught and released at the border, which could be a boon to Corrections Corporation of America, which contracts with federal officials to transport and house their immigrant charges."

As Russell Pearce once wrote, "Arizona did not make illegal, illegal, illegal was already illegal." "I've been in law enforcement most of my life," he told an interviewer in the aftermath of SB 1070 in 2010. "I like putting the bad guys in jail. I'm very vigilant, always have been. I never intended to run for office . . . and I never expected to be the icon on these issues from coast to coast. But I did expect to be vigilant in the defense of freedom and liberty and the Second Amendment and God-given rights. I've been vigilant on these issues for years, but when you do certain things all of a sudden it becomes a national story, a national issue."

Whether or not Pearce had been brought down as a national icon for Arizona's vigilance, the *Arizona Capitol Times* noted one key detail in the report on the record number of deportations Napolitano had overseen through Secure Communities: "Most of those had been convicted of driving under the influence."

"Illegal immigrants caught in traffic stops often are pressured into signing an agreement to leave the United States and to pay a fine or somehow acknowledge responsibility for the traffic offense and thereby end up in the statistics as criminals even though they never went to court," Marshall Fitz, immigration policy director at the liberal Center for American Progress think tank, told an ABC News reporter.

DUIs and other traffic violations had become the ticket to deportation, the new benchmark for our immigration policy.

WHEN ILLEGAL IS NOT ALWAYS ILLEGAL

On a summer evening in 1988, immigration paddy wagons probably would have roared by the car accident on the Phoenix patch of I-17. When the police arrived at the scene, the driver who had slammed into the van of an elderly man was "unsteady" on her feet. Her car had gone through a fairly significant bang-up. With her breath reeking of alcohol, unable to pass a couple of field sobriety tests on the side of the road, the driver was handcuffed and escorted to the Department of Public Safety station, according to *Arizona Republic* reports, where officers planned to test her blood-alcohol level.

Jan Brewer told the police she had only drunk one scotch. Well, actually, she admitted, make that two. When the officers realized her identity as a state legislator, they passed on the test and sent her home. Charges were dismissed because of her legislative immunity.

Attorney General Tom Horne had more of a problem with I-10 and Arizona Highway 51. In the course of one eighteen-month period, he had racked up six traffic violations in his beloved Jaguar, including a speeding ticket in a school zone. In his 2010 attorney general race, he admitted that he had openly lied on an Arizona Corporation Commission form from 1997 to 2000 about his history of bankruptcy on the East Coast; he had the distinction of being banned forever from the Securities and Exchange Commission after he "willfully aided and abetted" securities law violations as president of an investment firm that declared bankruptcy in 1970. In the spring of 2012, the FBI launched an investigation into Horne's alleged illegal "collaboration with an independent expenditure committee," which had bankrolled campaign ads against his opponent in 2010. The FBI also opened an inquiry into Horne's subsequent hiring of the campaign committee's chairwoman for an upper-level position in the attorney general's office. In denying the allegations, Horne claimed he had been "subjected to a major smear."

As the former head of the Motor Vehicle Division in Arizona, Pearce did not have the same driving trouble as his fellow colleagues; instead, he had been discharged from his position in 1999, after it was discovered that an employee under his supervision had altered a woman's drunk-driving record.

For Tea Party State Senator Lori Klein, who reintroduced Pearce's pet bill for the nullification of federal laws in 2012 and added to her viral online video collection by telling protesting Mexican Americans in Phoenix in the summer of 2011 to "go back to Mexico" if they didn't agree with her views, her own DUI-while-speeding ticket became a key fixture on her campaign website: "What good is learning a lesson the hard way if you can't share it and help others with the lesson learned?"

As Pearce had reasoned in the past over state laws, "I love government when it's in its proper role."

THE COURTROOM

The proper role of government, as it pertained to Arizona and its final showdown for states' rights, would ultimately be decided in the US Supreme Court: *Arizona v. United States.* By agreeing to hear Arizona's appeal of the Ninth Circuit Court decision, which had ruled that "states do not have the inherent authority to enforce the civil provisions of federal immigration law," the Supreme Court would determine whether federal immigration laws "preclude Arizona's efforts at cooperative law enforcement and impliedly preempt these four provisions of S.B. 1070 on their face." In brief: does Arizona have the right to be a state out of the union and carry out its own immigration policy?

Arizona openly chastised the Ninth Circuit Court's majority opinion, which warned that "the threat of 50 states layering their own immigration enforcement rules" could derail federal immigration policy. In fact, Arizona's case mocked such a conclusion by charging that "the disuniformity of federal immigration enforcement efforts" had actually "funneled unlawful entrants to Arizona and exacerbated the crisis that led to S.B. 1070's enactment."

Despite the fact that the Ninth Circuit Court concurred that Arizona faced an extraordinary immigration burden, Brewer's legal team doubled down on making the case that an "epidemic of crime, safety risks, serious property dam-

age, and environmental problems" was crossing the border under the control
of the most sophisticated organized crime network in the world. Forced to
bear a "seriously disproportionate share of the burden of an already urgent
national problem," Arizona accused federal enforcement efforts of focusing
"primarily on areas in California and Texas, leaving Arizona's border to suffer
from comparative neglect."

Brewer's attorneys understood, like all legal observers, that "the federal
government has exclusive authority to regulate immigration." In 2010, Center
for American Progress analyst Ian Millhiser reminded Arizonans that the Supreme Court had struck down a Pennsylvania law in 1941 requiring "every
alien 18 years or over" to register annually with the state. "As the Court explained, state laws which intrude on immigration policy can have grave consequences for US foreign policy: 'One of the most important and delicate of
all international relationships, recognized immemorially as a responsibility
of government, has to do with the protection of the just rights of a country's
own nationals when those nationals are in another country. Experience has
shown that international controversies of the gravest moment, sometimes
even leading to war, may arise from real or imagined wrongs to another's subjects inflicted, or permitted, by a government.'"

As *Hines v. Davidowitz* establishes, Millhiser added, "the supremacy of the
national power in the general field of foreign affairs, including power over immigration, naturalization and deportation, is made clear by the Constitution.
This is because the decision of a single rogue state to engage in abusive behavior towards immigrants reflects upon the United States as a whole."

Yet SB 1070, Arizona argued, "encourages the cooperative enforcement of
federal immigration laws throughout all of Arizona." Brewer's team insisted
that SB 1070 would only "supplement" the federal government's "inadequate
immigration enforcement," not replace it, and that the state was "acutely aware
of the need to respect federal authority to set the substantive rules governing
immigration."

Not that Arizona needed to ask permission in the first place. Drawing
heavily from the same conservative legal theories as did Russell Pearce and
his fringe Constitution Party stalwarts, Arizona's Supreme Court challenge
also invoked a notorious 2002 memo from the Justice Department's Office
of Legal Counsel to Attorney General John Ashcroft and asserted Arizona's
right as a "sovereign entity" to enforce federal laws. The Bybee memo claimed

that states have "inherent authority" to authorize police officers to make warrantless arrests for federal criminal violations: "We believe such arrest authority inheres in the States' status as sovereign entities."

Brewer's team added, for good measure: "The failure of federal law to authorize Arizona's efforts in express terms is beside the point. Arizona officials have inherent authority to enforce federal law and such cooperative law enforcement is the norm, not something that requires affirmative congressional authorization. SB 1070 does not impose its own substantive immigration standards, but simply uses state resources to enforce federal rules."

Although the Supreme Court's consideration of SB 1070's main provisions would go far in determining whether Arizona's law unconstitutionally usurps the federal government's authority to regulate immigration law and enforcement, Center for American Progress analyst Marshall Fitz added in an essay, "It bears noting that the Court's ruling will not resolve all concerns and legal challenges posed by the Arizona law or by other state laws currently being litigated. Other state laws also create restrictions on education, housing, and private contracting, none of which will be conclusively decided by the court's ruling in this case." Nonetheless, Fitz concluded, "The stakes are momentous, but the constitutional arguments seem clear-cut, so we remain optimistic that the Court will strike this measure down and send a clear signal to other states considering similar legislation. The credibility of the Court as the guardian of core constitutional principles that protect every resident of the nation hangs in the balance."

The Supreme Court's decision had "the power to shape American life" in an extraordinary election year, the *New York Times* noted. By accepting the case, the Court had thrust itself into one of the most politically charged debates of our time. Its decision, of course, went far beyond the Arizona border; similar federal court injunctions on copycat immigration laws in other states, such as Alabama, Utah, and Georgia, hinged on the Court's ruling, as well. Legislators from twenty states, ranging from Mississippi to Montana, filed *amicus curiae* briefs in support of Arizona's immigration law. A week after opening arguments on April 25, 2012, a Senate committee in New Hampshire debated a resolution based on SB 1070.

"With SB 1070, Arizona declared a war of attrition on immigrants," Puente human rights activist Carlos Garcia said in Phoenix on the eve of the Supreme Court hearing. "What was started in Arizona quickly led to the Arizonification of this country, one that treats undocumented immigrants as criminals and treats all Latinos as undocumented."

"What happens in Arizona doesn't stay in Arizona," Tucson human rights activist and attorney Isabel Garcia often said, referring to the state's vanguard role in states' rights and punitive immigration policy. Yet after the Pearce recall, the national outpouring of solidarity with Tucson's Mexican American Studies program, and now the ruling by the Supreme Court on SB 1070 and states' rights, that expression had more than one meaning.

"What happens in Arizona spreads," Carlos Garcia added. "Two years ago, we said, 'The best way to support Arizona is to fight the places where police are being enlisted as immigration officers in your own towns.' Since that call, hundreds of campaigns have been born challenging Arizonification and turning the tide from hate to human rights."

Indeed, when the Supreme Court struck down three out of four SB 1070 provisions on June 25, 2012, it notably allowed the controversial "papers, please" requirement for police to check the immigration status of suspects. "Arizona has paid a very high price for what amounts to a very limited, even Pyrrhic, victory today," said Thomas Saenz, president of MALDEF, who reminded observers of a separate case over constitutional claims by civil rights groups. He added: "We must take all steps to prevent any racial profiling and unconstitutional arrests from this terrible Arizona state intrusion on federal immigration policy."

THE COURT OF PUBLIC OPINION

When journalist and fifth-generation Tucsonan Mari Herreras expertly sorted fact from fiction in the Mexican American Studies fiasco for the *Tucson Weekly*, she debunked ten myths—"stories of mythical proportions have surrounded the fight for Mexican-American studies, with some truths sprinkled in between the lines," she wrote—in a way that displayed one of the most illuminating but tragic, if not obscene, realities in Arizona's education showdown. As the state celebrated its centennial in 2012, the families of its founding Mexican American pioneers—including the 60 percent of the students who made up Tucson Unified School District—still had to defend and justify the teaching of Mexican American history and literature, as if they were not part of the greater American experience.

In a harrowing crackdown on intellectual freedom and free speech, such an expulsion went beyond Tucson's classrooms and bookshelves. Having returned to his native Tucson to serve as editor of *La Estrella*, the *Arizona Daily Star*'s Spanish-language edition, the widely admired Ernesto Portillo Jr. chronicled his dismay at being banned from the schoolroom himself, as a reporter, in 2012: "The district would rather keep out reporters in the hope the issue will go away, so it seems." He added: "While MAS students and teachers never really had a chance, they didn't give up, even as their passion and goals were questioned and vilified. Neither will the students, their parents and teachers give up their fight in the wake of the governing board's decision to capitulate. For now, the students and teachers are banned."

With the impeccable timing that continued to cement Tucson's reputation as a hotbed of censorship, only two days after *The Daily Show* skewered inept Tucson school board member Michael Hicks for dismantling the Mexican American Studies program—in a cringe-worthy interview, Hicks had embarrassingly referred to civil rights icon Rosa Parks as "Rosa Clarks," insisted that Latino teachers provided free burritos to entice students to their radical classrooms, and admitted that he had based his extremist views on "hearsay of others"—and one day after MAS director Sean Arce was sacked, the online *Tucson Citizen* news site announced on April 4, 2012, that it had pulled the plug on the city's most popular Latino blogger and activist, David Morales, even though Three Sonorans drew more than 1.6 million visits to his take-no-prisoners blog.

Morales's termination placed him in good company in Arizona's history of Latino journalism. Nearly a half century ago, pioneering Chicano author and columnist Mario Suárez drew the wrath of Arizona Governor Howard Pyle for his investigative and biting columns in Tucson's *Prensa Mexicana* newspaper on corruption and discrimination. Faced with reprisals and threats against his family, Suárez had to end his column, "El Gavilan," but he went on to lead community and education efforts in Arizona and California.

Imbued with the local and national outrage over his dismissal, Morales launched his unrepentant and muckraking Three Sonorans blog on an independent site.

The final showdown in the extremist witch hunt to outlaw Mexican American Studies in Tucson continued in the courts; but the supremely American struggle for access to democratic education, freedom of expression, and local control of schools continued to play out on the state's bitterly divided sides, as it had for more than a century.

"Arizona's discrimination against Mexican American and Ethnic Studies is unconstitutional," said Vince Rabago, a lawyer representing the National Association for Chicana and Chicano Studies (NACCS) and twenty-six education and civil rights organizations, which filed an *amicus curiae* brief on behalf of the students' legal challenge. "The state is arguing that 'states' rights' allow them to restrict curriculum in a discriminatory manner against Mexican Americans. This is comparable to the days after desegregation where states tried to restrict efforts to reach equality. These organizations from across the country support the bedrock principles of Equal Protection and the First Amendment in an academic context."

While schools across the country joined annual celebrations of United Farm Workers leader Cesar Chavez's March 31 birthday in 2012, Tucson students reassigned from the recently outlawed Mexican American Studies program were forced to ignore Arizona's most famous native son. Four years earlier, presidential candidate Barack Obama had joined a campaign to make Chavez's birthday a national holiday. As part of the TUSD's indiscriminate sweep of all textbooks, videos, and Mexican American Studies curriculums from the classrooms, Chavez's powerful "Address to the Commonwealth Club of California" had been banished from any teacher-led discussions in Tucson.

With Arizona State Superintendent John Huppenthal declaring his intent that same month to launch an extraordinary new attack on Mexican American Studies at the university level, Chavez's prophetic speech had never seemed more timely–and more dangerous to the Arizona Tea Party and its enablers like TUSD Superintendent John Pedicone in Tucson.

"These trends are part of the forces of history that cannot be stopped," Chavez had admonished his listeners in 1984. "No person and no organization can resist them for very long. They are inevitable. Once social change begins, it cannot be reversed. You cannot uneducate the person who has learned to read. You cannot humiliate the person who feels pride. You cannot oppress the people who are not afraid anymore. Our opponents must understand that it's not just a union we have built. Unions, like other institutions, can come and go. But we're more than an institution. For nearly twenty years, our union has been on the cutting edge of a people's cause—and you cannot do away with an entire people; you cannot stamp out a people's cause."

Looking back at his longtime work with the United Farm Workers and their struggles, including campaigns for child labor protections, environmental justice, workplace safety, and basic civil rights, Chavez defiantly framed how the union workers had "sent out a signal to all Hispanics that we were fighting for our dignity, that we were challenging and overcoming injustice, that we were empowering the least educated among us—the poorest among us. The message was clear: if it could happen in the fields, it could happen anywhere—in the cities, in the courts, in the city councils, in the state legislatures."

Nearly three decades later, no one understood that reality more than the Tea Party–led legislature in Arizona and extremist state officials like Brewer, Pearce, Horne, and Huppenthal—and a new generation of Latinos and their allies across all ethnic lines and divisions. Flanked by the implacable Maricopa County Sheriff Joe Arpaio, Russell Pearce greeted a packed house of Tea Party activists in Mesa on March 19 and announced his campaign to reclaim a State Senate seat in the 2012 election. "One thing we need in this country are fighters," Arpaio said. "Never surrender." Standing outside the event in a symbolic protest, Randy Parraz and his Citizens for a Better Arizona ranks embodied that sentiment more than Arpaio, Pearce, or their Tea Party minions could ever realize.

"The consciousness and pride that were raised by our union are alive and thriving inside millions of young Hispanics who will never work on a farm," Chavez had concluded. "Like the other immigrant groups, the day will come when we win the economic and political rewards which are in keeping with our numbers in society. The day will come when the politicians do the right thing by our people out of political necessity and not out of charity or idealism. That day may not come this year. That day may not come during this decade. But it will come, someday!"

That day was now in Tucson, in Mesa, and across Arizona, where Chavez's very words were now outlawed. That day was now in the United States.

"Yet we are filled with hope and encouragement. We have looked into the future and the future is ours," Chavez declared. "History and inevitability are on our side."

THE BALLOT BOX

In the end, these combined showdowns clearly galvanized a new generation of inspired and motivated voters in Arizona and around the country.

"The crisis of Mexican American Studies and SB 1070 is not an isolated one," said Selina Rodriguez, who graduated from the MAS program and now directs a youth center in Santa Monica, California. "It will continue to affect our state and nation as a whole. I have witnessed firsthand how students and scholars from across the country have come in solidarity in support of MAS and the Tucson community. I have seen the passion in the eyes of students, teachers, family members, and those who have been touched by MAS strive to preserve and protect the program. MAS taught me to move forward—*adelante*—while making sure my community is right alongside me. My work and ideology will continue to hold these values close. To never forget the knowledge, traditions, and teachings of our community and to share what I learn with others."

Looking at the way the Pearce recall spurred new Latino voters to take to the polls, Voto Latino director Maria Teresa Kumar could barely hide her enthusiasm for future elections: "Arizona may well become a shining example of what happens to Republican candidates who try to win by demonizing Latinos."

As one Arizona Republican official noted, "immigration fatigue" had begun to sink the party. Or as Phoenix playwright and Hispanic Chamber of Commerce spokesperson James Garcia told the *New York Times,* "There has been a tangible, palpable momentum shift in the state, which is essentially saying, 'Well, that was a disaster, and what should we do about it?'"

Garcia's question underlined a slight shift in media perceptions, as well. When *Time* magazine nominated Governor Brewer for its "*Time* 100" poll of the most influential movers and shakers on the world scene in 2012, it reminded readers that "under the leadership of Republican Brewer, Arizona has faced off with the federal government like no other state in recent memory." Yet to the amazement of Arizonans—and the world—and in a bold forecast of the state's future, Brewer's singular role was nudged from the ranks of the people "that inspire us, entertain us, challenge us and change our world." Instead, in her place, *Time* selected Dulce Matuz, a twenty-seven-year-old undocumented immigrant from Mexico, who was an Arizona State University graduate in electrical engineering and cofounder of the Arizona Dream Act Coalition, and hailed her as the "finest of her generation."

"We are Americans," Matuz proclaimed, "and Americans don't give up."

Time also ran a cover story in February 2012 on "Why Latino Voters Will Swing the 2012 Election," including Arizona as a swing state that could tip toward President Obama thanks to Latino turnout. Western states, where the margin of victory often hung on one to three percentage points, the projected 8.7 percent increase in Latino voters emerged as crucial for Obama's reelection. In a breakdown of changing demographics, *Time* showed Latino voting ranks had grown in every one of those states, reminding its readership that fifty thousand new Latino voters came of age every month. According to the Pew Hispanic Center, Latinos were on pace to reach 30 percent of the total US population by 2050. In June, Obama embraced the Dream Act and issued an order to halt deportation of undocumented youth and to grant work permits.

"In Arizona, it is the marginalized youth who will (re)create and influence our cities and neighborhoods," Selina Rodriguez added. "Youth are our foundation and engine. It is their creativity and savvy that can keep a community, business, or political entity from thriving. According to the 2010 Census, Arizona's greatest growth appeared to be among relatively young 'Hispanics.' The majority of this population understands the concept of struggle and what it means to persevere. The battle over Mexican American Studies underscored the future generation of our state who will carry on the knowledge and culture of our community."

The key question, however, was not over the growing numbers or changing demographics, but the issues that would propel new voters to the polls in ranks that matter.

"This whole issue of trying to demonize the Latino population," said Georgia Democratic Representative John Lewis, one of the leaders of the civil rights movement, had effectively made "immigration the new civil rights movement." Lewis argued that such a movement had to go beyond Arizona's borders. "Too many of our brothers and sisters are being racially profiled because of their background, last name, or the language they may speak," he said. "The state of Georgia is copying the state of Arizona, and I think there will be other states to follow the same path. When you take on the immigrant population, you're taking on all of us. During the Freedom Rides, we were saying, in effect, you arrest one of us, you're going to arrest all of us. You beat fifteen or twenty of us, then you're going to have to beat more than four hundred of us. I see parallels between then and now. There must be a real movement to resist this attempt to say that people who come from another land are not one of us."

More than a half century ago, William Faulkner confronted the racism in Lewis's youth among his fellow Southerners who quietly allowed the South to "wreck and ruin itself in less than a hundred years." He warned Southerners to "speak now against the day when our Southern people who will resist to the last these inevitable changes in social relations, will, when they have been forced to accept what they at one time might have accepted with dignity and goodwill, will say: 'Why didn't someone tell us this before? Tell us this in time?'"

Writing in 1962, Arizona Republican Senator Barry Goldwater wrote a prediction for the state's centennial celebration: "Our ties with Mexico will be much more firmly established in 2012 because sometime within the next fifty years the Mexican border will become as the Canadian border, a free one, with the formalities and red tape of ingress and egress cut to a minimum so that the residents of both countries can travel back and forth across the line as if it were not there."

His camera fixed to the right side, as always, Three Sonorans blogger Morales understood Faulkner's admonition. In the aftermath of the outlawing of Mexican American Studies and the fallout over SB 1070, he sat down on Salomon Baldenegro Sr.'s couch and asked the veteran Chicano leader of Tucson how he managed to keep up his jovial and almost incorrigibly optimistic view, especially in the most despairing moments.

"Since 1848, when the war ended with Mexico, there have been attempts to marginalize us," Baldenegro said, sitting back in his armchair. "There have been laws passed that said we couldn't speak our language. Laws and policy passed that we couldn't practice our traditions, such as Cinco de Mayo, in public. There were laws passed that you couldn't live in a certain neighborhood, or that we couldn't vote. Even policies that prohibited Mexican kids— farmworker kids—from going to school. But if you study our history, you will see we have won every single time, we have won. We are resilient. Our history is not one of victimization. Our history is one of achievement. We have not only survived all manner of attacks, we have gone forward. And we're going to win again. This should give people resilience to fight the fight."

Baldenegro paused for a moment, looked away, and then turned back and faced the Tucson blogger.

"If Brewer, Pearce, Huppenthal, and Horne studied our history, they'd give it up, because they'd realize we're going to win again."

ACKNOWLEDGMENTS

Innanzitutto i miei ringraziamenti vanno a Carla per avermi trascinato nelle osterie bo-
hémien di Bologna e nelle prime linee del mio deserto di Sonora e per avermi fatto
conoscere, attraverso la bella canzone cantata da Nonna Gigia, "Laggiù nell'Arizona,"
il vero significato di famiglia, dei valori della terra e della patria. Uno speciale ringrazi-
amento a Diego e Massimo per aver dato futuro a queste parole e speranze.

Special thanks, as always, to my bro Doug and *mi cuñada* Katie Gannon, who
have provided me with the safe haven to write, hike, and keep myself rooted in the
Sonoran Desert for so many years. And to my folks, Jean and John, who may have
traded *la maravilla* of Pima County for the redrock country of Yavapai County, but
have always been part of my journey for a place called home.

Mil gracias, mis compañeros, for your time, support, ideas, and advice, especially
Jennifer DeMello, John Niecikowski, Royce Davenport, Roberto Bedoya, Leland
Scott, Carlos Muñoz, Marcelo Muñoz, Gregory McNamee, Tom Zoellner, Luis
Urrea, Luis Rodriguez, Mari Herreras, Hector Acuna, Salomon Baldenegro Sr. and
Cecilia Cruz, Becky Harvey, Kristel Foster, Sal Baldenegro Jr. and Wenona Benally
Baldenegro, Dan Buckley, Jessica Pacheco, Deyanira Nevarez and Richard Mar-
tinez, Christine Szuter, Lauren Kuby, Michael Wautier, Ruben Romero, Luke
Knipe, Laura Dent, Isabel Garcia, Gabe Schivone, Devon Peña, Rudy Acuña, Selina
Rodriguez Barajas, David Morales, and Diana Uribe. Thanks so much for your life's
work and courageous examples: Curtis Acosta, Rene Martinez, Sally Rusk, Sean
Arce, Jose Gonzalez, Lorenzo Lopez, Yolanda Sotelo, Maria Federico Brummer,
Salo Escamilla, Norma Gonzales, Nicholas Dominguez, Maya Arce, and Karina
Lopez. Special shout-out to all of the UNIDOS activists in Tucson for your inspiring
resistance, and to my fellow artists and writers at Word Strike/Culture Strike, Tony
Diaz and los Librotraficantes, Bill Bigelow with the Zinn Education Project, and
Deborah Menkart at Teaching for Change. Big thanks to Phoenician stalwarts Don
O'Neal, Brenda Rascon, Julie Jorgensen, Amanda Zill, Randy Parraz and Lilia Al-
varez, Chad Snow, Stephen Lemons, Dennis Gilman, Cindy Dachs, James Garcia,
and northern Arizonans Cheryl and Joe Bader, Erik and Cindy Bitsui, Mik Jordahl,

Stephanie Brown and Donn Johnson, Warren and Ellavina Perkins, Priscilla and Tim Aydelott, and so many others I deeply appreciate and admire in Arizona, in these times.

I would like to express my deep gratitude to Ellen Geiger and the Frances Goldin Literary Agency, and to my editor, Carl Bromley, associate editor Marissa Colón-Margolies, copy editor Mark Sorkin, project editor Sandra Beris, and Basic publisher John Sherer, Cassie Nelson, Michele Jacob, and the wonderful team at Nation Books for giving me the opportunity to return to Arizona's front lines.

Thanks to the editors at *Salon,* the *New York Times, The Nation, Huffington Post, Alternet, Common Dreams,* and *Word Strike,* where various excepts first appeared in different forms.

Finally, to the reader: for all its flaws and foibles and fights, Arizona remains a singular land. "The desert has gone a-begging for a word of praise these years," John Van Dyke wrote in 1901. "It has never had a sacred poet; it has in me only a lover." Nathan Allen, the wise O'odham poet, addressed all in the same way, visitors and transplants: *Sup un thun thuth mumth e tha da.* I'm so glad you have come.

BIBLIOGRAPHIC NOTES

Along with extensive interviews in 2010–2012 and my own news reporting in Arizona for *Salon, The Nation, Huffington Post,* the *New York Times, Alternet,* and *Common Dreams,* my research was largely based on primary and secondary historical documents; manuscripts; personal papers and correspondence; oral histories; governmental and nongovernmental reports; and online and digital archival sites at the Arizona Memory Project/Arizona State Archives; the Arizona Historical Society (Tucson, Tempe); the University of Arizona Library and Special Collections; the Arizona Collections at Arizona State University; the Mesa, Tucson, and Phoenix Public Libraries; and the Bisbee Mining and Historical Museum. I also drew from archival collections and news reports from the following newspapers and journals:

Arizona Capitol Times

Arizona Citizen
  (Tucson, 1870–1880)

Arizona Daily Citizen (Tucson)

Arizona Daily Miner (Prescott)

Arizona Daily Star (Tucson)

Arizona Republic (Phoenix)

Bisbee Daily Review

Copper Era (Clifton)

East Valley Tribune

El Tucsonense

Journal of Arizona History

Journal of the Southwest

Phoenix Gazette

Phoenix New Times

Prescott Courier

Tucson Citizen

Tucson Weekly

PREFACE: HOMECOMING

Allen, Nathan. "Keeper of the House." *Wicazo Sa Review* (Autumn 1993).

Benton-Cohen, Katherine. *Borderline Americans: Racial Division and Labor War in the Arizona Borderlands.* Cambridge: Harvard University Press, 2009.

Contreras, Guillermo. "Tribe Wants U.S. Citizenship for Members in Mexico." *Albuquerque Journal,* May 27, 2001.

"Culture of Cruelty." No More Deaths report, 2011. www.cultureofcruelty.org /documents/2011_report/.

Duarte, Carmen. "Tohono O'odham: Nation Divided." *Arizona Daily Star,* May 30, 2001.

Jaacks, Jason. "A Voice in the Desert." Cordellera Productions, April 25, 2011.

Jaramillo, Canela. "A Conversation with Ai." *Standards* 7, no. 2 (Spring-Summer 2001).

Kondracke, Morton. "'Nativist Lobby' Is Winning on Immigration." *Roll Call,* January 12, 2011.

McCormick, Richard. *Arizona: Its Resources and Prospects; A Letter to the Editor of the New York Tribune, reprinted from that Journal of June 26th, 1865.* Tucson: Territorial Press, 1968.

Nakashima, Ellen. "A Nation Divided, Indians Want to Traverse Freely." *Washington Post,* June 3, 2001.

Norrell, Brenda. "New Spy Towers Pitched for Sovereign Tohono O'odham Nation, After Billion Dollar Boondoggle." *Censored News,* November 23, 2011.

Otero, Lydia. *La Calle: Spatial Conflicts and Urban Renewal in a Southwest City.* Tucson: University of Arizona Press, 2010.

Pearce, Russell. "Obama Files to Stop Senator Russell Pearce from Speaking on State's Right to Control Casino Opening." Press release. Phoenix, AZ, October 28, 2010.

Roosevelt, Eleanor. "To Undo a Mistake Is Always Harder Than Not to Create One Originally." *Confinement and Ethnicity.* Washington, DC: National Park Service, 1999.

Sahagun, Louis. "Immigration Sweep Stirs Cloud of Controversy." *LA Times,* September 1, 1997.

Sheridan, Thomas. *Arizona: A History.* Tucson: University of Arizona Press, 1995.

Suárez, Mario. *Chicano Sketches: Short Stories.* Tucson: University of Arizona Press, 2004.

"U.S.-Mexico Border Crossing Deaths Are a Humanitarian Crisis, According to Report from the ACLU and CNDH." San Diego: American Civil Liberties Union, September 30, 2009.

Véa, Alfredo Jr.. *La Maravilla.* New York: Putnam, 1994.

For further reading on the O'odham and the Hohokam, I'd suggest:

Bahr, Don, William Smith Allison, Julian Hayden, and Juan Smith. *The Short, Swift Time of Gods on Earth: The Hohokam Chronicles.* Berkeley: University of California Press, 1994.

Fish, Paul and Fish, Suzanne. *The Hohokam Millennium.* Santa Fe: School for Advanced Research Press, 2008.

Fontana, Bernard. *Of Earth and Little Rain.* Tucson: University of Arizona Press, 1989.

Meeks, Erik. *Border Citizens: The Making of Indians, Mexicans, and Anglos in Arizona.* Austin: University of Texas Press, 2007.

Nabhan, Gary. *The Desert Smells Like Rain: A Naturalist in O'odham Country.* Tucson: University of Arizona Press, 2002.

O'odham Solidarity Project. solidarity-project.org.

Spicer, Edward. *Cycles of Conquest: The Impact of Spain, Mexico, and the United States on Indians of the Southwest, 1533–1960.* Tucson: University of Arizona Press, 1967.

Tohono O'odham Nation. "History." www.tonation-nsn.gov/ton_history.aspx.
Webb, George. *A Pima Remembers.* Tucson: University of Arizona Press, 1959.

INTRODUCTION: THE THREE SONORANS PROPHECY

Biggers, Jeff. "Arizona, Meet Yourself." *Salon,* January 7, 2012.
Morales, David. "The Rebirth of Arizona." Three Sonorans blog, *Tucson Citizen,* June 16, 2010.
———. "This is a story you should all know." MathGeneRation's Weblog, May 8, 2010. mathgeneration.wordpress.com/2010/05/08/this-is-a-story-you-should-all-know/.
"Richard C. McCormick." *Arizona Weekly Star,* May 6, 1880.

CHAPTER ONE: *ARIZONA V. UNITED STATES*

Aizenman, N. C. "Health-care Law: Arizona Tries New Approach to Get by Federal Medicaid Rules." *Washington Post,* January 23, 2011.
"Arizona and Interposition." *New York Times,* April 24, 2012.
"Arizona Divided: A Tale of Two Counties." *The Economist,* March 31, 2011.
Bennett, Brian. "Janet Napolitano Urges Officials to Stop Exaggerating Violence on U.S. Side of Border." *LA Times,* February 1, 2011.
Benson, Matthew. "Sen. Sylvia Allen Ridiculed for Earth Remark." *Arizona Republic,* July 11, 2009.
Biggers, Jeff. "On Eve of Martin Luther King, Jr. Memorial, Arizona Sues to Overturn Voting Rights Act." *Huffington Post,* August 26, 2011.
———. "The Other Arizona." *The Nation,* January 13, 2011.
Carson, Donald. *Mo: The Life and Times of Morris K. Udall.* Tucson: University of Arizona Press, 2000.
Davidson, Osha. "Showdown Looming Between Sheriffs and Feds?" *Forbes,* January 25, 2011.
Dwyer, Devin. "Obama's Record-High Deportations Draw Hispanic Scorn." ABC News, December 28, 2011.
Fitz, Marshall and Raul Hinojosa-Ojeda. "A Rising Tide or a Shrinking Pie: The Economic Impact of Legalization Versus Deportation in Arizona." Center for American Progress report, March 24, 2011.
Frey, William. "Will Arizona Be America's Future?" Up Front blog, Brookings Institution, April 29, 2010.
"Gov. Jan Brewer: Government Is a Necessary Evil," ABC News, February 27, 2011.
Hahnefeld, Laura. "SB 1070 Backlash: Lime Fresh Mexican Grill from Miami Takes a Jab at Arizona." *Phoenix New Times,* September 28, 2011.
Hunt, George. "Enlightened Industrialism." *Railway Carman's Journal* 21 (October 1916).
King, James. "Arizona Governor Jan Brewer Signs Wild West Gun Bills Into Law." *Phoenix New Times,* April 6, 2010.
Knaub, Mara. "Shooter Shows Up to Special Session in Costume." *Yuma Sun,* June 10, 2011.

"Law and Border." *Daily Show,* April 26, 2010.

Montini, E. J. "Arizona to Secede (Without Officially Doing So)." *Arizona Republic,* February 2, 2011.

Norris, Chuck. "Chuck Norris on Ben Quayle and Border Violence." March 22, 2011. sonoranalliance.com/2011/03/22/chuck-norris-on-ben-quayle-and-border-violence/.

Obama, Barack. Remarks at a memorial event, "Together We Thrive: Tucson and America." *Washington Post,* January 12, 2011.

Olbermann, Keith. "Worst Persons: Pat Robertson, Rick Perry, and Frank Antenori." *Countdown with Keith Olbermann,* August 2, 2011.

Pearce, Russell. "Arizona Takes the Lead on Illegal Immigration Enforcement." *The Social Contract,* Summer 2010.

Poston, Charles. *Building a State in Apache Land.* Kila, MT: Kessinger Publishing, 2004.

"Pundit Says 50,000 Hispanic Citizens Turn 18 and Become Eligible to Vote Every Month." PolitiFact Texas, October 7, 2011. www.politifact.com/texas/statements /2011/oct/07/ruben-navarrette-jr/pundit-says-50000-hispanic-citizens-turn-18 -and-be/.

Rau, Alia Beard. "Pearce, Lewis Mainly Split on Immigration Enforcement." *Arizona Republic,* October 7, 2011."

Robbins, Ted. "A 51st State? Some in Arizona Want a Split." National Public Radio, May 9, 2011.

Ruelas, Richard. "Guns in Arizona: Legislator's Gun Highlights Debate." *Arizona Republic,* July 10, 2011.

Sanchez, Andrea. "Author of SB-1070 Russell Pearce: 'Obama May Not Be Visiting Arizona Because We Require Papers.'" ThinkProgress, December 8, 2010. thinkprogress .org/politics/2010/12/08/134107/russell-pearce-obama-birther/?mobile=nc.

Sandburg, Carl. *Abraham Lincoln: The Prairie Years and the War Years.* New York: Mariner Books, 2002.

Santa Cruz, Nicole. "Arizona Rep. Raúl Grijalva Doesn't Back Down." *LA Times,* May 24, 2010.

"State Senate Should Kill Embarrassing Bill." *Arizona Republic,* April 17, 2012.

Verrilli, Donald. "No. 11-182. In the Supreme Court of the United States. State of Arizona, et al, Petitioners v. the United States of America. On Writ of Certiorari to the United States Court of Appeals for the Ninth Court. Brief for the United States." March, 2012.

Wagner, Dennis. "Violence Is Not Up on Arizona Border Despite Mexican Drug War." *Arizona Republic,* May 2, 2010.

CHAPTER TWO: TO BE OR NOT TO BE A STATE

Acuña, Rodolfo. *Corridors of Migration: The Odyssey of Mexican Laborers, 1600–1933.* Tucson: University of Arizona Press, 2007.

———. *Occupied America: A History of Chicanos.* New York: Harper & Row, 1988.

"Arizona Assumes Place Among State of Nation." *Arizona Daily Star,* February 15, 1912.

Arizona Daily Star, August 18, 1911.

"Arizona Will Don the Garb of Statehood." *Arizona Daily Star*, February 14, 1912.

Benton-Cohen, Katherine. *Borderline Americans: Racial Division and Labor War in the Arizona Borderlands*. Cambridge: Harvard University Press, 2009.

Beveridge, Albert. "In Support of an American Empire," in *A History of the U.S. Political System: Ideas, Interests, and Institutions*, edited by Richard A. Harris and Daniel J. Tichenor. Santa Barbara, CA: ABC-CLIO, 2009.

———. Congressional Record, Fifty-eighth Congress, Third Session, February 6, 1905.

"Bryan on Recall," *Arizona Daily Star*, February 9, 1911.

"Buying a Governor." *Brotherhood of Locomotive Firemen and Enginemen's Magazine* 62 (1917).

Bykrit, James. *Forging the Copper Collar: Arizona's Labor Management War of 1901–1921*. Tucson: University of Arizona Press, 1982.

"Certificate of the Governor, Chief Justice, and Secretary of Arizona Transmitting a Copy of the Constitution of Arizona and the Ascertainment of the Vote Adopting the Same." Washington, DC: Government Printing Office, 1911.

"Complete Verbatim Report, Arizona Constitutional Convention, 1910." Arizona. Constitutional Convention, 1910.

Congressional Record, vol. 27, part 2, 1911.

Dodge, Ida Flood. "Arizona Under Our Flag." *Arizona Daily Star*, February, 1928.

Ehrlich, Karen. "Arizona's Territorial Capital Moves to Phoenix." *Journal of the Southwest* 23, no. 3 (Autumn 1981).

Fitch, John. "Arizona Embargo on Strike-Breakers." *The Survey*, May 6, 1916.

"George Hunt," *Collier's Weekly*, April 15, 1916.

Globe Democrat, October 30, 1911.

Goff, John. *George W. P. Hunt and his Arizona*. Pasadena, CA: Socio Technical Publications, 1973.

Gompers, Samuel. "The Arizona Recall Story in a Nutshell." *The American Federationist* 19 (1912).

Gordon, Linda. *The Great Arizona Orphan Abduction*. Cambridge: Harvard University Press, 2001.

"Government Orders 1200 I.W.W. Taken." *Bisbee Daily Register*, July 16, 1917.

"G. W. P. Hunt: Phoenix to Inauguration." *Arizona Daily Star*, February 14, 1912.

Heard, Dwight. "Why Arizona Opposes Union With New Mexico." *The World To-Day* 10 (1906).

Hubbard, Howard. "Arizona's Enabling Act and President Taft's Veto." *Pacific Historical Review* (September 1934).

Hunt, George W. P. "Bisbee Deportations." Letter from Hunt to President Woodrow Wilson, July 1917. Reprinted in *Testimonio: A Documentary History of the Mexican American Struggle for Civil Rights*, edited by F. Arturo Rosales. Houston: Arte Publico Press, 2000.

———. "Diary," July 24, 1917. *Arizona Record*, July 1917.

————. "Message of Geo. W.P. Hunt: Governor of Arizona to the First Legislature of the State of Arizona," March 18, 1912. Arizona State Press, 1912.

Jones, Mary "Mother." *Autobiography of Mother Jones*. Chicago: Charles Kerr, 1925.

Kingsolver, Barbara. *Holding the Line: Women in the Great Arizona Mine Strike of 1983*. Cornell: ILR Press, 1996.

LaCagnina, Yolanda. *The Role of the Recall of Judges Issue in the Struggle for Arizona Statehood*. Dissertation. University of Arizona, 1951.

Lockwood, Frank. *Pioneer Portraits: Selected Vignettes*. Tucson: University of Arizona Press, 1968.

————. *Arizona Characters*. New York: Macmillan, 1928.

Martinez, Mariano. "Arizona Americans." Letter to the Editor. *New York Times*, October 31, 1904.

McClintock, James. *Arizona, Prehistoric, Aboriginal, Pioneer, Modern; The Nation's Youngest Commonwealth within a Land of Ancient Culture*. Chicago: S. J. Clarke, 1916.

McGinnis, True Anthony. "The Influence of Organized Labor on the Making of the Arizona Constitution." Master's Thesis. University of Arizona, 1931.

Mellinger, Philip. *Race and Labor in Western Copper: The Fight for Equality, 1896–1918*. Tucson: University of Arizona Press, 1995.

Munds, Frances Willard. "Arizona Campaign." Speech by Frances Willard Munds, Arizona State Library, Archives and Public Records, 1912.

Murphy, James. "Arizona's Constitutional Recall Provision." *Arizona Bar Journal* (September 1966).

Murphy, Nathan. "Report of the Governor of Arizona to the Secretary of the Interior, 1899." Washington, DC: Government Printing Office, 1899.

New Republic, January 22, 1916.

Noel, Linda. "I Am an American: Anglos, Mexicans, Nativos, and the National Debate Over Arizona and New Mexico Statehood." *Pacific Historical Review* (August 2011).

O'Neal, Bill. "Captain Harry Wheeler: Arizona Lawman." *Journal of Arizona History* 27, no. 3 (August 1986).

Otero, Lydia. *La Calle: Spatial Conflicts and Urban Renewal in a Southwest City*. Tucson: University of Arizona Press, 2010.

Owen, Robert. "Admission of Territories of New Mexico and Arizona." Testimony before the US Senate Committee on Territories. Washington, DC: Government Printing Office, 1911.

Park, Joseph F. "The History of Mexican Labor in Arizona During the Territorial Period." Master's Thesis. University of Arizona, 1961.

Parrish, Michael. *Mexican Workers, Progressives, and Copper: The Failure of Industrial Democracy in Arizona during the Wilson Years*. La Jolla, CA: Chicano Research Publications, 1979.

"President Taft Signs Proclamation Declaring Arizona a Sovereign State." *Arizona Daily Star*, February 15, 1912.

"Recall of Nothing." *Tucson Citizen*, July 25, 1911.

Robinson, William Henry. *The Story of Arizona*. Phoenix: The Berryhill Company, 1919.

Rosenblum, Jonathan. *Copper Crucible: How the Arizona Miners' Strike of 1983 Recast Labor*. Cornell: ILR Press, 1995.

Sacks, B. "The Creation of the Territory of Arizona." *Journal of the Southwest* 5, no. 1 (Summer 1963).

Sheridan, Thomas. *Arizona: A History*. Tucson: University of Arizona Press, 1995.

Tefft, Miriam. "The Last of the Vigilantes." Unpublished manuscript. Arizona Historical Society Biographical Files, 1982.

"The Completed State," *Arizona Daily Star*, February 14, 1912.

"The Test Oath Again," *Deseret Weekly*, October 10, 1891.

Vaughan, James. "All Women and Children Keep Off Streets Today." Unpublished manuscript. Arizona Historical Society Collections, 1962.

Wilson, Marjorie Haynes. "Governor Hunt, the 'Beast' and the Miners." *Journal of Arizona History* 15 (Summer 1974).

"Women and Children Keep Off Streets." *Bisbee Daily Register*, July 12, 1917.

CHAPTER THREE: MANUFACTURING THE CRISIS

Alonzo, Monica. "Phil Roberts Exaggerated the Phoenix PD's Kidnapping Statistics, Then Tried to Debunk His Own Numbers." *Phoenix New Times*, July 7, 2011.

———. "Phoenix Cops May Have Inflated Kidnapping Stats to Get Federal Bucks." *Phoenix New Times*, February 17, 2011.

"Arizona Gov. Jan Brewer Wrongly Claims Father Died Fighting Nazi Germany." Associated Press, June 2, 2010.

"Arizona Governor: GOP's Martin, Mills Lead Goddard." Rasmussen Reports, March 23, 2010.

"Arizona Lawmaker Circulated White Separatist E-mail." Associated Press, October 12, 2006.

Armbruster, Ben. "Gov. Brewer: 'Arizona has been under terrorist attacks' with 'all of this illegal immigration.'" ThinkProgress, April 30, 2010. thinkprogress.org/politics /2010/04/30/94663/brewer-terrorist-attacks/.

Barry, Tom. "Securing Arizona: What Americans Can Learn From Their Rogue State." *Boston Review*, March 2011.

"Beck runs with debunked Phoenix kidnapping claim." Media Matters, June 30, 2010. mediamatters.org/research/201006300072.

Beck, Glenn. "Arizona Makes Illegal Immigration Illegal." *The Glenn Beck Program* (radio), April 14, 2010. www.glennbeck.com/content/articles/article/198/39157/.

———. "The #2 City in World for Kidnapping Is. . . . " *The Glenn Beck Program* (radio), February 13, 2009. www.glennbeck.com/content/articles/article/196/21451/.

Beirich, Heidi. "John Tanton and the Nativist Movement." Southern Poverty Law Center Publications, February 2009.

Benen, Steve. "Not Intended to Be a Factual Statement." *Washington Monthly*, April 9, 2011.

Biggers, Jeff. "Bloody Monday: Glenn Beck, FOX News, Gov. Jan Brewer and the Louisville Massacre Anniversary." *Huffington Post,* August 2, 2010.

———. "Did Tea Party President Pearce Plagiarize (Again) for 'White Nationalist' Press?" *Huffington Post,* October 24, 2011.

———. "The Disturbing Copy-and-Paste Habits of Russell Pearce." *Salon,* August 3, 2011.

———. "How Arizona Wrote the GOP Platform." *Salon,* November 3, 2011.

Brewer, Jan. *Scorpions for Breakfast: My Fight Against Special Interests, Liberal Media, and Cynical Politics to Secure America's Borders.* New York: Broadside Books, 2011.

Bushman, Richard. *Joseph Smith: Rough Stone Rolling.* New York: Knopf, 2005.

Cawley, R. McGreggor. *Federal Land, Western Anger: The Sagebrush Rebellion and Environmental Politics.* Lawrence, KS: University Press of Kansas, 1993.

Davenport, Paul. "Brewer Says She Was Wrong About Beheadings." *Arizona Republic,* September 3, 2010.

"Fear and Loathing in Prime Time: Immigration Myths and Cable News." Media Matters Action Network, May 21, 2008.

Fernandez, Henry. "Know Your Sources: The Mainstream Press Keeps Finding Wacky Immigration 'Experts.'" Center for American Progress, September 19, 2007. americanprogress.org/issues/2007/09/know_your_sources.html.

Fischer, Howard. "Poll Shows SB 1070 Is Putting Brewer on Top in Gov Race." Capitol Media Services, October 29, 2010.

"Gov. Brewer's Beheading Claims to Cost Arizona $250,000." Change.org, July 7, 2010. news.change.org/stories/gov-brewer-s-beheadings-claim-to-cost-arizona-250-000.

"Gov. Jan Brewer Needs to Get Her Facts Straight." *Arizona Republic,* June 29, 2010.

Green, Linda. "Notes from the Arizona Borderlands: Immigration, Militarization, Inequality." *Lehman Today,* June 21, 2011.

Grimsted, David. *American Mobbing, 1828–1861: Toward Civil War.* New York: Oxford University Press USA, 2003.

"Huckabee Pushes Myth That Arizona Is "The Number One Kidnapping Capital in the World." Media Matters report, July 8, 2010. mediamatters.org/mmtv/201007080068.

"Immigrants Targeted: Extremist Rhetoric Moves into the Mainstream: Groups: The Federation for American Immigration Reform (FAIR)—Washington D.C." Anti-Defamation League report, 2007. www.adl.org/civil_rights/anti_immigrant/fair.asp.

"Jan Brewer: I Made 'Error' in Beheadings Claim." CBS News, November 2, 2010.

Jilani, Zaid. "Prison Lobbyists Working for AZ Gov. Brewer Are Set to Profit From Immigration Law She Signed." ThinkProgress, July 26, 2010. thinkprogress.org/politics/2010/07/26/109493/prison-brewer/.

"John McCain: Illegal Immigrants 'Intentionally Causing Accidents on the Freeway.'" *Huffington Post,* June 20, 2010.

Kaye, Jeffrey. "Enforcing Arizona's SB 1070: A State of Confusion." Immigration Policy Center, July 27, 2010.

Keane, John. "Arizona's Sagebrush Rebellion: Politics and Land Management." Master's Thesis. University of Arizona, 1981.

Kiefer, Michael and Richard Ruelas. "Neighbor Found Guilty in Man's Shooting Death: Pair Had Been Quarreling About SB 1070." *Arizona Republic,* April 14, 2011.

Kobach, Kris. "Why Arizona Drew a Line." *New York Times,* April 28, 2010.

Lemons, Stephen. "Joe Arpaio Partners with Nativist Extremist Kris Kobach, Arizona ADL Blasts Both." *Phoenix New Times,* February 10, 2010.

———. "Phoenix Hate Crimes Rise 125 Percent from 2006 to 2010." *Phoenix New Times,* June 6, 2011.

Maddow, Rachel. "Racist Roots of Arizona's Immigration Law." *The Rachel Maddow Show,* April 27, 2010.

Morales, David. "Brewer losing her head over new lies?" Three Sonorans blog, *Tucson Citizen,* July 1, 2010.

"Past and Future." *Arizona Daily Star,* February 14, 1970.

Pitzl, Mary Jo. "Brewer Tells Budget Directors to Tighten Belts." *Arizona Republic,* December 21, 2009.

Rau, Alia Beard. "Arizona GOP Tried to Make Most of Supermajority." *Arizona Republic,* May 5, 2012.

Reyes, Raul. "Arizona Pols Stoke Immigration Myths." *USA Today,* July 22, 2010.

"Russell Pearce: Brewer Owes Me." 3TV News (Phoenix), November 3, 2010.

Schlangen, Les. "Sagebrush Bill Breaks Babbitt's Veto String." *Prescott Courier,* April 15, 1980.

Selby, Gardner. "Phoenix As Kidnapping Capital Tops Reader Favorites." *Austin-American Statesman,* December 30, 2010.

Sterling, Terry Greene. *Illegal: Life and Death in Arizona's Immigration War Zone.* Guilford, CT: Lyons Press, 2010.

Sullivan, Laura. "Prison Economics Help Drive Ariz. Immigration Law." National Public Radio, October 28, 2010.

———. "Shaping State Laws With Little Scrutiny." National Public Radio, October 29, 2010.

"The Sagebrush Rebellion: Issues for the Arizona Legislature." Tucson: University of Arizona, College of Agriculture, 1981.

Walsh, Jim. "Mesa Man Pushes to Keep Brother's Name on Sept. 11 Memorial." *Arizona Republic,* April 2, 2011.

CHAPTER FOUR: FEAR AND LOATHING
IN A LAND OF CARPETBAGGERS

"American Troops Are Ready to Cross the Line into Mexico." *Arizona Daily Star,* February 25, 1912.

Arizona Citizen, April 2, 1872.

———, May 22, 1875.

———, October 27, 1877.

"Arizona Fears the Rebels; Gov. Hunt Says Americans in Sonora Are Hard Press by Them." *New York Times,* April 26, 1914.

Barney, J. M. "Early Days in Tucson: Some Historical Notes." Arizona Municipality, 1940.

Biggers, Jeff. "A Mexican Immigrant's Act of Honor." *New York Times,* February 14, 2012.

"Border Army Ready to Clash with Mexico." *New York Times,* November 30, 1919.

Jackson, Orick. *The White Conquest of Arizona.* Los Angeles: West Coast Magazine, 1908.

Jacoby, Karl. *Shadows at Dawn: A Borderlands Massacre and the Violence of History.* New York: Penguin, 2008.

Lamar, Howard. "Carpetbaggers Full of Dreams: A Functional View of the Arizona Pioneer Politician." *Arizona and the West* 7 (1965).

Lockwood, Frank. *Pioneer Portraits.* Tucson: University of Arizona Press, 1968.

"Minute Men Revived After Indian Scare." *Arizona Republic,* April 10, 1940.

Poston, Charles. *Building a State in Apacheland.* Kila, MT: Kessinger Publishing, 2004.

———. "Twas Thirty Years Ago." *Sunshine and Silver.* Tucson. January 4, 1885.

———. Unpublished manuscript. Address given in 1896. Arizona State Historian, Phoenix, AZ.

"Preserve the Old Landmarks," *Arizona Daily Star,* December 29, 1910.

"Rebellion in Mexico Spreads Fast." *Arizona Daily Star,* February 14, 1912.

"Rebels Carry the War into All Sections." *Arizona Daily Star,* February 14, 1912.

Sacks, B. "The Creation of the Territory of Arizona." *Journal of the Southwest* 5 (Summer 1963).

Sheridan, Thomas. *Los Tucsonenses: The Mexican Community in Tucson, 1854–1941.* Tucson: University of Arizona Press, 1986.

Sonnichsen, C. L. *Tucson: The Life and Times of an American City.* Norman, Oklahoma: University of Oklahoma Press, 1982.

———. *Pioneer Heritage: The First Century of the Arizona Historical Society.* Arizona Historical Society, 1984.

"The Maligning of Mexico." *Arizona Daily Star,* July 9, 1912.

"The War of the Rebellion: A Compilation of the Official Records of the Union and Confederate Armies." Washington, DC: GPO, 1897.

Trimble, Marshall. *Arizona: A Panoramic History of a Frontier State.* New York: Doubleday, 1977.

CHAPTER FIVE: THE DANGED FENCE

Alonzo, Monica. "Paul Babeu's Mexican Ex-Lover Says Sheriff's Attorney Threatened Him With Deportation." *Phoenix New Times,* February 16, 2012.

"American Legion Post 41." Arizona Stories Series. PBS (Arizona), December 3, 2010.

Archibold, Randal. "A Border Watcher Finds Himself Under Scrutiny." *New York Times,* November 24, 2006.

"Arizona Launches Fundraising Website for Border Fence." Associated Press, July 19, 2011.

"Arizona Sheriff Takes on Obama in Letter." ABC News (Phoenix), May 26, 2011. www .abc15.com/dpp/news/state/arizona-sheriff-takes-on-obama-in-letter.

"Ariz. Sheriff Scoffs at Critics of Border Crackdown." Fox News, February 16, 2011.

Arpaio, Joe and Len Sherman. *Joe's Law: America's Toughest Sheriff Takes on Illegal Immigration, Drugs and Everything Else That Threatens America.* New York: AMACON, 2008.

"AZ Sheriff Babeu Appears on a White Nationalist Program, Invites Listeners to Join His 'Posse.'" Media Matters report, July 19, 2010. mediamatters.org/blog/201007 190033.

Ball, Larry. "Frontier Sheriffs at Work." *Journal of Arizona History* 27, no. 3 (1986).

Biggers, Jeff. "Alleged Gunman's GOP Pal." *Salon,* May 2, 2012.

———. "Arizona Launches $50 Million Border Wall Campaign." *Huffington Post,* July 20, 2011.

———. "Arizona's Next Scandal? Tea Party State Official Says Ethnic Studies Violates Ban." *The Nation,* June 15, 2011.

———. *In the Sierra Madre.* Chicago: University of Illinois Press, 2006.

———. "Sheriff Arpaio Showdown: Resignation Demands Grow Amid Child Sex Crimes Debacle." *Huffington Post,* December 7, 2011.

———. "Sheriff Takes Another Hit." *Salon,* December 15, 2011.

Browne, Devin. "Freshman Senator Takes on Enduring Immigration Issues." KPBS Radio, July 28, 2011.

Castro, Raúl. *Adversity Is My Angel: The Life and Career of Raúl H. Castro.* Ft. Worth: Texas Christian University Press, 2009.

Collem, Lindsey. "Arizona Border Mayors Ask Pinal Sheriff to Tone It Down." *Arizona Republic,* February 16, 2011.

Cooper, Michael. "McCain Makes Appeal to Hispanics." *New York Times,* July 9, 2008.

"Curriculum Audit of the Mexican American Studies Department, Tucson Unified School District." Miami Lakes, FL: Cambrium Learning, 2011.

Fischer, Howard. "Brewer Unaware of Napolitano Visit Due to Staff Error." *Yuma Sun,* Capitol Media Services, July 8, 2011.

"Fox News, the Preferred Anti-Immigrant Network for Anti-Immigrant Sheriff Paul Babeu." Media Matters, October 27, 2011. mediamatters.org/blog/201110270009.

"Fox Pushes AZ Efforts to Build Border Fence Despite Its Predicted High Cost and Unproven Effectiveness." Media Matters, December 1, 2011. mediamatters.org/research /201112010015.

Gabrielson, Ryan and Paul Giblin. "Reasonable Doubt." *East Valley Tribune,* July 8, 2008.

Gans, Herbert. *The Urban Villagers: Group and Class in the Life of Italian-Americans.* New York: Free Press, 1962.

"Glenn Spencer." Southern Poverty Law Center, Intelligence Files. www.splcenter.org /get-informed/intelligence-files/profiles/glenn-spencer.

Gomez, Alan, Jack Gillum, and Kevin Johnson. "U.S. Border Cities Prove Havens from Mexico's Drug Violence." *USA Today*, July 18, 2011.

Green, Terry Sterling. "Arizona's Other Shooting Horror." *Daily Beast*, January 20, 2011.

Hensley, J. J. "Arpaio Deposition Reveals He Hasn't Read His Own Book." *Arizona Republic*, January 4, 2010.

———. "Arpaio Unveils Obama Birth-Certificate Probe." *Arizona Republic*, March 1, 2012.

———. "Wallow Fire: 2 Arizona Cousins Are Facing Federal Charges." *Arizona Republic*, August 24, 2011.

Holthouse, David. "Arizona Showdown." Southern Poverty Law Center, *Intelligence Report*, Summer 2005.

"How the GOP and Fox News Make Anti-Immigrant Ideas 'Mainstream.'" Media Matters, October 27, 2011. politicalcorrection.org/mobile/blog/201110270003.

Hunt, Kasie. "John McCain Tacks Right on Immigration." Politico.com, April 19, 2010. www.politico.com/news/stories/0410/36022.html.

"John McCain Border Shift: 'Complete Danged Fence.'" ABC News, May 11, 2010.

"John McCain: Immigrants Caused Arizona Wildfires." *Huffington Post*, June 19, 2011.

Johnson, Kevin. *The "Huddled Masses" Myth: Immigration and Civil Rights*. Philadelphia: Temple University Press, 2004.

"Justice Department to Sue Arizona Sheriff After Talks Fall Through." CNN News, April 5, 2012.

Kelly, Erin. "Arizona Border Security to Get an Upgrade." *Arizona Republic*, July 7, 2011.

Kim, Seung Min. "Grijalva: McCain Comments a 'New Low' in Discourse." Politico.com, June 20, 2011. www.politico.com/blogs/glennthrush/0611/Grijalva_McCain_comments_a_new_low_in_discourse.html.

Lacey, Marc. "As Arizona Fire Rages, So Does Rumor on Its Origin." *New York Times*, June 1, 2011.

Lemons, Stephen. "Glenn Spencer, Nativist Anti-Semite, Lectures State Senate Border Security Committee." *Phoenix New Times*, March 1, 2012.

———. "Neo-Nazis Patrol the Vekol Valley; J. T. Ready Calls 'Border Ops' for Saturday." *Phoenix New Times*, June 16, 2010.

———. "Russell Pearce Versus J. T. Ready in Dennis Gilman's New Video." *Phoenix New Times*, January 3, 2011.

———. "Shawna Forde, Alleged Kid Killer, Extremist, Phoenix Tea Party Attendee, and Ghost of Tea Parties Future." *Phoenix New Times*, June 22, 2009.

———. "Will the $100 Million Hole Joe Arpaio Dug Kill Him in the 2012 Election?" *Phoenix New Times*, April 21, 2011.

Louis, Bill. "Sheriff Arpaio Failed Victims of El Mirage." *Arizona Republic*, December 8, 2011.

Luo, Michael. "McCain Says Immigration Reform Should Be Top Priority." *New York Times*, May 22, 2008.

Magloff, Spencer. "McCain on Immigration: The Border Is Broken." CBS News, April 27, 2010.

McCombs, Brady. "US Plan on Border Drugs Leans More on Prevention." *Arizona Daily Star,* July 8, 2011.

McGirk, Tim. "Border Clash." *Time,* June 26, 2000.

Miller, Joshua R. "Arizona Sheriff: Wildfires Likely Started by Mexican Drug Traffickers, Smugglers." Fox News, June 22, 2011.

Morgan, Lee, II. *The Reaper's Line: Life and Death on the Mexican Border.* Tucson: Rio Nuevo Press, 2011.

Peralta, Eyder. "Arizona Sheriff Uses a Tank and Steven Seagal to Arrest Cockfighting Suspect." The Two-Way blog, National Public Radio, March 23, 2011.

Perez, Thomas. "Notice of Intent to File Civil Action." US Department of Justice. Letter to Sheriff Joseph M. Arpaio, May 9, 2012.

Phoenix Gazette. July 15, 1882.

Riccardi, Nicholas. "Court Upholds Verdict Against Arizona Rancher Who Detained Illegal Immigrants on His Land." *LA Times,* February 4, 2011.

Rivera, Geraldo. *The Great Progression: How Hispanics Will Lead America to a New Era of Prosperity.* New York: New American Library, 2009.

Sandoval, Anthony. "Manu Chao Stands in Solidarity with Sheriff Joe Arpaio." *Phoenix New Times,* September 21, 2011.

Schlegel, Paul. "Southern Arizona and the Mexican Revolution: An Example of How Events South of the Border Affected the Southwest." Unpublished manuscript. Northern Arizona University, 1990.

Steller, Tim. "Babeu Is New Face of Arizona Sheriffs." *Arizona Daily Star,* May 23, 2010.

Sterling, Terry Greene. *Illegal: Life and Death in Arizona's Immigration War Zone.* Guilford, CT: Lyons Press, 2010.

Todd, Cece. "SB 1070 Upsets Arizona's Only Hispanic Governor." *East Valley Tribune,* May 7, 2010.

"Use Amnesty, Guest Worker Plans, McCain Urges Ridge." *Tucson Citizen,* April 10, 2003.

CHAPTER SIX: RECALL: THE FIRST SHOWDOWN

Bagley, Will. *Blood of the Prophets: Brigham Young and the Massacre at Mountain Meadows.* Norman, OK: University of Oklahoma Press, 2004.

———. *Innocent Blood: Essential Narratives of the Mountain Meadows Massacre.* Norman, OK: Arthur C. Clark, 2008.

Bair, JoAnn and Richard Jensen. "Prosecution of the Mormons in Arizona Territory 1880s." *Arizona and the West* 19 (Spring 1977).

Berry, Jahna and Alia Beard Rau. "Supreme Court Upholds Arizona Employer Sanctions Law." *Arizona Republic,* May 27, 2011.

Biggers, Jeff. "Arizona's Shock Doctrine? Children Call Out Legislators on Immigration Bills Defeat." *Huffington Post,* March 17, 2011.

————. "Arizona Topples Senate President Russell Pearce, SB 1070 Immigration Law Architect, in Historic Recall Vote." *Huffington Post,* November 8, 2011.

————. "Arizona Turns the Tide." *The Nation,* May 31, 2011.

————. "Facing Tight Recall Race, AZ Tea Party President Pearce Double Downs on Extremists." *Huffington Post,* October 11, 2011.

————. "In the 19th Century, the Romneys Fled the Law." *Salon,* September 9, 2011.

————. "Tea Party Love Boat Going Down." *Huffington Post,* October 17, 2011.

————. "Tea Party Scandal Explodes in Arizona Recall Election." *Huffington Post,* September 25, 2011.

————. "What Happens in Arizona, Doesn't Stay in Arizona." *Salon,* November 9, 2011.

Buck, Ed. 'It's Real, But 'Leaders' Lack Courage to Address It." *Arizona Republic,* August 16, 1987.

Bull, Bart. "Antihero." *Spin,* May 1988.

Burchell, Joe. "Meacham Announces He'll Make His Fifth Run for Governorship." *Arizona Daily Star,* July 2, 1986.

BusinessWeek, August 19, 1972.

"Cesar Chavez Fasts in Arizona." *El Macriado,* June 9, 1972.

Chavez, Cesar. Address to the Commonwealth Club of San Francisco, November 9, 1984. California Department of Education. chavez.cde.ca.gov.

Chu, Dan. "Arizona's Outspoken New Governor, Evan Mecham, Seems to Enjoy Diving Straight into Political Hot Water." *People,* August 24, 1987.

Epps, Garrett. "Stealing the Constitution." *The Nation,* January 20, 2011.

Gorman, Anna. "Arizona Immigration Law an Unpleasant Reminder of Chandler's Past." *LA Times,* June 6, 2010.

"Guerrero Named City's No. 1 Citizen." *Mesa Journal Tribune,* January 9, 1942.

Hart, Bill. "A Politico's Comeback." *Arizona Republic,* February 2, 2003.

Hernandez, Kelly Lytle. "The Crimes and Consequences of Illegal Immigration: A Cross-Border Examination of Operation Wetback, 1943–1954," *Western Historical Quarterly* 37 (Winter 2006).

"How to Overthrow a Governor." *The New American,* March 28, 1988.

Hull, John. "Evan Mecham, Please Go Home." *Time,* November 9, 1987.

"Immigration: Church Issues New Statement." Church of Jesus Christ of Latter-day Saints, June 10, 2011. www.mormonnewsroom.org/article/immigration-church-issues-new-statement.

Jensen, Richard and John C. Hammerback, eds. *The Words of Cesar Chavez.* College Station: Texas A&M University Press, 2002.

Kramer, Eric. "Romneys, Udalls Have Ties to Ariz. Territorial Polygamy Trials." *Tri-Valley Dispatch,* June 8, 2011.

"Kris Kobach, Who Helped Write SB 1070, Endorses Romney." *Arizona Republic,* January 11, 2012.

Lemons, Stephen. "Joe Arpaio on Glenn Beck Re: Mexican Migrants, 'They Like to Fight Each Other.'" *Phoenix New Times,* October 10, 2009.

"Letter from Arizona by Cesar Chavez." *El Macriado,* June 9, 1972.

Levy, Jacques. *Cesar Chavez: Autobiography of La Causa.* Minneapolis: University of Minnesota Press, 2007.

Lopez, Larry. "Pressure On: Mecham May Force Barr to Work Harder, Demos Say." *Tucson Citizen,* July 2, 1986.

Lyons, Sarah. "Pearce Calls for Deportations." *East Valley Tribune,* September 29, 2006.

Marin, Christine. "Cesar E. Chavez in Phoenix, 1972 Fast at the Santa Rita Hall." *Barriozona.* www.barriozona.com/cesar_chavez_in_phoenix.html.

Mecham, Evan. "Positive Achievements Tell the Story." *Arizona Republic,* August 16, 1987.

Melvin, Hollard. "A History of Mesa." Master's Thesis. University of Arizona, 1933.

Merrill, W. Earl. *One Hundred Steps Down Mesa's Past.* Mesa, AZ: 1970.

Miroff, Nick. "In Besieged Mormon Colony, Mitt Romney's Mexican Roots." *Washington Post,* July 23, 2011.

Montini, E. J. "Gutierrez on What Happens AFTER the March." *Arizona Republic,* May 30, 2010.

Morales, David. "Who Is Randy Parraz?" Three Sonorans blog, *Tucson Citizen,* July 7, 2010.

Nelson, Gary. "Distorted Book Is Bad History, Poses Its Own Tyranny." *Arizona Republic,* September 19, 2010.

Nevins, Joseph. *Operation Gatekeeper: The Rise of the 'Illegal Alien' and the Remaking of the U.S.-Mexico Boundary.* New York: Routledge, 2001.

Novak, Shannon and Lars Rodseth. "Remembering Mountain Meadows: Collective Violence and the Manipulation of Social Boundaries." *Journal of Anthropological Research* 62 (Spring 2006).

"Obama Calls for Cesar Chavez National Holiday." Press Media Wire. March 31, 2008.

Otis, Reta Reed. *Mesa: Desert to Oasis.* Mesa Historical Society, 1996.

"Our Town." Mesa Public Schools, 1949.

Pearce, Russell. "One Battle in Arizona Immigration War." Politico.com, March 26, 2011. www.politico.com/news/stories/0311/51971.html.

"Reagan Wants Mecham." Mecham for Governor Committee newsletter, 1986.

"Recall Governor Williams. Si Se Puede." *El Macriado,* June 9, 1972.

Reinhart, Mary. "Governor Stirs Outrage with 'Pickaninnies' Book." Associated Press, March 26, 1987.

"Rep. Trent Franks: Obama Is 'Enemy of Humanity.'" CBS News, September 29, 2009.

Riccardi, Nicholas. "Arizona's Relentless Conservative Voice." *LA Times,* January 17, 2011.

Roberts, Laurie. "Hendershott Demands $21 Million. Really." *Arizona Republic,* August 31, 2011.

Romney, Mitt. *Turnaround: Crisis, Leadership, and the Olympic Games.* New York: Regnery Publishing, 2004.

Rueles, Richard. "Son's Shooting Drives Rep. Pearce's Efforts." *Arizona Republic,* February 7, 2005.

Sanghani, Zarana. "Students, Teachers Press Lawmaker to Save Adult Classes." *East Valley Tribune,* February 23, 2003.

Schultheis, Emily. "Parraz Suing Arpaio for '08 Wrongful Arrest." Politico.com, August 19, 2010. www.politico.com/news/stories/0810/41260.html.

Sherwood, Robbie. "Border Debate Splits Arizonans." *Arizona Republic,* July 10, 2005.

———. "Outraged Defender of Border." *Arizona Republic,* July 10, 2005.

Snider, Burr. "Evan Mecham." *San Francisco Examiner,* November 22, 1987.

Sonmez, Felicia. "Russell Pearce, Arizona Immigration Law Author, Says Romney's 'Policy Is Identical to Mine.'" *Washington Post,* April 5, 2012.

Templar, Le. "Stirring the Melting Pot." *East Valley Tribune,* September 20, 2005.

———. "Pearce: Relic or reformer?" *East Valley Tribune,* March 16, 2003.

"Temporary Admission of Illiterate Mexican Laborers." Hearings before the House Committee on Immigration and Naturalization, Sixty-sixth Congress, Second session on HJ 271 . . . January 23, 27, 28, 30, and February 2, 1920.

Thompson, Hunter S. "No Paranoia. Mecham." *Boston Globe,* January 27, 1988.

Udall, David. *Arizona Pioneer Mormon: David King Udall: His Story and His Family, 1851–1938.* Tucson: Arizona Silhouettes, 1959.

Weisman, Alan. "Up in Arms in Arizona." *New York Times,* November 1, 1987.

"Wetbacks: Can the States Act to Curb Illegal Entry?" *Stanford Law Review* 6, no. 2 (March 1954).

Wilentz, Sean. "Confounding Fathers." *New Yorker,* October 18, 2010.

Willis, Chad. "Early Mesa: Outpost in Babylon." Master's Thesis. Arizona State University, 2001.

Young, Daniel Webster. *Forty Years Among the Indians: A True Yet Thrilling Narrative of the Author.* Los Angeles: Westernlore Press, 1960.

Zaitchik, Alexander. "The making of Glenn Beck." *Salon,* September 21, 2009.

CHAPTER SEVEN: OUTLAWING HISTORY: THE SECOND SHOWDOWN

Arizona Citizen, April 24, 1875.

———, May 22, 1875.

"Arizona Schools Chief Says Ethnic Studies Law Takes Focus off Race." CNN, May 14, 2010.

"Arizona's Tom Horne Blasts NCLB at the Heritage Foundation." *Education Week,* April 24, 2007.

Baldenegro, Salomon Sr. "My Tucson: Chicano Movement Improved Tucson." *Tucson Citizen,* July 28, 2006.

"Beck Fearmongers Again About Arizona School's Ethnic Studies Program." Media Matters, May 5, 2011. mediamatters.org/mmtv/201105050042.

Biggers, Jeff. "Arizona's Attorney General Says Ethnic/Mexican American Studies 'Must Be Destroyed.'" *Huffington Post,* September 21, 2011.

———. "Arizona's Choice Today: Tucson Students Lead New Civil Rights Movement." *The Nation,* May 3, 2011.

———. "Arizona's Dirty Lessons: Is Tucson School District Dismantling Ethnic Studies to Appease Tea Party?" *Huffington Post,* August 8, 2011.

———. "Arizona's Next Scandal? Tea Party State Official Says Ethnic Studies Violates Ban." *The Nation,* June 15, 2011.

———. "Arizona's Precious Knowledge." *Huffington Post,* June 13, 2011.

———. "Arizona Unbound: National Actions on Mexican American Studies Banishment." *Huffington Post,* January 25, 2012.

———. "Arizona Uprising: Chained Ethnic Studies Students Take Over School Board in Tucson." *The Nation,* April 27, 2011.

———. "As Teachers Heal Tucson, Will Extremist Officials Escalate Crisis This Week?" *The Nation,* June 7, 2011.

———. "AZ School Chief Compares Mexican-American Studies to Hitler Jugend." *Huffington Post,* September 28, 2011.

———. "Day After in Tucson." *Huffington Post,* January 11, 2012.

———. "Did Arizona Education Chief Huppenthal Commit a Felony in Growing Ethnic Studies Scandal?" *Huffington Post,* June 17, 2011.

———. "The Madness of the Tucson Book Ban: Interview with Mexican American Studies Teacher Curtis Acosta." *Huffington Post,* January 25, 2012.

———. "Tucson Says Banished Books May Return to Classrooms." *Salon,* January 18, 2012.

———. "Tucson's Mexican American Studies Director Sean Arce Wins National Zinn Education Award." *Huffington Post,* April 3, 2012.

———. "Who's Afraid of the Tempest?" *Salon,* January 13, 2012.

Blanco, Maria. "Before *Brown*, There Was *Mendez*: The Lasting Impact of *Mendez v. Westminster* in the Struggle for Desegregation." Immigration Policy Center, March 25, 2010.

"Books with Borders." *New York Times,* March 15, 2012.

Ceasar, Stephen. "Tucson Students Confront Loss of Their Chicano Studies Class." *LA Times,* January 11, 2012.

"Did Protesters Really 'Kill' Tom Horne?" Facebook entry, Save Ethnic Studies, May 15, 2010.

Franklin, Benjamin. "Observations Concerning the Increase of Mankind, 1751," in *Autobiography and Other Writings.* Cambridge: Oxford University Press, 1999.

Goldwater, Barry. "Three Generations of Pants and Politics in Arizona." Arizona Historical Society, 1962.

Harte, John Bret. "Charlie Meyer Was Bulwark of Law Here." *Tucson Citizen,* July 9, 1985.

"Horne Resigns from Board of ADL." Jewish News of Greater Phoenix (online), March 5, 2010.

Horne, Tom. "What Does Being Jewish Have to Do with Being an Elected Official?" Jewish News of Greater Phoenix (online), June 9, 2006.

Hughes, Emmet John. "Goldwaterism." *Newsweek,* July 27, 1964.

Huicochea, Alexis. "TUSD Argues for Appeal of Horne Finding." *Arizona Daily Star,* January 22, 2011.

Hull, Tim. "Students, Not Teachers, Can Fight Ban on Ethnic Studies." Courthouse News Service, January 11, 2012.

Johnson, P. J. "They Said Clean Up the Streets . . . So Charlie Did." *Tucson Citizen,* May 9, 1981.

Kimble, Mark. "Immigration: What Would Barry Do?" *Tucson Citizen,* January 5, 2008.

Lewin, Tamar. "Citing Individualism, Arizona Tries to Rein in Ethnic Studies in School." *New York Times,* May 13, 2010.

Martinez, Richard. "Plaintiffs Motion for Preliminary Injunction. No. CV 10-623 TUC AWT." United States District Court for the District of Arizona, November 14, 2011.

Morales, David. "Barrio Destruction: Will the City of Tucson Continue to Be Part of the Problem or Own Responsibility?" Three Sonorans blog, *Tucson Citizen,* July 6, 2011.

———"Did You Watch Barrios and Barriers on PBS Last Night and See Who John Pedicone from SALC Had Arrested?" Three Sonorans blog, *Tucson Citizen,* May 10, 2011.

———. "Profiles of the Tucson Right-Wing: Fearful Christian Men with Guns Who Are Ready to Kill." Three Sonorans blog, *Tucson Citizen,* August 11, 2011.

———. "Students Take Over TUSD Board Chambers, Wisconsin-style." Three Sonorans blog, *Tucson Citizen,* April 27, 2011.

———. "Teachers to Call for John Pedicone's Resignation This Thursday." Three Sonorans blog, *Tucson Citizen,* June 1, 2011.

———"TUSD Board Member Speaks Out: We Are BANNING Books and PICTURES." Three Sonorans blog, *Tucson Citizen,* January 31, 2011.

———. "VIDEO: John Pedicone Orders the Arrest of Mexican-American History Professor While Attacking Mexican-American History Classes." Three Sonorans blog, *Tucson Citizen,* May 6, 2011.

———. "VIDEO: John Pedicone and Mark Stegeman Treat the White Man Differently." Three Sonorans blog, *Tucson Citizen,* August 10, 2011.

Paz, Octavio. "In Search of the Present." The Nobel Foundation, 1990. www.nobelprize.org/nobel_prizes/literature/laureates/1990/paz-lecture.html.

Pedicone, John. "Adults Used Students As Pawns in TUSD Ethnic Studies Protest." *Arizona Daily Star,* May 1, 2011.

"Recent Efforts Show Pattern of Recklessness." *Arizona Republic,* March 25, 2011.

Santa Cruz, Nicole. "Arizona Bill Targeting Ethnic Studies Signed into Law." *LA Times,* May 12, 2010.

Sleeter, Christine. "Ethnic Studies and the Struggle in Tucson." *Education Week,* February 15, 2012.

Stern, Ray. "Tom Horne Promotes Video by Raza Studies Supporter, Decries 'Thuggish Behavior' of Crowd." *Phoenix New Times,* March 17, 2011.

Stocker, Joseph. "Arizona's Century of Jewish Life." *Arizona Days and Ways,* November 14, 1954.

Sutter, John. "Tucson Battles Wild West Image After Shooting." CNN, January 13, 2011.

"The New Thrust in American Politics: Goldwater Accepting Nomination," *Time,* July 24, 1964.

"Tucson's Mexican American Studies Ban." *Daily Show,* April 2, 2012.

EPILOGUE: WHAT HAPPENS IN ARIZONA
DOESN'T STAY IN ARIZONA

Biggers, Jeff. "At Supreme Court, Arizona Leaves Affected Voices at Home." *Huffington Post,* April 24, 2012.

———. "Silencing Chavez." Wordstrike.net, March 25, 2012. wordstrike.net/silencing -chavez.

———. "Tucson Citizen Shuts Down Popular Latino Blogger Three Sonorans." *Alternet,* April 4, 2012.

"Brewer Suspected of DUI in 1988 Crash; Case Not Pursued." *Arizona Republic,* October 27, 2010.

Castillo, Guadalupe. "Tucson History de *la Calle.*" Three Sonorans blog, November 22, 2010.

Clement, Paul and Sciarotta, Joseph. "No. 11-182. In the Supreme Court of the United States. STATE OF ARIZONA and JANICE K. BREWER, Governor of the State of Arizona, in her official capacity, v. United States of America. Writ of Certiorari to the United States Court of Appeals for the Ninth Circuit. Brief for Petitioners." August 11, 2011.

"Corrected Driving Record Leads to Firing of Motor Vehicle Officials." *Arizona Daily Star,* August 19, 1999.

"Deportations of Immigrants Hits Record Number Under Obama Administration." Associated Press, July 22, 2011.

Duda, Jeremy. "FBI Investigating Tom Horne for Campaign Violations." *Arizona Capitol Times,* April 2, 2012.

———. "Horne Uses Accuser's Words Against Him." *Arizona Capitol Times,* April 4, 2012.

"Educators Ask Federal Court to Declare Arizona's Ban on Ethnic Studies Unconstitutional." PR Newswire, March 7, 2012.

Egerton, John. *Speak Now Against the Day: The Generation Before the Civil Rights Movement in the South.* Chapel Hill: University of North Carolina Press, 1995.

Fitz, Marshall. "*Arizona v. United States* in the U.S. Supreme Court. A Primer on the Legal Arguments in Landmark States' Rights Case." Center for American Progress, April 4, 2012. americanprogress.org/issues/2012/04/az_us_supreme_court.html.

Garia, Uriel. "Deportations in 2011 Set Record High for Third Straight Year." *Arizona Capitol Times,* October 20, 2011.

Gavette, Gretchen. "Why Three Governors Challenged Secure Communities." *Frontline* (PBS News), October 18, 2011.

"Goldwater's Crystal Ball." *Arizona Republic,* March 24, 2012.

Gonzales, Daniel. "Border Patrol's New Plan Will Use Existing Resources." *Arizona Republic,* May 8, 2012.

———. "Report: 22% of Deportees Have U.S.-Born Children." *USA Today,* April 6, 2012.

Gordy, Cynthia. "Rep. John Lewis: Immigration Is the New Civil Rights Battle." *The Root,* May 20, 2011. www.theroot.com/views/rep-john-lewis-immigrations-new-civil-rights-battle.

Greene, Terry. "Jan Brewer, Other Arizona Officials Weigh Wider Impact of New Border Strategy." *Daily Beast,* May 9, 2012.

Herreras, Mari. "Ethnic Studies Myths." *Tucson Weekly,* November 17, 2011.

Hoyt, Joshua. "What Do 396,906 Deportations Mean? 654,895 Children Lose a Parent." *Huffington Post,* October 24, 2011.

"Jan Brewer." *Time,* March 29, 2012.

Klasfeld, Adam. "ICE Changed Its Tune on 'Secure Communities.'" Courthouse News Service, August 9, 2011.

Klein, Lori. "Lessons Learned." Lori Klein for State Senate (website). networkedblogs.com/67boc.

Kumar, Maria Teresa. "Losing Arizona." *Huffington Post,* March 1, 2012.

Lemons, Stephen. "Does Russell Pearce Believe in the Holy Lie?" *Phoenix New Times,* September 22, 2011.

Longoria, Eva. "Dulce Matuz: Advocate." *Time,* April 1, 2012.

Markon, Jerry. "Memo from 2002 Could Complicate Challenge of Arizona Immigration Law." *Washington Post,* May 18, 2010.

Millhiser, Ian. "Why International Opposition to SB1070 Proves That the Arizona Law Is Unconstitutional." ThinkProgress, July 23, 2010. thinkprogress.org/security/2010/07/23/176179/sb1070-declaration/.

Morales, David. "Regeneration and Renewal—Tucson 2012." Three Sonorans blog, April 8, 2012. threesonorans.com/2012/04/08/regeneration-and-renewal-tucson-2012/.

———. "We Are Resilient and We Will Win—Sal Baldenegro, Sr." Three Sonorans blog, *Tucson Citizen,* January 20, 2012.

Nagourney, Adam. "Across Arizona, Illegal Immigration Is on Back Burner." *New York Times,* February 26, 2012.

Newton, Casey. "Attorney-General Candidate Tom Horne Denied 1970 Bankruptcy." *Arizona Republic,* June 20, 2010.

Pitzl, Mary Jo. "Horne Has Gotten 6 Speeding Tickets in Past 1 1/2 years." *Arizona Republic,* August 21, 2009.

"Politics and the Supreme Court." *New York Times,* February 4, 2012.

Portillo, Ernesto Jr. "Neto's Tucson: Mex. American Studies Teachers, Students Are Left in Lurch." *Arizona Daily Star,* January 22, 2012.

Rivas, Jorge. "Arizona Gov. Jan Brewer Visits Alabama, Praises Immigration Law." *Colorlines,* October 31, 2011.

Suárez, Mario. *Chicano Sketches: Short Stories.* Tucson: University of Arizona Press, 2004.

"Why Latino Voters Will Swing the 2012 Election." *Time,* March 5, 2012.

INDEX